FOOD SECURITY IN AN UNCERTAIN WORLD
An International Perspective

FRONTIERS OF ECONOMICS AND GLOBALIZATION

15

Series Editors:

HAMID BELADI
University of Texas at San Antonio, USA

E. KWAN CHOI
Iowa State University, USA

FRONTIERS OF ECONOMICS AND GLOBALIZATION
VOLUME 15

FOOD SECURITY IN AN UNCERTAIN WORLD

An International Perspective

Edited by

Andrew Schmitz
University of Florida, Gainesville, FL, USA

P. Lynn Kennedy
Louisiana State University, Baton Rouge, LA, USA

Troy G. Schmitz
Arizona State University, Mesa, AZ, USA

United Kingdom – North America – Japan
India – Malaysia – China

Emerald Group Publishing Limited
Howard House, Wagon Lane, Bingley BD16 1WA, UK

First edition 2015

Copyright © 2015 Emerald Group Publishing Limited

British Library Cataloguing in Publication Data
A catalogue record for this book is available from the British Library

ISBN: 978-1-78560-213-9
ISSN: 1574-8715 (Series)

ISOQAR certified
Management System,
awarded to Emerald
for adherence to
Environmental
standard
ISO 14001:2004.

Certificate Number 1985
ISO 14001

INVESTOR IN PEOPLE

CONTENTS

LIST OF CONTRIBUTORS

Roshan Adhikari	Oregon State University, Corvallis, OR, USA
John Antle	Oregon State University, Corvallis, OR, USA
Miroslav Batka	International Food Policy Research Institute (IFPRI), Washington, DC, USA
Patrick Bell	United States Military Academy, West Point, NY, USA
Eleonora Canigiani	Food and Agriculture Organization of the United Nations (FAO), Rome, Italy
Lisa F. Clark	University of Saskatchewan, Saskatoon, SK, Canada
Eugenio Díaz-Bonilla	International Food Policy Research Institute (IFPRI), Washington, DC, USA
Claudia Diaz Carrasco	University of California Cooperative Extension, Riverside, CA, USA
Mandiaye Diagne	Africa Rice Center (AfricaRice), Regional Station Saint Louis, Senegal
Alvaro Durand-Morat	University of Arkansas, Fayetteville, AR, USA
Dwayne J. Haynes	University of Florida, Gainesville, FL, USA
Shida Rastegari Henneberry	Oklahoma State University, Stillwater, OK, USA
Jill E. Hobbs	University of Saskatchewan, Saskatoon, SK, Canada
Darren Hudson	Texas Tech University, Lubbock, TX, USA
Maros Ivanic	International Finance Corporation, Washington, DC, USA
Nicholas Kalaitzandonakes	University of Missouri, Columbia, MO, USA
P. Lynn Kennedy	Louisiana State University, Baton Rouge, LA, USA

William A. Kerr	University of Saskatchewan, Saskatoon, SK, Canada
Won W. Koo	North Dakota State University, Fargo, ND, USA
Ekaterina Krivonos	Food and Agriculture Organization of the United Nations (FAO), Rome, Italy
Prithviraj Lakkakula	North Dakota State University, Fargo, ND, USA
Jorge Lara-Álvarez	Fideicomisos Instituidos en Relación con la Agricultura (FIRA), Morelia, Michoacán, Mexico
David Magaña-Lemus	Fideicomisos Instituidos en Relación con la Agricultura (FIRA), Morelia, Michoacán, Mexico
Will Martin	International Food Policy Research Institute (IFPRI), Washington, DC, USA
William H. Meyers	University of Missouri, Columbia, MO, USA
Dragan Miljkovic	North Dakota State University, Fargo, ND, USA
Donna Mitchell	Texas Tech University, Lubbock, TX, USA
Jamie Morrison	Food and Agriculture Organization of the United Nations (FAO), Rome, Italy
Siwa Msangi	International Food Policy Research Institute (IFPRI), Washington, DC, USA
Riley Post	US Special Operations Command Central (USSOCCENT), MacDill AFB, Florida, USA
Stephanie Price	Oregon State University, Corvallis, OR, USA
Andrew Schmitz	University of Florida, Gainesville, FL, USA
Troy G. Schmitz	Arizona State University, Tempe, AZ, USA
Richard Taylor	North Dakota State University, Fargo, ND, USA
Eric J. Wailes	University of Arkansas, Fayetteville, AR, USA
Ryan B. Williams	Texas Tech University, Lubbock, TX, USA

1

Food Security: Starvation in the Midst of Plenty

Andrew Schmitz[a] and P. Lynn Kennedy[b]

[a]*Food and Resource Economics Department, University of Florida, Gainesville, FL, USA*
[b]*Department of Agricultural Economics and Agribusiness, Louisiana State University,
6261 Morgan Bend Drive, Baton Rouge, LA, USA*
E-mail address: aschmitz@ufl.edu and lkennedy@agcener.lsu.edu

Abstract

Purpose — The purpose of this analysis is to determine the impact of various factors, including population growth, income growth, and research and development on food security. This chapter also seeks to better understand the role of relative food prices in consumers' selection of foods to meet their nutritional needs.

Methodology/approach — We utilize a welfare economic framework to provide a theoretical examination of the impact of various factors (including income growth, population growth, and research and development) on food security among the poor. A minimum nutritional diet is specified as a baseline for the evaluation of these scenarios.

Findings — Scenarios show the impacts that income, population growth, and research and development have on food security through their price and quantity impacts. Also, we highlight the difficulty in formulating an optimal diet that meets the recommended dietary requirements for only calories and protein, as different foods contain calories, proteins, and micronutrients in differing proportions. This indicates that changes in relative food prices will often alter consumers' nutrient intake with respect to the minimum nutritional diet.

Social implications — Research and development is critical in guaranteeing food availability. Trade-based, production-based, and own-labor entitlements are key factors in determining food security. Consumption subsidies and income supplements can be used to assist those who do not have entitlements sufficient to meet their minimum nutritional diet.

Keywords: Entitlements, availability, R&D, calories, protein, nutrients

Frontiers of Economics and Globalization
Volume 15   ISSN: 1574-8715
DOI: 10.1108/S1574-871520150000015001

1. Introduction

Inadequate food supply is just one of many factors that can result in insufficient access to food. While food availability has long been recognized as a factor in food security (Malthus, 1798), poverty and famine result from a lack of entitlements (Sen, 1981). The entitlement set contains all possible combinations of goods and services that a person can legally obtain using their endowments (Osmani, 1993). The endowment set includes all resources legally owned by an individual. Entitlement relationships in a market economy can be categorized as (1) trade-based entitlements (the right to trade what one owns with a willing party); (2) production-based entitlements (the right to arrange production using what one owns or with resources hired from a willing party); (3) own-labor entitlements (the right to one's own labor power and the resulting trade-based and production-based entitlements); and (4) inheritance and transfer entitlements (the right to what is willingly given by its legitimate owner). The lack of entitlements and corresponding access to food give rise to starvation in a food-abundant world.

Sen (1981) used a number of examples involving famines in India and Africa to make his case. He could have used examples from food-abundant countries, such as the United States, where starvation and poverty exist amid plenty. This phenomenon in the United States led the President's Commission on Income Maintenance Programs to publish the report *Poverty Amid Plenty: The American Paradox* (President's Commission, 1969). Despite agricultural exports exceeding agricultural imports in the United States since 1960, the Commission's study showed that of the 15% of Americans living in poverty, approximately 63% of these did not have adequate access to food.

For our purposes, we assume a recommended daily required nutrient intake that specifies the minimum level of calories, protein, and other nutrients necessary for an average individual to maintain a healthy lifestyle. We also assume a generic food commodity that contains calories, protein, and other nutrients in the correct proportion so that sufficient consumption will result in the fulfillment of the minimum daily requirements. While these levels vary across cultures and countries, the US government suggests a daily intake of 2,400 calories and 56 grams of protein for a 19- to 30-year-old male and 2,000 calories and 46 grams of protein for a 19- to 30-year-old female (CDC, 2012; USDA, 2015). These recommended levels are for active adults.

We examine several different scenarios to determine the impact of various factors (including income growth, population growth, and research and development) on food security among the poor. A minimum nutritional diet is defined as a baseline for the evaluation of these scenarios. Whether the status quo finds the poor in a state of malnourishment, at the minimum nutritional diet threshold, or if the poor have food consumption at levels exceeding the minimum daily requirements, our analyses demonstrate the impact of select factors on the ability of society's poor to achieve a minimum nutritional diet.

2. Model I – income effect

Consider Figure 1, where S is supply, D_p is demand for food by the poor, D_r is demand for food by the rich and total demand is TD. At equilibrium price p^0, total consumption is q^0, the poor consume q_p, and the rich consume q_r.

Assume that at a consumption level of q_p, the poor are malnourished. Given the above mentioned USDA caloric needs, q_p represents a caloric intake of less than 2,400 calories. Based on data from Koo and Taylor (2015), the average per capita caloric supplies in India and sub-Saharan Africa were below the 2,400 calorie level in 2012. Other regions in the Koo and Taylor study had over 2,400 carlories available on a per capita basis. However, as this model shows, adequate overall supply of calories does not guarantee that each group receives sufficient levels to meet their dietary requirements.

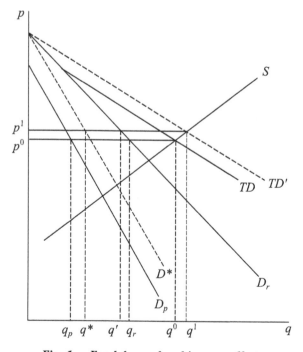

Fig. 1.   Food demand and income effect.

Because an adequate overall supply of food does not necessarily result in the fulfillment of the caloric needs of all groups, we now examine the effect of income growth for the poor. To do this, consider an increase in the income of the poor by whatever means. For example, in the United States, this is accomplished through the distribution of Electronic Benefit Transfer (EBT) cards to welfare recipients, providing supplemental funds to increase their food purchasing ability (USDA/FNS, 2015). This will result in a shift in the demand curve of the poor from D_p to D^* and likewise shift total demand from TD to TD'. This increase in total demand causes the price to increase to p^1. Although the price increases, the shift in demand due to increased income causes food consumption by the poor to increase to q^*. In this case, q^* represents a per capita consumption level of 2,400 calories, indicating that the increase in income was sufficient to bring the poor up to the minimum required intake of calories. Simultaneously, because of the price increase, food consumption by the rich decreases to q', a level still greater than the minimum required caloric intake. Total consumption is now q^1. It is important to note that as a result of this income effect, expenditures on food by the poor increase despite higher prices, while expenditures on food by the rich may increase or decrease due to the higher prices depending on their price elasticity of demand. Clearly, if q^* satisfies the minimal food requirement constraint, then it is met by income growth by the poor.

3. Model II – research and development

The example of research and development (R&D) examines food security from a standard supply-side perspective. Consider Figure 2, where R&D impacts food prices and food levels. Initial supply is given by S and total demand by TD. At the equilibrium price p^0, the poor consume q_p of food given demand D_p, the rich consume q_r given demand by the rich of D_r, and the total consumption is q^0. Assume that q_p is below the minimum required caloric intake level of 2,400 calories.

The effect of R&D is to shift supply from S to S'. As a result of this R&D-induced shift, the price of food decreases from p^0 to p^1. The quantity of food consumed by the poor increases to q^*, which is the minimum nutritional diet with respect to caloric intake. The new total consumption is q^1.

Of significance here is the impact of R&D without changes in demand. As R&D shifts the supply curve to S', the poor are able to meet their minimum caloric requirement. However, as other factors impact demand, these R&D impacts may be negated. Another important point is the impact on the rich. While the rich consume in excess of the minimum caloric requirement prior to the R&D supply shift, their consumption is even greater afterward.

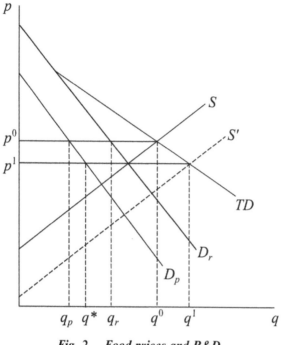

Fig. 2. Food prices and R&D.

4. Model III: R&D and population growth

In Figure 3, we discuss R&D in the context of population growth. R&D causes supply to shift from S to S' as in Model II, but at the same time the population of the poor increases, shifting their demand from D_p to D^* causing total demand to increase from TD to TD'. However, on a per capita basis, food consumption by the poor need not increase even though total food consumption has increased.

Because of the R&D effect, the food price remains at p^0 in the presence of an output increase from q^0 to q^1. Because of population growth, R&D cannot narrow the so-called food gap in Model III. In fact, Koo and Taylor (2015) show a world per capita calorie surplus in 2012 of 5.1 calories, and then forecast per capita deficits of 48.4 in 2025 and 361.1 in 2050. Their forecast is consistent with the Malthusian prediction that population growth would eventually outstrip that of R&D, eventually resulting in food deficits. Even in the case of food deficits, Model III shows that those with entitlements (the rich) can access food, while those without entitlements (the poor) cannot access adequate calories.

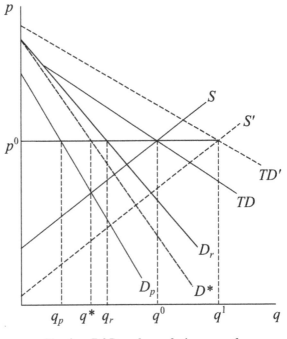

Fig. 3. R&D and population growth.

5. Model IV: calories and protein

In Figure 4, the price for calories is P^0 and total consumption is Q^1. The nutritionally required amount of calories needed by the poor is Q^0 (Figure 4A). While Koo and Taylor (2015) discuss calorie supply and demand, they do not include protein and other elements that make up the nutritional diet. Consider, for example, the protein requirement for a nutritional diet, wherein the equilibrium price is p^1, and q^1 is consumed by the poor (Figure 4B). Suppose that Q^0 in Figure 4A is 2,400 calories and q^* in Figure 4B is 56 grams of protein, the respective nutritional requirements for calories and protein. In this case, the poor have adequate calories but are deficient in protein. To achieve the optimal protein intake of q^*, the price of protein would have to fall to p^1. This could come about through the use of subsidies, income supplements, or other mechanisms.

As noted, we assume that q^* denotes the 56 grams of protein recommended according to US standards for the nutritional diet of a 19- to 30-year-old male. Subsidization of protein-rich foods for the poor consumer shifts his demand outward from D_p to D^* and simultaneously shifts total demand outward from TD to TD'. Although this increases

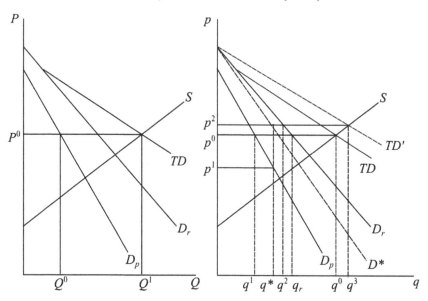

Fig. 4. Calories combined with protein: (a) calories; (b) protein.

the market price of protein-rich products to p^2, the consumption level of the poor consumer increases from the suboptimal level of q^1 to the recommended level of q^*. The rich consumer decreases his consumption of protein-rich foods from q_r to q^2 given the higher market price.

6. Optimizing nutrient intake

Optimizing individual nutrient intake has to consider combinations of food groups, substitution possibilities, and factors such as age and activity level. For example, a 19- to 30-year-old male needs approximately 2,400 calories and 56 grams of protein per day in addition to other vitamins and minerals, but this is not necessarily the case for a 70-year-old male. If a food subsidy is put in place, the increased intake of protein-rich foods also adds excess calories to the consumer's diet. The same dilemma is faced with respect to increasing consumption of fresh fruits and vegetables to achieve an adequate intake of vitamins and nutrients. The interdependence of food groups in simultaneously providing an adequate diet (with respect to energy, proteins, and other vitamins and nutrients) highlights the fragile nature of existence for those living in poverty.

This is not unlike the approach that has been taken in balancing rations in the animal husbandry industry (Henry & Morrison, 1916). Livestock rations are constructed based on an understanding of the required nutrients for a particular animal given the desired objective. For example, a 660-pound feeder calf requires a different set of calories, proteins, and nutrients to achieve a particular level of growth in a maintenance ration than is the case for a ration for a lactating dairy cow. Examples of these types of rations are presented in Tables 1 and 2. Along with these requirements, the nutrient makeup of the available feedstuffs must be known. Various different roughages, grains, and other nutrient sources are available to the producer to achieve the desired nutrient mix. Given that the nutrient makeup of each of the sources will vary across regions and over time, care must be taken to continually evaluate these nutrient sources to ensure achieving the appropriate ration. As can be seen, meeting the basic technical requirements of either the appropriate

Table 1.   Ration for 660-pound feedlot calves and yearlings (expected daily gain of 2.0 to 2.5 pounds)[a]

Ingredient	Ration Number			
	1	2	3	4
Corn, cracked	10	–	20	53
Ground ear corn	–	60	–	–
Corn silage	86	–	65	–
Legume–grass hay[b]	–	36	11	44
Protein supplement[c]	4	4	4	3
Total	100	100	100	100
Calculated analysis				
(1) As-fed basis				
Crude protein (%)	4.50	10.30	6.10	10.90
Total digestible nutrients (%)	30.30	64.90	39.00	66.50
Net energy – maintenance (Mcal/kg)	0.67	1.45	0.88	1.52
Calcium (%)	0.42	0.87	0.54	0.92
Net energy – growth (Mcal/kg)	0.19	0.42	0.26	0.42
Phosphorus (%)	0.16	0.30	0.20	0.32
Dry matter (%)	40.80	88.20	52.60	88.90
(2) Dry matter basis				
Crude protein (%)	11.00	11.70	11.60	12.30
Total digestible nutrients (%)	74.30	73.60	74.10	74.80
Net energy – maintenance (Mcal/kg)	1.64	1.64	1.67	1.71
Calcium (%)	1.03	0.99	1.03	1.03
Net energy – growth (Mcal/kg)	0.47	0.48	0.49	0.47
Phosphorus (%)	0.39	0.34	0.38	0.36

Source: Jurgens (1982, p. 293).

[a]Formulations are on an as-fed basis. Calves and yearlings should consume approximately 2.25%–2.75% of their body weight as daily dry matter. Yearling stocker cattle will generally consume greater quantities of daily dry matter (resulting in greater daily gain) than grain-background calves. Salt may be fed free choice with all rations.

[b]A typical legume–grass hay mixture may be alfalfa-brome or Clover–Timothy. Haylage will substitute for hay on an equal basis if corrected for moisture content.

[c]Protein supplement should contain approximately 30%–35% crude protein (up to one-third of the protein may be derived from nonprotein nitrogen), 2.75%–3.25% calcium, and 1.5%–2.0% phosphorus.

Table 2.   Ration for lactating dairy cows[a]

Ingredient	Ration Number			
	1	2	3	4
Corn, ground	–	70	–	–
Ground ear corn	92	–	85	74
Oats, ground or rolled	–	28	–	–
Urea[b]	–	–	1	–
Soybean meal[c]	6	–	12	–
Soybeans, cracked	–	–	–	24
Dicalcium phosphate[d]	1	1	1	1
Trace mineral salt and vitamin premix	1	1	1	1
Total	100	100	100	100
Calculated analysis				
(1) As-fed basis				
Crude protein (%)	9.90	9.50	14.80	15.20
Total digestible nutrients (%)	71.70	74.60	71.10	73.90
Net energy – lactation (Mcal/kg)	1.60	1.74	1.58	1.67
Calcium (%)	0.29	0.25	0.30	0.32
Phosphorus (%)	0.45	0.50	0.47	0.51
Dry matter (%)	87.40	88.50	87.70	88.40
(2) Dry matter basis				
Crude protein (%)	11.30	10.70	16.90	17.20
Total digestible nutrients (%)	82.00	84.30	81.10	83.60
Net energy – lactation (Mcal/kg)	1.83	1.97	1.80	1.89
Calcium (%)	0.33	0.28	0.34	0.36
Phosphorus (%)	0.52	0.56	0.54	0.58

Source: Jurgens (1982, p. 317).
[a]Formulations are on an as-fed basis.
[b]Urea may be included up to 1% of the concentrate mix to supply protein.
[c]Other high-protein feeds or commercial supplements can be substituted for soybean meal on a protein basis.
[d]Other high Ca-P mineral mixes as steamed bone meal or commercial mixtures can replace dicalcium phosphate.

growth or maintenance ration is an ongoing task. An added consideration for the producer is to achieve this minimum set of nutrients at a least cost basis.

Dieticians apply the same basic principles when seeking to guarantee that at-risk groups receive the minimum nutritional diet given their respective stages of life. For example, federally subsidized school lunch programs are designed to guarantee that school-aged youth receive the energy, protein, and nutrients necessary for their growing bodies. However, if the menu contains foods that children will not eat, alternatives must be found that will still achieve the dietary objectives. This is similar to the use of molasses to increase the palatability of a livestock ration. The sweetener ingredient can encourage consumption of the ration, yet it must be added in concert with other inputs to guarantee that all nutrient levels fall within desired parameters.

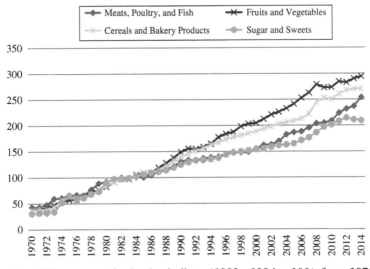

Fig. 5. ***US consumer food price indices (1982–1984 = 100) from 1970 to 2014. Source: USBLS (1985).***

Food prices play an important role in determining what kinds of foods consumers choose. This is especially true for those consumers who are at or below the poverty line. An example of the role of prices in either encouraging or discouraging the contribution of a particular food group in a consumer's diet is provided in Figure 5. US consumer price indices from 1970 to 2014 are provided for four food groups: (1) meats, poultry, and fish; (2) fruits and vegetables; (3) cereals and bakery products; and (4) sugar and sweets. During this period, the fruits and vegetables group becomes relatively more costly than the other food groups. This would suggest that consumers near or below the poverty line likely found it more difficult to obtain the necessary vitamins and nutrients provided by this food group. Simultaneously, as the sugar and sweets category has become relatively less expensive, those same consumers may have shifted consumption to a more affordable food category, thereby failing to obtain the complete range of vitamins, minerals, and other nutrients necessary for the recommended nutritious diet.

7. Summary, conclusions, and future considerations

The food security of an individual, household, or country is influenced by both effective demand for and availability of food. This chapter has examined simultaneously the impact of food demand on food security through income growth, the impact of food supply on food security through R&D, and has modeled population growth and technological development to determine their impacts on food security.

Model I shows the impact of an income supplement for the poor, in which a rightward shift in food demand by the poor increases their per capita consumption. However, this causes prices to increase for all consumers. Provided the number of poor does not increase, an increase in income will move those portions of society within the food insecure group toward food security. A sufficient increase in income would allow them to achieve food security.

Model II shows the impact of a food supply shift resulting from R&D. A rightward shift in the supply of food results in downward pressure on food supply to both the rich and poor. While this moves those who are food insecure toward or even beyond food security, those previously food secure groups can now consume at levels in excess of a secure level.

Model III considers the impact of population growth combined with an investment in R&D. Although population growth tends to put upward pressure on food prices, R&D tends to mitigate those effects. While our example shows levels of population growth and R&D that had no impact on food prices, proportionally different levels of growth in population and R&D will impact prices positively or negatively depending on whether R&D trails or outstrips population growth.

These three scenarios provide an indication as to the impacts of income, population growth, and R&D on food security. But these models fail to provide any indication as to the impact these factors have on the dietary makeup of the population with respect to calories, proteins, and other micronutrients. Model IV highlights the difficulty in formulating an optimal diet that meets the minimum nutritional diet for only calories and protein. Different foods contain calories, proteins, and micronutrients in differing proportions. This means that changes in relative food prices will often alter consumers' nutrient intake with respect to the minimum nutritional diet; sometimes this may be for the better, but sometimes it is for the worse.

Diverse needs and preferences within families, communities, and populations preclude the formulation of a one-size-fits-all diet in respect to adequate nutrition. This highlights the challenge to policy makers as they consider the means to provide food and nutrition security to the populace. This dilemma can be seen through the controversy related to EBT cards in the United States (USDA/FNS, 2015). Welfare recipients are given supplemental funds to increase their food purchasing ability, increasing their demand. However, many question whether purchases with these funds should be limited to specific food categories that best meet the nutritional needs of the recipients.

It is clear that entitlements and availability are key elements that influence food security. While their relationship to availability has been recognized since the time of Malthus (1798), entitlements also constrain the possible fulfillment of food security. While the availability component of food security can never be guaranteed, continued investments in agricultural R&D (along with a well-functioning agricultural economy) remain an important part in achieving sufficient food availability. At the same time, while the entitlement component of food security can never be guaranteed, a healthy and growing economy should provide access to trade-based, production-based, and own-labor entitlements to the greatest percentage of the population possible. As Sen (1981) discussed with respect to transfer entitlements, consumption subsidies and income supplements can and should be used to assist the portion of society that does not have entitlements sufficient to meet their minimum nutritional diet. Guaranteeing access to a minimum nutritional diet for all, particularly children, contributes to the development of human capital which, in turn, contributes to future economic vitality, entitlements, and food security.

It is interesting to place this chapter within the context of recent population projections by the United Nations (UN). The UN now predicts that India will surpass China's population growth by 2022, rather than by 2028, as previously forecasted (Gladstone, 2015). In its 2015 revision, the UN Department of Economic Social Affairs stated that China's population is 1.38 billion compared with 1.3 billion in India. In 7 years, the population of each of these countries is expected to reach 1.4 billion. The report also said that the global population of 7.3 billion is expected to reach 9.7 billion by 2050, slightly larger than the 9.6 billion forecasted just 2 years ago. Much of the overall increase in population is expected in countries with high child birth rates, mainly in Africa, or in countries with already large populations. Half of the growth is expected to come from nine countries, including India, Nigeria, Pakistan, and Ethiopia. By contrast, the populations of 48 countries are expected to decrease during the same time period, mainly in Europe. Our chapter clearly raises questions as to the low probability of an adequate food supply matching population growth. It would perhaps take a miracle for productivity to increase as fast as population growth. And if it did, there would still be a food shortage as there is now. If there were an increase in per capita consumption of nutritional foods by the poor that coincided with the population increase, the food would have to come from a reduction in consumption of food in rich countries.

References

Centers for Disease Control and Prevention [CDC]. (2012). *Nutrition for everyone: Basics: Protein*. Retrieved from http://www.cdc.gov/nutrition/%20everyone/basics/protein.html

Gladstone, R. (2015). UN sees an earlier lead in India's population rise. *New York Times*, July 30, p. A4.

Henry, W. A., & Morrison, F. B. (1916). *Feeds and feeding: A handbook for the student and stockman*. Englewood Cliffs, NJ: Prentice-Hall Press.

Jurgens, M. A. (1982). *Animal feeding and nutrition* (5th ed.). Dubuque, IA: Kendall Hunt.

Koo, W. W., & Taylor, R. (2015). Who will feed the growing populations in the developing nations? Implications of bioenergy production. In A. Schmitz, P. L. Kennedy, & T. G. Schmitz (Eds.), *Food security in an uncertain world: An international perspective* (Vol. 15). Frontiers of Economics and Globalization. Bingley, UK: Emerald Group Publishing Limited.

Malthus, T. R. (1798). *An essay on the principle of population.* London: J. Johnson Publishing.

Osmani, S. R. (1993). *The entitlement approach to famine: An assessment.* Helsinki: United Nations University World Institute for Development Economics Research (UNU/WIDER). Retrieved from http://www.wider.unu.edu/publications/working-papers/previous/en_GB/wp-107/

President's Commission. (1969). *Poverty amid plenty: The American paradox.* Washington, DC: Government Printing Office.

Sen, A. (1981). *Poverty and famines: An essay on entitlement and deprivation.* Oxford: Oxford University Press.

United States Bureau of Labor Statistics [USBLS]. (1985). *US consumer food price indices: 1982–1984.* Washington, DC: USBLS.

United States Department of Agriculture [USDA]. (2015). *How many empty calories can I have?* Washington, DC: USDA. Retrieved from http://www.choosemyplate.gov

United States Department of Agriculture, Food and Nutrition Service [USDA/FNS]. (2015). *Supplemental nutrition assistance program (SNAP).* Retrieved from http://www.fns.usda.gov/snap/supplemental-nutrition-assistance-program-snap

2

Trade and Food Security: Links, Processes, and Prospects [☆]

Ekaterina Krivonos, Jamie Morrison and Eleonora Canigiani

Trade and Markets Division, Food and Agriculture Organization of the United Nations (FAO), Rome, 00153, Italy
E-mail address: ekaterina.krivonos@fao.org, jamie.morrison@fao.org and eleonora.canigiani@fao.org

Abstract

Purpose — We examine the links between trade and food security, the processes that shape countries' trade-related interventions in pursuit of food security objectives, and the prospects for better situating trade and food security in debates related to the use of trade policy.

Methodology/approach — Building on the previous and ongoing work of Food and Agriculture Organization of the United Nations and others, this chapter revisits the interaction between trade and food security, with the objective of contributing to a more informed discussion of policy choices and improved incorporation of food security concerns into trade-related decision-making processes.

Findings — The linkages between trade and food security have been subject to intense debate both at the national and international level. Furthermore, these linkages have become central to many trade-related discussions, including the ongoing multilateral trade negotiations at the World Trade Organization. However, the specific context of the relationship between trade and food security, and of the role of trade in securing improvements in food security, have made it difficult to craft a global framework that ensures that the pursuit of national objectives is compatible with reducing food insecurity at the global level.

Practical implications — As the global governance system undergoes a transition, the roles and responsibilities for food security are being

---

[☆] The views expressed herein are those of the authors and do not necessarily reflect the views of Food and Agriculture Organization of the United Nations (FAO).

Frontiers of Economics and Globalization
Volume 15   ISSN: 1574-8715
DOI: 10.1108/S1574-871520150000015002

redefined within a more complex and interconnected global landscape whose contours are still to be fleshed out. This calls for a reflection on the multilateral trading system and on the need to strengthen the synergies with nontrade processes to enhance the role of trade in contributing to food security.

Keywords: Trade, food security, WTO

1. Introduction

A multitude of factors influence the complex relationship between increased engagement in global agricultural trade and changes in levels of food security, making it difficult to identify the relative merits of different approaches to managing trade and/or supporting agricultural sectors. The challenge remains to define exactly what countries seek when arguing for greater recognition of food security in the formulation of trade agreements. At the same time, other global processes, like those related to the post-2015 Sustainable Development Goals (SDGs), have experienced serious challenges in creating a coherent global framework that adequately addresses food security. The global governance system is undergoing a transition whereby roles and responsibilities are being redefined within a much more complex and interconnected global landscape whose contours are still to be fleshed out.

In this chapter, we examine (1) the changing trends in agricultural markets and trade; (2) the links between trade and the four dimensions of food security (availability, access, utilization, and stability), focusing on the risks and potential benefits of an expansion in trade; (3) the appropriateness of different trade and related policy measures in improving food security at different stages of development; and (4) an overview of the contentious issues in the global trade negotiations relating to agriculture as well as other global processes that are significant in ensuring that trade works for food security.

2. The changing landscape of agricultural markets

Driven by new factors affecting the demand and supply of agricultural products – most notably the rapid growth of emerging economies – agricultural markets have undergone profound changes since the early 1990s. These changes have major implications for global demand for food, rapid urbanization, climate change, biofuel policies, and elevated food prices.

The higher level of food prices since 2006 has marked a new context for agriculture and food security (Figure 1). Food prices increased steeply

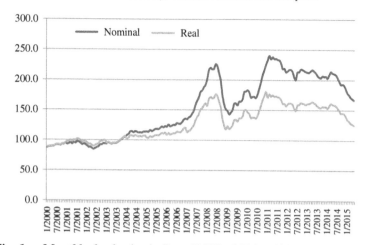

Fig. 1. Monthly food price indices (2002–2004 = 100). Source: FAO (http://www.fao.org/worldfoodsituation/foodpricesindex/en/).

during 2006–2008, followed by other spikes in 2010 and 2011, contributing to growing food import bills of developing countries that engage in net food importing.

Population growth in developing regions and economic expansion of the major emerging economies are two key factors driving the increasing global demand for food. World population is expected to grow from 7.2 billion in 2015 to 9.5 billion by 2050, which according to the Food and Agriculture Organization of the United Nations (FAO) requires the production of 60% more food (Alexandratos & Bruinsma, 2012). Coupled with rising incomes, this growth has led to higher food demand and a shift in consumption patterns toward higher protein diets.

However, the positive trend of reduced food insecurity in most parts of the world coincides with a greater concern for nutritional aspects as the massive growth in the consumption of cheaper food oils (such as soy and palm oils) and processed foods raises concerns about increasing obesity and related diseases (Hawkes, 2015).

On the supply side, a remarkable transformation in patterns of production and trade is occurring, with developing countries accounting for an increasingly larger share of agricultural production, value-added, and trade. Between 1995 and 2012, the share of high-income countries in the world's value-added agriculture declined from 39.9% to 31.7% (World Bank, 2015).

As shown in Figure 2, Africa, Asia, Eastern and Central Europe, Latin America, and the Caribbean are all projected to continue increasing agricultural production, while growth rates in Western Europe and North America are expected to decrease (Organisation for Economic Co-operation Development and Food and Agriculture Organization of the United Nations [OECD-FAO], 2015). Latin America has become the

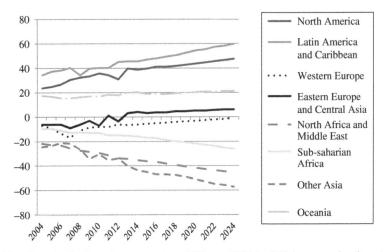

Fig. 2. *Agricultural net exports, billions (2014–2024 are projections).*
Source: *OECD/FAO agricultural outlook, 2014–2024 (Embargoed until July 1, 2015).*

largest net exporter of food with significant production growth outstripping increases in consumption. Driven primarily by grain and oilseed exports from Russia, Ukraine, and Kazakhstan, Eastern Europe and Central Asia have shifted from being net-importing regions to being net-exporting regions.

Primarily due to a high population growth rate, sub-Saharan Africa is becoming a rapidly growing net-importing region. In the Middle East and North Africa, where domestic agricultural production cannot keep pace with demand, these countries are also becoming rapidly growing net-importing regions. Driven by China's evolution to net-importing status for agricultural commodities, Asia is the fastest growing net importer, with a sharp increase after 2007.

3. Trade and food security: conceptual linkages

Through imports and exports, trade has direct implications for food security. Imports can stimulate productivity-enhancing changes and innovations in domestic production and associated supply chains, while exports can improve incomes through forward and backward linkages. Table 1 examines the links and effects of trade on food security availability, access, utilization, and stability (Shaw, 2007).

Greater involvement in trade can have both positive and negative consequences for food security through the effect on relative prices of goods

Table 1. Four dimensions of food security

Availability	Physical availability of food. Food availability addresses the supply side of food security and is determined by the level of food production, stock levels, and net trade.
Access	Economic and physical access to food. Economic access is determined by disposable income, food prices, and the provision of and access to social support.
Utilization	Commonly understood as the way the body makes the most of various nutrients in the food. Sufficient energy and nutrient intake by individuals are the result of good care and feeding practices, food preparation, diversity of the diet, and intrahousehold distribution of food.
Stability	Stability of the other three dimensions over time.

Source: Shaw (2007).

and factors of production (Table 2). Domestic production, total food supply, price, employment, income, and government revenue are the key variables directly affected by trade and play important roles in determining physical and economic access to food by populations experiencing malnutrition. They also affect the quality and nutritional value of food available to consumers. These linkages and the associated transmission channels depend on the characteristics of a country's economy, including level of economic and institutional development, comparative advantage in agriculture (specifically, whether the country is a net food importer or exporter), the structure of the domestic market, and traits of agricultural producers. The latter characteristics are important in differentiating between countries in which smallholders account for the majority of the agricultural output and those in which large commercial farms drive production (FAO, 2003, 2006).

With regard to food availability, an important question is whether food imports displace or complement domestic production. As countries become more open to international trade in agricultural products, they become more exposed and potentially more vulnerable to sudden changes in global agricultural markets. For example, import surges (sudden increases in volumes of imports from one year to the next) could trigger a disruption of domestic production with disastrous impacts on domestic farmers and workers (loss of jobs, reduced incomes, and foregone multiplier effects in the economy that can have negative consequences for food security). The potential for disruptions has been used in supporting arguments both for a more cautious approach to agricultural trade liberalization and for the establishment of effective safeguards in new trade agreements.

A contrasting view is that increases in imports are largely demand driven. An analysis of production and imports in developing countries by Diaz-Bonilla (2015) indicates that causality runs from changes in

Table 2. ***The possible effects of trade on the four dimensions of food security***

Availability	*Possible positive effects*	*Possible negative effects*
	• Trade liberalization boosts imports and increases the quantity and variety of food available.	• For net food exporting countries, higher prices in international markets divert part of production previously available for domestic consumption to exports, potentially reducing domestic availability of staple foods.
	• Dynamic effects on domestic production: greater competition from abroad may trigger improvements in productivity through greater investment, R&D, technology spillover.	• For net food importers, domestic producers unable to compete with imports are likely to curtail production, reducing domestic supplies, foregoing important multiplier effects of agricultural activities in rural economies.
Access	*Possible positive effects*	*Possible negative effects*
	• For net food importing countries, food prices typically decrease when border protection is reduced.	• For net food exporters, the domestic prices of exportable products may increase.
	• In the competitive sectors, incomes are likely to increase as the result of greater market access for exports.	• Employment and incomes in sensitive import-competing sectors may decline.
	• Input prices are likely to decrease.	
	• Macroeconomic benefits of trade openness such as export growth and inflow of foreign direct investment support growth and higher employment which boost incomes.	
Utilization	*Possible positive effects*	*Possible negative effects*
	• Greater variety of available foods through imports may promote a more balanced diet and accommodate different preferences and tastes.	• Greater reliance on imported foods is often associated with an increase in consumption of cheaper and more readily available high-calorie/low nutritional value foods.
	• Food safety and quality may improve if exporters have more advanced national control systems in place or if international standards are applied more rigorously.	• Prioritization of commodity exports diverts land and resources from traditional and indigenous foods, often superior from a nutritional point of view.
Stability	*Possible positive effects*	*Possible negative effects*
	• Imports reduce seasonal effect on food availability and prices to consumers.	• Open trade policies reduce policy space to deal with short-term market shocks.
	• Imports mitigate local production risks.	• Vulnerability to changes in trade policy by exporters, such as export bans.
	• Shallow versus deep markets: global markets are less prone to policy or weather-induced shocks.	• Sectors at earlier stages of development may become more susceptible to price shocks and/or import surges.

Source: FAO, IFAD, and WFP (2015).

production to changes in imports in Least Developed Countries (LDCs) and Low-Income Food-Deficit Countries (LIFDCs) (the data fail to support reverse causality). This lends support to the hypothesis that trade has a stabilizing effect on supplies: shortfalls in production are compensated by increased imports to stabilize domestic consumption while, in periods of abundant domestic output, imports diminish (Diaz-Bonilla, 2015).

Primarily determined by the purchasing power of consumers, access to food is affected by trade through its impact on prices, employment, income, and government budgets for social protection. One of the most direct effects for net food importing countries is the decrease in food prices from reductions in border protection. However, a common concern is that employment opportunities in sensitive import-competing sectors may also decline and that the role of the sector in supporting the processes of structural transformation will become weakened.

The critical question in relation to utilization, which primarily concerns nutritional aspects, is how trade and globalization affect diets. While some argue that the prevalence of cheaper, less nutritious foods such as vegetable oils, sugars, and flours — as well as highly processed foods and drinks — has worsened the nutritional status of populations in both developed and developing countries, others argue that globalization has led to greater food variety and better food safety (Hawkes, 2015). Understanding the relationship between trade and nutrition will help clarify whether adjustments are needed in the way food systems operate to make trade more conducive to better nutrition and healthier lives.

Stability is an issue closely linked to volatility in agricultural markets. Beyond the narrow understanding of shallow versus deep markets and the pooling of risks associated with production shortfalls (weather, conflict, or policies), the critical question remains whether or not trade makes markets more volatile. This means understanding the impacts of trade on overall economic and political instability and the likelihood of crises. A separate inquiry would analyze the risks of trade-induced specialization for environmental sustainability and plant health (e.g., as a result of trade triggering a move away from diversified crop production and toward monoculture-dominated agriculture).

4. Trade policy from the national perspective

Country case studies help shed light on the different ways trade openness can affect food security. An analysis undertaken by FAO (2006) has assessed the impact of economic reforms affecting agricultural trade on food security in developing countries. The analyses of individual countries such as Ghana, Nigeria, Uganda, China, Chile, Guyana, and Peru show fairly positive food security outcomes, while the consequences in other countries such as Cameroon, Malawi, and India appear more ambiguous.

For the remaining countries (Kenya, Morocco, Senegal, Tanzania, and Guatemala), food security outcomes appear to be disappointing.

The mixed evidence is confirmed in a comprehensive review by McCorriston et al. (2013) on trade liberalization and food security. The authors conclude that of the 34 studies, 13 report improvements in the utilized food security indicators, 10 show declines, and the other 11 produce mixed results, with food security varying across populations, regions, and time. McCorriston et al. (2013) conclude that the results are mixed because trade liberalization is part of a broader policy program of reforms.

Indeed, research shows that countries supporting the primary sector tend to be better off in most dimensions of food security (availability, access, and utilization), while taxation is detrimental to food security (Magrini, Montalbano, Nenci, & Salvatici, 2014). However, the research also shows that excessive protection leads to poor performance in all dimensions of food security.

4.1. Food price spikes and policy reactions

As food import bills increased significantly following the 2008 increases in food prices and the waning of confidence in global markets as a reliable source of affordable food, many developing countries adopted policies in an attempt to influence domestic prices directly through border measures and price controls as well as to create incentives for increasing domestic supply. These policies were coupled with social protection measures to reach poor consumers.

Among trade policy instruments, export restrictions and the elimination of import tariffs were the preferred policies to address food security concerns following the first food price spike. Border measures are particularly attractive for policy makers because they quickly contain the negative effects of global price increases on domestic consumers. Moreover, export taxes are seen as measures for boosting fiscal revenues, especially for countries experiencing account difficulties as a result of the global recession triggered by the 2008 financial crisis.

Tariff reduction or elimination can help lower the domestic price of an imported good. However, in most net food importing countries, tariffs on food products are already low, so reducing such tariffs has only a minimal impact on domestic prices.

Export restrictions (export taxes or quantitative restrictions) have been introduced by some net food exporting countries to guarantee sufficient supplies to domestic markets in the short term. These measures can constrain increases in domestic prices, at least in the short run, by reducing or banning exports, even while increasing supplies to the domestic market. However, by reducing producer prices, these measures also create disincentives to expand production, and thus can reduce supplies in the medium term. Moreover, at the global level and when put in place by several exporters simultaneously, export restrictions reduce global supplies and exacerbate the uncertainty and volatility in global food markets (FAO, 2009).

The experience in developing countries (e.g., Latin America) shows that policy consistency and transparency play an important role in determining the outcomes of trade policies applied during periods of higher global food prices (FAO, 2014a). In some developing countries, export restrictions initially put in place for a temporary period of time have been extended, undermining producers in their ability to make informed production and marketing decisions. This contributes to an uncertain policy environment, reducing incentives and ultimately leading farmers away from growing crops affected by frequent policy changes.

4.2. The changing patterns of domestic support

In the decades leading up to the Uruguay Round, high levels of producer support in OECD countries contributed to the long period of suppressed world food prices. The Uruguay Round focused on reducing distortions in the global agricultural markets by curbing domestic support in the OECD countries. However, the burden on government budgets was reduced as these countries reduced more distortive forms of domestic support as part of their commitments to the WTO. Driven by the larger fiscal space created by growth as well as the greater priority given to the agricultural sector as an important element for food security, developing countries (particularly emerging economies) increased their levels of support (Figure 3).

Measured by the Nominal Rate of Assistance, the percentage of domestic prices received by farmers exceeded those in the international markets. Developing countries on the whole turned taxation of agriculture into various levels of subsidization (Figure 4) (Nelgen, 2015).

Price supports and input subsidies have had a major impact on world agriculture. Developing countries use input subsidies to alleviate constraints on farmers' access to credit and technology as well as constraints on their access to risk management instruments. Both of these constraints lead to suboptimal levels of production (Dorward & Morrison, 2015).

However, both price support and the subsidization of inputs have constituted arguably inefficient approaches to supporting producer incomes. Conventional wisdom says targeted nontrade policies for stimulating agricultural production and improving food security are preferable. However, there are concerns that many countries, in particular low-income ones, may not have the institutional capacity to apply such instruments. Some recourse to the levers of trade policy or subsidies might be necessary,

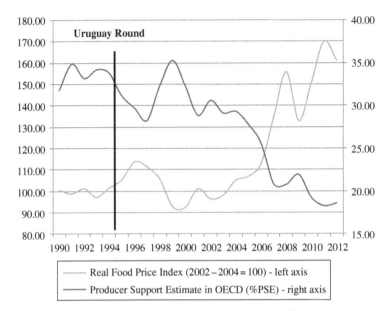

Fig. 3. *Food price index and producer support in OECD.* **Source:** *Authors' calculations based on FAO and OECD data.*

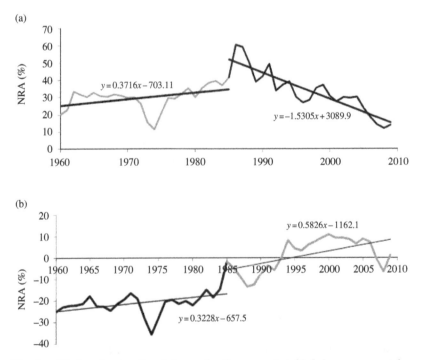

Fig. 4. *National rate of assistance for farmers: (a) high-income countries; (b) developing countries.* **Source:** *Nelgen (2015).*

particularly if the objective is to boost productivity and achieve higher levels of agricultural development. Dorward and Morrison (2015) argue that price support and input subsidies can provide incentives for increasing production and investments in agriculture as well as in rural infrastructure, triggering market transformations.

To address their development needs in a consistent and systematic manner, countries must take a better overview of available policy instruments and weigh the pros and cons of the different measures, including cost and the relative ease of implementation and monitoring.

With regard to agriculture, the policy mix will need to take into account the specific situation of each country. For example, the policy set in countries where the rural population accounts for a large proportion of the inhabitants, and where agricultural production is dominated by smallholder farmers, will need to be quite different than in countries where the agricultural sector is more concentrated in large farms and is both more capital- and technology-intensive. Similarly, measures that provide opportunities and incentives to increase production are preferable if smallholder producers constitute the majority of food insecure households, whereas measures that provide trade openness and targeted income support for producers are preferable if the urban poor constitutes the majority of food insecure households.

Understanding the ultimate objectives of policies (trade, agricultural, or other) is paramount. Expected gains, as well as distributional effects, should be ex ante clarified, with winners and losers clearly identified along with adjustment measures (such as skill development and job placement for those negatively affected). For example, when undertaking reforms as part of trade negotiations, countries must have evidence concerning the specific consequences of assuming new trade or regulatory obligations. This is necessary for making the process of reforms as transparent as possible and for making policy choices on the basis of sound analysis.

5. Trade and food security in global processes

5.1. Food security in international trade negotiations

Agriculture provides both direct and indirect benefits to society that go beyond merely producing commodities. These benefits include food security, ecological service, employment, and rural lifestyle (Clapp, in press). Within the international trade rules, agriculture is treated as an exceptional sector of society (WTO, 1995).

The WTO Agreement on Agriculture (AoA) sets the rules for agricultural trade, covering market access, domestic support, and export subsidies (WTO, 1995). With regard to market access, many developing countries retain relatively high-bound tariff rates in basic foodstuffs, although the applied rates are low. While the option of applying tariffs to the bound levels is compatible with WTO commitments, in practice this policy may have limitations, especially for net food importing countries – while protecting domestic producers of similar products, higher tariffs imply a welfare loss for domestic consumers, who pay a higher price. However, such measures could be justified if customs revenues generated by tariffs provide social protection to food insecure households while allowing domestic producers to benefit from higher domestic prices, generating sufficient volumes and improving the quality of their products.

The domestic support provisions in the AoA and commitments made by individual countries with regard to the Aggregate Measurement of Support (AMS) have implications for the range of policies these countries can pursue. Some policies are exempted from the commitments to limit agricultural support, subject to the rules and criteria set out in the relevant provisions of the AoA. Exempted support includes green box measures that meet the fundamental requirement that they have no – or at most minimal – trade-distorting effects or effects on production and that they satisfy the specific criteria outlined in Annex 2 of the AoA. Some examples of policies exempted from AMS commitments under the green box include general services,[1] public stockholding for food security purposes, domestic food aid, decoupled income support, income insurance, and income safety nets. Developing countries enjoy additional flexibilities under the development provisions (Article 6.2, AoA).

Nonetheless, some developing countries have expressed concerns that the current trade rules place too many restraints on their ability to achieve both the agricultural development and the food security objectives. To what extent WTO agreements provide sufficient and appropriate policy space for developing countries to fight malnutrition is the subject of intense discussion.

One of the debated food security issues is domestic support for public stockholding. India has argued that the procurement of public stocks from low-income, resource-poor farmers at prices higher than the market price[2] constitutes an essential part of a government's effort to address food security. As a result of intense negotiations, the Bali decision on public stockholding for food security purposes has ruled (as a so-called

---

[1] This includes research, training, pest and disease control, marketing and promotion, infrastructure, farmer settlement, land reform, rural development, and rural livelihood security.

[2] Under the current rules, AoA allows an exemption from AMS calculations for expenditures on food stockholding for products that form an integral part of a food security program identified in national legislation. To become exempt food purchases by the government must be made at current market prices while sales from food security stocks must be made at no less than the current domestic market price for the product and quality in question. Otherwise, a price gap calculation involving the administered price has to be included in AMS calculations.

peace clause) that until a permanent solution is found, WTO members cannot challenge the compliance of a developing country member state. A number of transparency obligations and safeguard provisions have been introduced in an effort to limit the negative effects that acquired stocks might have on the food security of other WTO members and on global markets. As a condition, countries must ensure that stocks procured under such programs do not adversely affect the food security of other WTO members, although it is unclear how compliance will be monitored and enforced (FAO, 2014b).

Another issue for developing countries that has not yet been resolved in the WTO is the Special Safeguard Mechanism (SSM), which allows developing countries to raise tariffs temporarily to prevent sudden and potentially harmful import surges. The disruptions caused by import shocks have been used in supporting arguments both for a more cautious approach to agricultural trade liberalization and for the establishment of effective safeguards in new trade agreements. Negotiations on the modalities for the SSM have been particularly difficult, with some countries arguing for an effective user-friendly instrument and other countries arguing that without significant constraints such an instrument could be used in ways that disrupt trade. Moreover, some countries are seeking exemptions from tariff reductions for products they see as important for their food security (Special Products).

Multilateral trade rules have not yet fully addressed other issues related to food security. For example, disciplines on export restrictions are rather weak and leave substantial space for exporting countries to curtail exports when food prices increase. These actions contribute to further increases in world prices and force countries that initially did not consider doing so to adapt insulating measures (Martin, 2015).

More generally, what one country perceives as a right to defend its own interests could become another country's trade distortion (Matthews, 2015). The policy one country uses to protect its agricultural sector from price volatility (and specifically the aggregate effect of all individual country actions) could have a destabilizing effect on world markets, leading to detrimental effects on poverty and food security. Martin (2015) estimates that the aggregate effects of insulating policies increase world price volatility and poverty rates.

5.2. Connecting trade and food security in global processes

The post-2015 development agenda, which includes the SDGs and the financing for development (FfD) initiatives, places great emphasis on both trade and food security. However, the linkages between trade and food security remain poorly articulated. Governance over trade and food security continues to suffer from weak connections among policy processes at all levels. Such weak connections reinforce the lack of coherence between priorities and approaches, exacerbating an already polarized policy debate.

For example, in the post-2015 global development process, food security is clearly identified as part of the SDGs, whereas trade is identified as an enabler of the SDGs while also being included among the means of implementation (MOI). The MOI specify the tasks and resource commitments for the implementation of the SDGs and are negotiated in the FfD process. This creates a potential disconnect between trade and food security in the global process, and this disconnect is also reflected in the institutional architecture that governs these issues. The SDGs are designed to create common and shared goals across sectors in an increasingly interconnected world.

The situation becomes even more complicated if we examine other relevant processes that may directly or indirectly impact the relationship between trade and food security. Direct processes include those that address the rules of international trade, international reserves, and stocking policies; the use and expansion of biofuels; the management of fisheries; investments in agricultural land; commodity speculation; and international assistance during crises and emergencies. Indirect processes include international environmental regimes, the international human rights regime, climate policies, and energy market regulation (Matthews, 2015).

Building a more coherent global framework for trade and food security is closely linked to a broader reform of global governance and the institutional architecture that supports it. Greater synergy among institutions, as well as the mechanisms and processes established to address social, economic, and environmental issues at all levels, is fundamental to achieving an ambitious agenda of shared, global goals.

The WTO occupies a distinct space in this emerging architecture of global governance, but it is unrealistic and inappropriate to expect the WTO to expand its responsibilities to cover all relevant issues. It is thus important to examine how nontrade processes might be used to agree on shared objectives and to identify the mix of policies for enhancing the role of trade in contributing to food security. In such a context, making trade policies work better for food security is a political as well as an economic challenge.

The lack of coordination and coherence among sectoral processes plays an important role in the deadlock in international policy negotiations and reinforces the polarization of views and approaches, thus making it difficult for countries to take advantage of trade agreements. Bridging policy processes across sectors and levels (i.e., building horizontal and vertical linkages) may help improve understanding and optimize the availability and use of policy space for food security in trade agreements. Stronger synergies among processes can also increase policy coherence and predictability, therefore ensuring a greater stability of policy objectives over the long term. This will help national governments define common objectives across sectors and help them decide how to balance different factors in the context of agreed global frameworks.

6. Conclusions

Those involved in the negotiation of key accords affecting trade and food security have struggled to adequately deal with the complexity and context specificity of the relationship between trade and food security. At the global level, negotiators have been unable to agree on the degree of flexibility required by countries in using trade, and related trade policies, to support national food security objectives. Negotiators have also been unable to agree on how to limit trade policies that detrimentally impact global markets and the food security status of trading partners. At the national level, the separation of policy processes related to both trade and agriculture sector development continues to limit the design and implementation of trade policies supportive of improved food security.

In this chapter, we have set out the key components of the relationship between trade and food security, the types of policies that may or may not be supportive of improved food security, and the policy processes that could influence such policies in the future. Our objective has not been to suggest a specific approach to overcome the challenges of using trade to assist in reducing food insecurity; rather, our objective has been to highlight differences of opinion about, and aspects related to, such challenges that are worthy of further research and debate.

References

Alexandratos, N., & Bruinsma, J. (2012). *World agriculture towards 2030/ 2050: The 2012 revision*. ESA Working Paper No. 12-03. FAO, Rome.

Clapp, J. (2015). *Food security and international trade: Unpacking disputed narratives*. Rome: FAO.

Diaz-Bonilla, E. (2015). *Lost in translation: The fractured conversation about trade and food security*. Rome: FAO.

Dorward, A. R., & Morrison, J. A. (2015). Heroes, villains and victims: Agricultural subsidies and their impacts on food security and poverty reduction. In G. Robinson & D. Carson (Eds.), *Handbook on the globalisation of agriculture*. Cheltenham: Edward Elgar.

Food and Agriculture Organization of the United Nations [FAO]. (2003). *Trade reforms and food security: Conceptualizing the linkages*. Rome: FAO.

Food and Agriculture Organization of the United Nations [FAO]. (2006). *Trade reforms and food security: Country case studies and synthesis.* Rome: FAO.

Food and Agriculture Organization of the United Nations [FAO]. (2009). *Guide for policy and programmatic actions at country level to address high food prices.* Rome: FAO.

Food and Agriculture Organization of the United Nations [FAO]. (2014a). *Policy responses to high food prices in Latin America and the Caribbean − Country case studies.* Rome: FAO. Retrieved from http://www.fao.org/3/a-i3909e.pdf

Food and Agriculture Organization of the United Nations [FAO]. (2014b). *The Bali package − Implications for trade and food security (FAO Trade Policy Briefs, 16).* Rome: FAO.

Food and Agriculture Organization of the United Nations, International Fund for Agricultural Development, and World Food Program [FAO, IFAD, & WFP]. (2015). *State of food insecurity in the world. The multiple dimensions of food security.* Rome: FAO.

Hawkes, C. (2015). Diet, chronic disease, and the food system: Making the links, pushing for change. In Advancing health and well-being in food systems: Strategic opportunities for funders. Compendium, Global Alliance for the Future of Food, Toronto.

Magrini, E., Montalbano, P., Nenci, S., & Salvatici, L. (2014). *Agricultural trade policies and food security: Is there a causal relationship?* Working paper n. 9/2014, Dipartimento di scienze sociali ed economiche, Sapienza Universita di Roma. Retrieved from http://www.diss.uniroma1.it/sites/default/files/GPS_Montalbanoetal_FS_9_14.pdf

Martin, W. (2015). *Food price changes, price insulation, and poverty food price changes, price insulation, and poverty.* Rome: FAO.

Matthews, A. (2015). *Articulating trade-related concerns related to food security in processes at the global levels.* Rome: FAO.

McCorriston, S., Hemming, D. J., Lamontagne-Godwin, J. D., Parr, M. J., Osborn, J., & Roberts, P. D. (2013). *What is the evidence of the impact of agricultural trade liberalization on food security in developing countries?* Retrieved from http://r4d.dfid.gov.uk/PDF/Outputs/SystematicReviews/Q11-Agri-liberalisation-2013McCorriston.pdf

Nelgen, S. (2015). *Positive or negative trends in support to agriculture?* Rome: FAO.

OECD & Food and Agriculture Organization. (2015). *OECD-FAO agricultural outlook for 2015−2024.* Paris: OECD.

Shaw, D. J. (2007). *World food security: A history since 1945.* New York, NY: Palgrave Macmillan.

World Bank. (2015). *World development indicators data.* Retrieved from http://data.worldbank.org/data-catalog/world-development-indicators

World Trade Organization [WTO]. (1995). *Agreement on agriculture.* Geneva: WTO.

3

Macroeconomic Policies and Food Security

Eugenio Díaz-Bonilla

Markets, Trade, and Institutions Division, International Food Policy Research Institute (IFPRI), Washington, DC, 20006, USA
E-mail address: e.diaz-bonilla@cgiar.org

Abstract

Purpose — This chapter places the discussion of trade and food security in a more general macroeconomic context.

Methodology/approach — This chapter uses historical analysis to briefly trace the debate on economy-wide policies, starting with the 1943 United Nations (UN) Conference on Food and Agriculture that led to the creation of the Food and Agriculture Organization of the United Nations in 1945. A general economic framework is used to organize the different channels through which macroeconomic policies may affect food and nutrition security.

Research implications — Examples of monetary, financial, fiscal, and exchange rate policies are presented, along with their implications for food and nutrition security.

Practical implications — The current debates about trade and food security must be placed in the context of the overall macroeconomic framework: a single trade policy may have different impacts depending on its interactions with other macroeconomic policies and structural factors.

Keywords: Macroeconomics, trade, food security, nutrition, developing countries

1. Introduction

The links between trade and food security have been controversial for many decades, with opposing views on a wide range of issues: for instance, some experts argue that trade and trade openness cause hunger

Frontiers of Economics and Globalization
Volume 15   ISSN: 1574-8715
DOI: 10.1108/S1574-871520150000015003

(Madeley, 2000), while others argue that complete liberalization of trade is best for food security (Griswold, 1999). There have been comprehensive reviews of case studies analyzing the links between trade and food security (FAO, 2003; McCorriston et al., 2013; Thomas, 2006), but these reviews have not abated the controversies (Díaz-Bonilla, 2015b).

This chapter places the discussion of trade and food security in a more general macroeconomic context. It uses historical analysis to briefly trace the debate on economy-wide policies, starting with the 1943 United Nations (UN) Conference on Food and Agriculture that led to the creation of the Food and Agriculture Organization of the United Nations (FAO) in 1945. A general economic framework is used to organize the different channels through which macroeconomic policies may affect food and nutrition security. The current debates about trade and food security must be placed in the context of an overall macroeconomic framework: a single trade policy may have different impacts depending on its interactions with other macroeconomic policies and structural factors.

2. Historical background

In its final declaration, the 1943 UN Conference on Food and Agriculture stated that the goal of food security could be achieved. It recognized that

> the first cause of malnutrition and hunger is poverty. It is useless to produce more food unless men and nations provide the markets to absorb it. There must be an expansion of the whole world economy to provide the purchasing power sufficient to maintain an adequate diet for all. With full employment in all countries, enlarged industrial production, the absence of exploitation, an increasing flow of trade within and between countries, an orderly management of domestic and international investment and currencies, and sustained internal and international economic equilibrium, the food which is produced can be made available to all people. (Shaw, 2007, pp. 3–4)

Several aspects in that statement anticipated future discussions about food security. First, its focus was on nutrition at the individual level (freedom from want[1]). Second, the declaration clearly stated that poverty leads to hunger and malnutrition. Third, as envisioned in the 1943 UN Declaration, the program to end hunger and malnutrition included (1) macroeconomics (e.g., world growth, full employment, enlarged industrial production, adequate management of capital flows and exchange rates,

---

[1] US President Franklin Roosevelt convened the 1943 UN Conference. The theme of the conference was related to his 1941 State of the Union address in which Roosevelt identified four essential freedoms, which included freedom from want (Shaw, 2007).

increased trade) and (2) microeconomics (e.g., value judgments on the proper behavior of economic agents and markets).

This expansive view of the issues and policies eventually concentrated on the discussion of production, trade, and food security. Some of the issues were related to concerns about food shortages linked to the reconstruction of Europe and Japan after the Second World War.

The price shocks of the early 1970s led to fears about scarcity of production. During the 1974 World Food Conference (WFC) in Rome (Italy) to confront the 1973/1974 global food crisis, an international system of managing food trade was proposed after discussions identified inadequate food production in developing countries and problems with key commodity markets in international trade. The 1974 WFC defined food security from the supply side to sustain global food consumption and to offset fluctuations in production and prices.

The 1974 WFC program to confront food problems at the world level envisioned five components: (1) to increase food production in developing countries; (2) to implement policies and programs for ensuring adequate food availability on a global scale; (3) to improve emergency relief and food aid; (4) to develop specific objectives and measures in international trade to stabilize markets, ensure access for importing countries, and expand markets for exporting countries; and (5) to make arrangements for implementing the recommendations of the conference (Shaw, 2007).

Because they affected all commodities, the price spikes in the 1970s clearly had a large macroeconomic component linked to the steep devaluation of the US dollar after the breakdown of Bretton Woods, expansive monetary and fiscal policies, and strong global economic growth (Díaz-Bonilla, 2010). However, the 1974 WFC basically concentrated on production and trade policies. The broader view of the 1943 UN Conference that concentrated on macroeconomic concerns had largely disappeared in the 1974 WFC.

World markets in the second half of the 1980s were oversupplied partly due to the agricultural policies in the European Union and the United States that expanded trade-distorting support for agriculture. This occurred while global demand was weak due to slow world growth and the debt crisis in developing countries. The export subsidy war between the European Union and the United States created agricultural trade conflicts that eventually led to the creation of the World Trade Organization (WTO). The focus was again on trade.

From the point of view of food security, some experts argued that subsidized agricultural and food production — while perhaps helping consumers and the developing countries that were net importers of those products — likely negated the positive employment effects from expanded production. Considered the main economic activity in many low-income countries, agriculture had significant growth multipliers for the whole economy (Haggblade, Hazell, & Dorosh, 2007). Thus, the level of non-realized dynamic benefits for those countries may have been substantial. The subsidized food exports which appeared to have converted several developing countries into food importers led to further specialization in other tropical agricultural products, thus increasing the external vulnerability of those countries (Díaz-Bonilla, Thomas, & Robinson, 2003).

The collapse of commodity prices during the second part of the 1980s suggested a common macroeconomic cause (Díaz-Bonilla, 2010) and indicated that production was not the main limitation to achieving food security. The focus then moved from food availability at global and national levels toward economic access and utilization at the household and individual levels. The point made by the 1943 UN Conference was reevaluated when it became obvious that the main obstacle to access was poverty and lack of income opportunities rather than food availability (Sen, 1981). Variability of food supply and access, as well as their sustainability over time, were increasingly highlighted. Another point made in 1943 was that food intake goes beyond simple survival to include an active and healthy life.

The 1996 World Food Summit stated that food security existed when everyone had food security to ensure a healthy life (FAO, 2003; Maxwell & Frankenberger, 1992). To accomplish this goal, four dimensions (physical availability, economic access, adequate utilization, and stability) of food security were established at the 1996 Summit. As a side note, debates about food security at the 1999 Seattle Ministerial of the WTO focused mainly on trade and WTO operations. It can be argued that the concept of trade in the debates about food security has at least three meanings. First is the notion of trade as the physical and economic exchange of goods and services. For many critics of globalization, the expansion of trade has been a proxy for the expansion of a capitalist system they consider flawed. Second, for some economists trade policies are largely border measures applied by governments for the influence of economic and physical flows of trade. Here, the debate within civil society and among policy makers has focused on whether open-liberalized or closed-protected trade regimes are better from the perspective of growth, stability, poverty, and food security. A third meaning has WTO trade policies encompassing not only measures at the border but also domestic policies and regulations. This debate is about national sovereignty and policy space, both of which are supposed to be limited by the WTO and similar international arrangements.

Meanwhile, the notion of food security keeps evolving. Physical availability and economic access are only preconditions for the adequate utilization of food, and they may not unequivocally determine the more substantive issue of malnutrition or nutrition insecurity at the individual level (Smith, 1998; Smith & Haddad, 2000).

In this vein, recent definitions clearly differentiate food security and nutrition security. For example, a report by the FAO, IFAD, and WFP (2013, p. 50) uses the following definitions:

• Food insecurity: a situation that exists when people lack secure access to sufficient amounts of safe and nutritious food for normal growth and development, and an active and healthy life. It may be caused by the unavailability of food, insufficient purchasing power, inappropriate distribution, or inadequate use of food at the household level.

• Nutrition security: a situation that exists when secure access to an appropriately nutritious diet is coupled with a sanitary environment and adequate health services and care to ensure a healthy and active life for all household members. Nutrition security differs from food security in that it also considers the aspects of adequate caring practices, health, and hygiene in addition to dietary adequacy.

The latter definition acknowledges the fact that the world now suffers from what is called the triple burden of malnutrition affecting households and individuals (Pinstrup-Andersen, 2007): undernutrition (the traditional focus of food insecurity − insufficiencies in calories and proteins), overnutrition (which creates health problems including obesity, diabetes, and cardiovascular problems), and micronutrient deficiencies. It should be noted that both undernutrition and overnutrition may coexist within the same family (Garret & Ruel, 2003; IFPRI, 2014).

3. Macroeconomic policies and food security

Considering that trade involves a variety of market and policy issues and that food and nutrition security is a multidimensional concept, it is no surprise that the debate about trade and food security continues with strong views on both sides of the argument (Díaz-Bonilla, 2015b). Discussions about economy-wide policies and food security in developing countries primarily emphasize trade issues, keeping more general macroeconomic topics out of the debate.[2]

In this section, several aspects of that larger context are discussed based on the framework presented in Figure 1 (Díaz-Bonilla, Thomas, Robinson, & Cattaneo, 2000; Smith, 1998). Figure 1 shows the different

---

[2] Analyses of the agricultural sector and macroeconomic policies in developing countries have been conducted in the context of partial equilibrium analysis (Bautista & Valdes, 1993; Krueger, Schiff, & Valdes, 1988). An econometric model with macroeconomic variables that allows discussion of growth over time has been applied to Argentina (Mundlak, Cavallo, & Domenech, 1989) and Chile (Coeymans & Mundlak, 1993). Extensive literature exists on macroeconomic policies and poverty (Díaz-Bonilla, 2008).

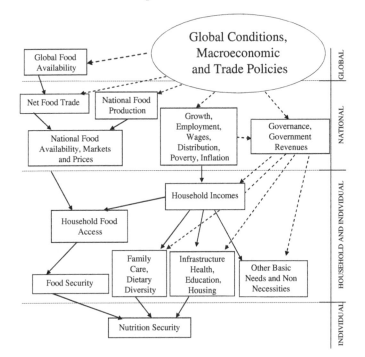

***Fig. 1.   How macroeconomic factors may influence food and nutrition
security.***

channels through which macroeconomic factors may influence the four
components of food security (availability, access, utilization, and stability) while separating food and nutrition security.

3.1. Availability and related issues

Macroeconomic policies influence domestic food production and food net
trade (i.e., food availability, the first component of the definition of food
security). While the exchange rate and the alignment of aggregate demand
and supply may have a larger influence than trade policies, the latter can
influence the composition of trade.

For instance, consider the basic national account equation
$GDP = C + I + G + EX - IM$,[3] or $GDP - (C + I + G) = EX - IM$
(usually $C + I + G$ is called Absorption, A). If a country experiences a

---

[3] GDP is gross domestic product, C is private consumption, I is total investment, G is governmental consumption, EX is exports, and IM is imports.

trade deficit (EX − IM < 0), then the country is absorbing (C + I + G = A) at a greater level than its level of production (GDP) (i.e., GDP − A < 0). This may be due to excessive expansionary monetary and fiscal policies (strong capital inflows or high levels of remittances may lead to trade deficits). Trade policies designed to expand exports EX or restrict imports IM − but not designed to modify the relationship between production (GDP) and absorption (A) − will not change the trade balance. Furthermore, with the balance between GDP and A unchanged, further reductions in IM (trying to increase the number of goods produced internally) will lead to parallel declines in EX at an unchanged trade deficit. The final effect depends on how much productive slack (unused resources) exists in that economy (as discussed below).

These macro balances are important to bear in mind when discussing proposals for food self-sufficiency/protection as a way of achieving food security. For instance, a government seeking to attain self-sufficiency in agricultural goods can use several potential trade interventions, including quotas that impose a maximum level of imports (IMmax) and import tariffs that make imports more expensive compared to the domestic good.

Now we disaggregate imports into agricultural (IMa) and nonagricultural (IMna), and do the same for exports (EXa and EXna), to obtain

$$GDP - (C + G + I) = GDP - A = EXa + EXna - IMa - IMna$$
$$= (EXa - IMa) + (EXna - IMna)$$

where (EXa − IMa) is the net agricultural trade balance and (EXna − IMna) is the net nonagricultural trade balance.

For example, assume that GDP = 100 units, A = 100, EXa = IMa = 10, and EXna = IMna = 30. The overall GDP − Absorption is in balance (100 − 100 = 0); the agricultural balance is also zero (EXa − IMa = 10 − 10 = 0), and the same holds for the nonagricultural balance (EXna − IMna = 30 − 30 = 0).

The first impact of restrictive trade policies on agricultural goods diminishes imports, which is the intended effect. Assume a country imposes a trade ban on agricultural imports to achieve complete self-sufficiency: IMa = 0. An accounting identity must always balance, but in this case the equation becomes imbalanced: GDP − A will still be zero (100 − 100 = 0), but now EXa − IMa = 10 − 0 = 10, while EXna − IMna is still zero (30 − 30 = 0). So the equation on the left-hand side is zero and on the right-hand side (RHS) is 10. How can the equation be balanced?

Mechanically, there are four basic options: GDP may increase by 10 units; Absorption may be reduced by 10; EXa may be reduced by 10 units; and the nonagricultural trade balance may turn negative in 10 units (−10). Obviously, there exists a large number of potential combinations across those basic options; for example, GDP may increase by 3 units, Absorption may decline by 6 (which would lead to 103 − 94 = 9); and

EXa may decline by 1 (now $9 - 0 = 9$). In each case, the nonagricultural trade remains in balance (EXna $-$ IMna $= 30 - 30 = 0$).

The implied preferred outcome for those suggesting self-sufficiency seems to be that the previously imported products are fully compensated by more production (GDP moves to 110), and that Absorption does not decline ($A = 100$). However, this is possible on two conditions. First, the country has unemployed domestic factors of production or other resources that can be mobilized to produce the previously imported goods without the need to take from other activities resources already employed in those alternative production activities. Second, the increase in incomes from those previously unemployed factors now producing the substituted imports should be enough to maintain the absorption of goods (A) at the same level.

However, if all factors of production are employed, the overall GDP will not change even though it may change the composition of GDP. For example, there may be more production of the protected good and less of other agricultural and nonagricultural goods. Because the protected good is now more expensive, there will be less consumption of the protected good. Likewise, if people keep consuming the good even with its higher price (because it may not have substitutes and is therefore price inelastic), then there will be less consumption of other goods. In both cases, A will likely decrease.

If this reduction in A is not enough to balance the equation, there may be more adjustments on the RHS as well. Either EXa or (EXna $-$ IMna) or both must decrease to rebalance the equation. The economic mechanisms that equilibrate the accounting identity may function as follows: with increases in protection for import-producing sectors, domestic prices of those goods would increase and resources (in this case fully employed) would move from previous activities oriented toward exports and/or the domestic market to the production of previously imported goods (in this case, the food commodities for which the government desires self-sufficiency). In substituting for imports, the movement of productive resources toward the domestic good decreases the supply of exports (for instance, land is now oriented toward the protected good). Exportable products coming principally from the agricultural sector (e.g., nonfood cash crops) would suffer the impact of the self-sufficiency policy; other agricultural goods may also be affected.[4] Therefore, with domestic factors fully employed (or some other restriction that does not allow the expansion of GDP), the adjustments in the case of IMa that move toward zero (self-sufficiency) constitute a reduction in consumption (decreasing A), in

---

[4] In fact, other food crops may also be displaced. For instance, there is some anecdotal evidence that the policy of self-sufficiency for wheat in Bolivia may be limiting the production of potatoes.

agricultural exports (EXa), or in the nonagricultural trade balance (EXna – IMna).

Actual conditions in developing countries fall between extremes of unemployed and readily available factors of production and resources, on the one hand, and fully employed domestic production capabilities, on the other. In these intermediate cases, GDP may expand due to the use of previously unutilized productive resources in the domestic production of the previously imported goods, but other activities and the associated GDP may decrease due to the transfer of domestic resources and factors of production to the domestic production of import substitutes. Although import substitution activities may grow, this expansion may occur without significantly increasing net employment or GDP, likely causing a decline in some exports and in the consumption of the more expensive good. If that expensive good is food, then the impact on poor consumers will need to be taken into account. This means society needs to consider the benefits of the policy (more employment of domestic factors) as well as the potential costs (more expensive products) that may negatively affect production and employment in other sectors. Still, the employment and expansion of GDP may be positive in a scenario of significantly unused resources, provided that they can be adequately mobilized for the production of traded goods.

Trade protection introduced with the objective of reducing a trade deficit will not have the intended results if the internal balance of demand and supply is not modified by other macroeconomic policies. The focus should be on excessive expansionary monetary and fiscal policies and an overvalued exchange rate. Furthermore, if capital inflows or remittances generate the trade deficit, then trade policies will not change the underlying imbalance. Therefore, like all broad public measures, trade policies must be analyzed in the context of the entire macroeconomic program and account for the complete array of general equilibrium effects.

3.2. Access, stability, and related issues

Beyond their impact on national food availability, macroeconomic policies also influence the rate, variability, and quality of growth (i.e., employment, income distribution, and poverty effects). Broad employment and income opportunities define economic access, which along with food availability defines food security conditions at the household level.

Avoiding economic crises and providing adequate management are central to stability (the third component of the definition of food security) so that physical and economic access are available at all times. In addition, considering that higher unemployment – and its persistence over time as generated by economic crises – deteriorates human capital, economic crises affect future economic access. Furthermore, usually a crisis decelerates or reverses improvements in health, nutrition, and education

indicators through its negative impact on the human capital of the poor
and its contribution to the persistence of poverty. A decline in the human
capital of the poor affects the performance of the economy. In particular,
crises compromise the limited productivity and human capital of the rural
poor if assets (e.g., livestock) must be sold to help small farmers survive
economic shocks or if poor children are removed from school to work on
the farm (Lipton & Ravallion, 1995).

Crises can also worsen income distribution, making it difficult for the
growth recovery to reduce poverty. Because crises produce risky economic environments that can lead the poor to engage in low-return activities, a high degree of macroeconomic volatility can cause poverty traps.
For instance, the Inter-American Development Bank (1995) estimates
that if Latin America and the Caribbean had a level of macroeconomic
stability similar to industrialized countries, the poverty headcount would
be reduced by 25%. Episodes of hyperinflation have been accompanied
by large increases in poverty and food insecurity (Díaz-Bonilla, 2008).
Most of these problems are linked to broader macroeconomic imbalances
that usually exceed the scope of trade policies.

3.3. Exchange rate policies

Economic crises vary in relation to inconsistent economic policies and
external shocks. Crises in developing countries are caused by exchange
rate misalignments related to the dual policy role of the exchange rate as
a real price in the real exchange rate approach. This approach emphasizes
the balance between tradable and non-tradable goods as well as the influence of the real exchange rate on production, trade, and employment
(Balassa, 1977, 1985). It also emphasizes the real exchange rate as a financial variable in the nominal anchor approach (which highlights the role of
the nominal exchange rate in the inflationary process and its relationship
with interest rates and capital flows) (Corden, 1990). In the nominal
anchor approach, the exchange rate has important effects on the assets
and liabilities of domestic economic agents and sectors, particularly the
banking system. Many economic crises in developing countries have
resulted from failed economic programs that do not properly articulate
this dual role. Policy makers need to have one instrument for each goal; it
would be very difficult for a government to attain external competitiveness (using the real exchange approach) and low inflation (using the nominal anchor approach) with just one instrument (such as the exchange
rate). Therefore, it is necessary to define exchange rate, monetary, fiscal,
and trade policies through a consistent economic program.

Ethiopia's policies during the 2008 price shocks offer an example of
macroeconomic factors being more of a determinant than world price
jumps. This example demonstrates the economic and social costs of foreign exchange rationing, a measure that governments sometimes utilize to
avoid a devaluation, which usually takes place anyway.

Before 2008, Ethiopia received capital inflows to finance investments. Those capital inflows increased the money supply and exacerbated inflationary pressures. The domestic currency began to appreciate, affecting exportable commodities and increasing imports. The increase in world prices of food and fuel led to greater balance-of-payment problems. The government of Ethiopia then started rationing foreign exchange and limiting imports, including food items. The result was that the domestic price of some staples (e.g., wheat) rose above world prices (Dorosh, Robinson, & Ahmed, 2009; Rashid & Lemma, 2011). Rashid and Lemma (2011) noted that Ethiopia's domestic prices did not follow the world prices before, during, or after the 2008 food crisis.

Due to the government's desire to avoid a depreciation of the domestic currency, the rationing of foreign exchange exacerbated the effects of the negative external shocks. Other estimations by Dorosh et al. (2009) through a computable general equilibrium model for Ethiopia showed that the exchange rate appreciation and the policy response to rationing foreign exchange negatively affected growth (through reduced incentives for the production of tradables) and worsened Ethiopia's income distribution. The country would have fared better in terms of growth, exports, and equity with a managed exchange rate that was allowed to depreciate in addition to a reduction in economic rents.

The main policy conclusion is the necessity of avoiding the overvaluation of the exchange rate, which then leads to abrupt and damaging adjustments in parity. Sharp devaluations or other financial disruptions that affect the financial/banking system have the largest negative impacts on the economy and society, leading to increases in poverty and food insecurity. Concerns about the poor and the vulnerable should make avoiding macroeconomic crises the main policy priority. Once the exchange rate is overvalued, delaying adjustment due to concerns about the poor and vulnerable tends to increase the imbalance and force even more damaging adjustments later on. Therefore, it is better to correct the exchange rate as soon as possible. In any case, it is crucial to implement safety nets for the poor and the vulnerable, including food stamps, food-for-work, school lunches, and supplementary feeding for mothers and infants. Those programs should be instituted during less turbulent times and expanded during periods of economic distress.

One of the most important things a policy maker can do to improve food security is to avoid economic crises that are usually related to broader macroeconomic policy problems than those related to trade policies.

3.4. Monetary policies

Beyond avoiding economic crises, another important economic objective is maintaining high growth with price stability (low inflation). The best monetary policy framework will (1) align growth, inflation, and

competitiveness in ways that support the economy, agricultural development, and food security during smooth economic periods; and (2) maintain growth, employment, and stable prices while avoiding sharp increases
in poverty and food insecurity during external or internal shocks. The four
main monetary frameworks are monetary targeting (MT), exchange rate
anchors (ERA), inflation targeting (IT), and "Other" (IMF, 2013). Most
lower-income developing countries are in the ERA and MT categories,
while most higher-income developing countries and industrialized countries are in the IT and Other categories (Díaz-Bonilla, 2015a).

While IT regimes seem to decrease the level of inflation and the volatility of output and inflation, empirical studies do not appear to discuss
their impact on growth. Calvo (2006) uses a theoretical model to show
that if the credibility of the central bank is limited, IT can lead to underutilization of capacity and appreciation of the exchange rate (meaning
lower growth). If IT regimes lead to less volatility at the expense of lower
average growth (perhaps because the country has selected a very low
inflation target), then the benefits of smoothing consumption may be
minimal compared to the greater significance of differences in the long-
term growth for a country's economic welfare (Lucas, 1982, 2003).

The selection of an inflation target is crucial for providing price stability without compromising growth and without generating overvalued
exchange rates. It could be argued that a 2% annual inflation rate is too
low for a developing country since reaching that target may require high
real interest rates that affect growth and capital flows that appreciate the
local currency. However, inflation at 25% or higher would likely have a
negative effect on growth and would generate an appreciation of the
domestic currency through other channels (e.g., a devaluation rate lower
than inflation to control inflationary pressures). These concerns also
apply to agriculture, making it necessary to analyze the impact of the
selected target level for inflation on agricultural performance. One must
consider whether macroeconomic policies used to reduce inflation to targets that are too low might simultaneously decelerate growth, increase
unemployment, and appreciate the real exchange rates in ways that could
offset the positive impact of lower inflation on agriculture.

Repercussions for poverty and food security may occur if the inflation
target is too high. The poor cite inflation as a central concern (Easterly &
Fischer, 2000[5]), and with larger shares devoted to food, inflated prices for

---

[5] Using household data for 38 countries, Easterly and Fischer (2000) found that both in perception (the poor are more likely to mention inflation as a concern) and in reality (several
measures of welfare negatively correlate with inflation, with high inflation increasing poverty
by lowering the share of the bottom quintile and the real minimum wage), inflation is a real
problem for the poor.

these products may be more relevant to food security than overall inflation. Thus, a (somewhat) higher inflation in commodities might benefit both producers and poor consumers. In the end, the proper alignment of inflation targets must not suffocate growth and employment generation nor affect the poor and the vulnerable in ways for which higher growth cannot compensate.

From the viewpoint of food security, high and persistent food inflation (which most likely requires treatment with macroeconomics rather than sectoral policies) is likely more relevant than price volatility (the problem agricultural price stabilization schemes attempt to solve).

3.5. Government and fiscal issues affecting all components of food and nutrition security

Another important channel of influence for macroeconomic policies is government revenues, which affect the implementation of transfer policies (e.g., food subsidies), the financing of public services, and investments in health and education. All these policies support food security.

The reciprocal effects between macroeconomics policies and food and nutrition security programs must be taken into account. On the one hand, appropriate macroeconomic policies help with overall growth and stability to sustain a healthy fiscal position while supporting food and nutrition security programs. On the other hand, these programs may have destabilizing fiscal effects, leading to macroeconomic crises that cause food insecurity.

For instance, Scobie (1988) traced some of the macroeconomic effects of food subsidies. He estimated that in Egypt during the 1980s, the fiscal deficit occurred when a 10% increase in food subsidies resulted in a 5% increase in the rate of inflation. In some cases, cuts in other agricultural and social investments financed increases in food subsidies (Scobie, 1988). In other cases, funding the subsidy program shifted the costs to producers through forced procurement of food items at below-market prices (Scobie, 1988).

Finally, there are general equilibrium effects on international trade and exchange rates, real wages, real incomes and income distribution, and agricultural and nonagricultural production. Food consumption subsidies may contribute to the deterioration of the trade balance by increasing imports while also decreasing exports of the subsidized products (Pinstrup-Andersen, 1988a, 1988b). The secondary effects depend on policies dealing with the deficit in the trade balance. In some cases, governments resort to devaluations of the domestic currency, placing pressure on domestic inflation and food prices and countering the effects of food consumption subsidies. In other cases, governments use import controls, ration the availability of foreign currency, or use multiple exchange rates that affect production in other sectors.

Regarding the latter measures, Scobie (1988) noted the cases of Chile, Indonesia, Tanzania, and Egypt in the 1980s, where worsening trade and foreign exchange conditions led to rationing of other imports, thus affecting general economic activity. More specifically, he estimated that in Egypt during the 1980s, a decline of 1 dollar in foreign exchange availability reduced food imports by only 5 cents, while raw materials and machinery fell by 15 and 30 cents, respectively. Because food imports crowded out the imports needed for industrial production, a 10% increase in the price of commercial food imports meant a 1%−2% decline in output and new investment in the industrial sector.

In summary, those food and nutrition security programs have economy-wide effects that must be analyzed, whether they are funded within the budget through mechanisms that create secondary effects (such as inflationary financing of deficits or increased indebtedness) or whether they are financed off-budget by shifting the implicit costs from general taxpayers to specific economic agents. As with all public expenditures, these programs use fiscal resources that may have a better alternative use for growth and equity as well as for poverty alleviation and food security.

3.6. Utilization and related issues

Figure 1 emphasizes the significance of the impact of policies at the individual level (nutrition security in Figure 1). Availability and access are only preconditions for adequate utilization of food. They do not unequivocally determine malnutrition (or nutrition insecurity) at the individual level (Smith, 1998; Smith & Haddad, 2000). Therefore, while macroeconomic policies affect directly food availability and economic access at the household and individual levels, macroeconomic policies only have an indirect effect on other factors such as the quality and quantity of family care related to the societal status of women (Díaz-Bonilla, 2015b).

4. Conclusions

This chapter argues that an exclusive focus on trade and food security, although a relevant policy topic, may omit significant economy-wide issues and policies that affect food and nutrition security. After a brief historical discussion of the creation of the FAO, this chapter presents a general framework and offers examples of the links between macroeconomic policies and food and nutrition security. A single trade policy may have different impacts depending on its interactions with other macroeconomic policies and structural factors. For instance, a reduction of agricultural tariffs will have a different impact if a country has an overvalued exchange rate as opposed to neutral or undervalued parity. Therefore, discussions of trade and food and nutrition security need to be placed in the context of the overall framework of monetary, financial, fiscal, and exchange rate policies.

References

Balassa, B. (1977). *Policy reform in developing countries.* Oxford: Pergamon Press.

Balassa, B. (1985). *Change and challenge in the world economy.* New York, NY: St. Martin's Press.

Bautista, R., & Valdes, A. (1993). *The bias against agriculture: Trade and macroeconomic policies in developing countries.* San Francisco, CA: ICS Press.

Calvo, G. (2006). *Monetary policy challenges in emerging markets: Sudden stop, liability dollarization, and lender of last resort.* IADB Working Paper No. 596. Inter-American Development Bank, Washington, DC.

Coeymans, J. E., & Mundlak, Y. (1993). Sectoral growth in Chile. 1962–1982. Research Report 95. IFPRI, Washington, DC.

Corden, W. (1990). *Exchange rate policy in developing countries.* Policy Research Working Paper No. 412. World Bank, Washington, DC.

Díaz-Bonilla, E. (2008). Global macroeconomic developments and poverty. Discussion Paper No. 00766. Washington, DC: IFPRI.

Díaz-Bonilla, E. (2010). Globalization of agriculture and food crises: Then and now. In B. Karapinar & C. Häberli (Eds.), *Food crises and the WTO* (pp. 49–80). Cambridge: Cambridge University Press.

Díaz-Bonilla, E. (2015a). *Macroeconomics, agriculture, and food security: A guide to policy making in developing countries.* Washington, DC: IFPRI.

Díaz-Bonilla, E. (2015b). *Lost in translation: The fractured dialogue on trade and food security.* Washington, DC: IFPRI.

Díaz-Bonilla, E., Thomas, M., & Robinson, S. (2003). Trade, food security, and the WTO negotiations: Some reflections on boxes and their contents. In *Agricultural trade and poverty: Making policy analysis count* (pp. 59–103). Compendium, OECD, Paris.

Díaz-Bonilla, E., Thomas, M., Robinson, S., & Cattaneo, A. (2000). Food security and trade negotiations in the World Trade Organization: A cluster analysis of country groups. Discussion Paper 59. IFPRI, Washington, DC.

Dorosh, P., Robinson, S., & Ahmed, H. (2009). Economic implications of foreign exchange rationing in Ethiopia. ESSP2 Discussion Paper 009. IFPRI, Washington, DC.

Easterly, W., & Fischer, S. (2000). *Inflation and the poor.* Policy Research Working Paper Series No. 2335. World Bank, Washington, DC.

Food and Agriculture Organization of the United Nations [FAO] (2003). *Trade reforms and food security: Conceptualizing the linkages.* Rome: FAO.

Food and Agriculture Organization of the United Nations, International Fund for Agricultural Development, and World Food Program [FAO, IFAD, & WFP] (2013). *The state of food insecurity in the world 2013: The multiple dimensions of food security.* Rome: FAO.

Garret, J., & Ruel, M. (2003). *Stunted children—overweight mother pairs: An emerging policy concern?* IFPRI Discussion Paper 148. IFPRI, Washington, DC.

Griswold, D. T. (1999). *Bringing economic sanity to agricultural trade.* Retrieved from http://www.cato.org/publications/commentary/bring ing-economic-sanity-agricultural-trade

Haggblade, S., Hazell, P., & Dorosh, A. (2007). Sectoral growth linkages between agriculture and the rural non-farm economy. In S. Hagblade, P. Hazell, & T. Reardon (Eds.), *Transforming the rural non-farm economy* (pp. 141–182). Baltimore, MD: Johns Hopkins University Press.

Inter-American Development Bank (1995). *Informe del progreso económico y social en Latinoamérica y el Caribe.* Washington, DC: Inter-American Development Bank.

International Food Policy Research Institute [IFPRI] (2014). *Global nutrition report 2014.* Washington, DC: IFPRI.

International Monetary Fund [IMF] (2013). *Annual report on exchange arrangements and exchange restrictions.* Washington, DC: IMF. Retrieved from https://www.imf.org/external/pubs/nft/2013/areaers/ar2013.pdf

Krueger, A., Schiff, M., & Valdes, A. (1988). Agricultural incentives in developing countries: Measuring the effects of sectorial and economy-wide policies. *World Bank Economic Review, 2*(3), 255–271.

Lipton, M., & Ravallion, M. (1995). Poverty and policy. In J. Behrman & T. Srinivasan (Eds.), *Handbook of development economics* (pp. 2551–2657). Amsterdam: North-Holland.

Lucas, R. (1982). Interest rates and currency prices in a two country world. *Journal of Monetary Economy, 10*(3), 335–359.

Lucas, R. (2003). Macroeconomic priorities. *American Economic Review, 93*(1), 1–14.

Madeley, J. (2000). *Trade and hunger: An overview of case studies on the impact of trade liberalization on food security.* Retrieved from http://www.agriculturesnetwork.org/magazines/global/go-global-or-stay-local/trade-and-hunger-the-impact-of-trade/at_download/article_pdf

Maxwell, S., & Frankenberger, T. R. (1992). *Household food security: Concepts, indicators, measurements: A technical overview.* New York, NY: UNICEF.

McCorriston, S., Hemming, D. J., Lamontagne-Godwin, J. D., Parr, M. J., Osborn, J., & Roberts, P. D. (2013). *What is the evidence of the impact of agricultural trade liberalization on food security in developing countries? A systematic review.* London: EPPI Centre, University of London.

Mundlak, Y., Cavallo, D., & Domenech, R. (1989). Agriculture and economic growth in Argentina, 1913–1984. IFPRI Research Report 76. IFPRI, Washington, DC.

Pinstrup-Andersen, P. (Ed.). (1988a). *Food subsidies in developing countries: Costs, benefits, and policy options.* Baltimore, MD: Johns Hopkins University Press.

Pinstrup-Andersen, P. (1988b). The social and economic effects of consumer-oriented food subsidies: A summary of current evidence. In P. Pinstrup-Andersen (Ed.), *Food subsidies in developing countries: Costs, benefits, and policy options* (pp. 3–18). Baltimore, MD: Johns Hopkins University Press.

Pinstrup-Andersen, P. (2007). Agricultural research and policy for better health and nutrition in developing countries: A food systems approach. *Agricultural Economics, 37,* 187–198.

Rashid, S., & Lemma, S. (2011). *Strategic grain reserves in Ethiopia: Institutional design and operational performance.* IFPRI Discussion Paper 01054. IFPRI, Washington, DC.

Scobie, G. (1988). Macroeconomic and trade implications of consumer-oriented food subsidies. In P. Pinstrup-Andersen (Ed.), *Food subsidies in developing countries: Costs, benefits, and policy options* (pp. 49–76). Baltimore, MD: Johns Hopkins University Press.

Sen, A. (1981). *Poverty and famines: An essay on entitlement and deprivation.* Oxford: Clarendon Press.

Shaw, D. J. (2007). *World food security: A history since 1945.* New York, NY: Palgrave Macmillan.

Smith, L. C. (1998). Can FAO's measure of chronic undernourishment be strengthened? *Food Policy, 23*(5), 425–445.

Smith, L. C., & Haddad, L. (2000). Explaining child malnutrition in developing countries: A cross-country analysis. IFPRI Research Report 111. IFPRI, Washington, DC.

Thomas, H. (Ed.). (2006). *Trade reforms and food security: Country case studies and synthesis.* Rome: FAO.

4

Food Security Measurement: An Empirical Approach

David Magaña-Lemus and Jorge Lara-Álvarez

Economic Research, Fideicomisos Instituidos en Relación con la Agricultura (FIRA), Morelia, Michoacan, 58342, Mexico
E-mail address: dmagana@fira.gob.mx and jlara@fira.gob.mx

Abstract

Purpose – Food security is an essential measure of welfare, especially for low-income families in developing countries. Policy makers should be aware of the harm food insecurity has on vulnerable households. This chapter empirically addresses the problems of measuring and monitoring food security in Mexico.

Methodology/approach – We identify the macro and micro approaches for measuring food security. The macro approach uses variables at the country level. Usually, this information is available on a yearly basis, is easy to implement, and can be compared across countries. The micro approach uses household questionnaires to collect food security information. Our analysis suggests that a macro approach will not be as precise as the micro approach due to inequality (agroclimatic, social, and economic).

Findings – Empirical experience suggests that food insecurity and its severity can be captured at the household level using the Food Insecurity Experiences Questionnaire. This questionnaire allows us to calculate food security measurements that closely follow the food security definition.

Originality/value – From a public policy perspective, the different methodologies for measurement do not consider all the dimensions of food security as defined by the term. This chapter examines which approach provides the best measurement of food security.

Keywords: Food security, food insecurity, macro approach, micro approach

Frontiers of Economics and Globalization
Volume 15   ISSN: 1574-8715
DOI: 10.1108/S1574-871520150000015004

1. Introduction: food security concept

The concept of food security has evolved over time. In the 1970s, food security meant having enough food to meet basic consumption requirements (Clay, 2003). This definition was expanded in 1996 and 2002 (Food and Agriculture Organization of the United Nations [FAO], 1996). The current consensus has food security measured according to the individual's access to food and food knowledge (nutrition and sanitation).

Food security possesses an inherent relationship with an individual's well-being. Brown (1987) lists potential outcomes of food insecurity, including premature births, impaired cognitive functioning, and low resistance to infection and illness. Vulnerable groups such as children (Aungst, 2013) and the elderly (Ziliak, 2011) often have chronic health conditions. Food insecurity also has social implications that affect human development and social interactions (Hamelin, Habicht, & Beaudry, 1999). It can affect macroeconomic outcomes, including diminished work productivity and increased public healthcare expenditures.

Food security has many dimensions and there are different approaches to measure it (Anderson, 1990). The term is sometimes used interchangeably with poverty and malnutrition (Food and Agriculture Organization of the United Nations [FAO], the International Fund for Agricultural Development [IFADS], & World Food Program [WFP], 2014). Some research studies claim to measure food security but instead focus on proxy variables like hunger. For instance, Meade and Rosen (2002) argue that a good threshold for food security is having enough money to buy food. FAO (2002) presents innovative methods to measure food security. Hales and Blakely (2002) study anthropometric results and poverty. Kuhnlein et al. (2002) measure access to nutrients for indigenous populations. The best measurement of food security is a methodology that includes all the dimensions listed in the definition of food security.

Since the 1990s, there has been a major development of methodologies that encapsulate all dimensions of food security. A proper measurement of food security should summarize the dimensions established in its definition from a series of observed facts. For policy makers, it is useful to have repeated measurements to reveal relative positions or to show positive or negative changes for setting targets and monitoring their achievement. Should policy makers prefer any one methodology among the overall set of food security methods?

This chapter examines the main methods to measure food security (macro and micro approaches). There is a discussion on advances in the macro and micro approaches and why the Food Insecurity Experiences Questionnaire (FIEQ), a household survey on food security, is our preferred method. We provide an empirical example of a household survey of food security experiences. The conclusions summarize the main findings, implications, challenges, and opportunities in using the FIEQ method.

2. Food security measurement classifications

To understand the implications of each food security measurement, a classification of each measurement is needed. We divide the methodologies into macro and micro, depending on the variables used. The macro category comprises food security measurements that use macro-aggregated (country-level) variables, while the micro category includes only micro-level variables (individual/household). Despite possessing the same goal, these indicators have different implications for public policies.

Studies by Coates (2013) and Jones, Ngure, Pelto, and Young (2013) arrive at the same conclusions: (1) the FAO (1996, 2002) definition is correct, and (2) there is no widely accepted single methodology to measure food security. The lack of a unique methodology clouds the setting of targets and the monitoring of their achievement. Therefore, it is important to discuss which methodologies best measure food security.

The level of food security is affected by macro variables such as unstable social and political environments, lack of economic growth, trade imbalances, natural resource constraints, social and economic inequality, lack of infrastructure, and corruption in social programs. While food security is important to policy makers, confusion persists concerning the relationship between commonly used food security proxy variables and the well-established food security definition. Over the years, researchers have relied heavily on hunger and malnutrition as proxies to food security, but neither of these variables captures the complex nature of food security. A proper measurement of food security needs to include the financial, physical, and social dimensions of food access at the macro and micro levels.

From a public policy perspective, classifying food security situations in terms of severity and duration is preferable to classifying each food security situation. The Integrated Food Security Phase Classification provides two types of classification: (1) the degree of severity of food insecurity at the moment of measurement and (2) the duration and persistence of food insecurity (chronic food insecurity). FAO (2000) has a similar classification based on chronic (long-term) and transitory (short-term) causes of food insecurity.

3. The macro approach

This food security measurement uses variables at the country level. The first step is to select the variables. Often, these variables are related to food access, food safety, food quality, government involvement, and infrastructure. The next step is to combine all the variables.

After selecting the variables, a macro food security index is constructed by normalizing each of the observations (i.e., they are assigned a 0–100 score, based on a best-possible outcome for each variable) and then a weighted average of those normalized observations is calculated.

For each country i, K variables are used to measure food security. Each observation X_{ik} (k = 1 to K) is normalized; that is, each observation is transformed into a 0–100 score (where 100 is the best outcome and 0 is the worst outcome). We denote $\tilde{X}_{ik}$ as this normalized observation. Finally, each variable has a weight that depends on its relevance to food security. Then, a weighted average[1] is estimated.

$$FS_i = \tilde{X}_{i1}w_1 + \tilde{X}_{i2}w_2 + \cdots + \tilde{X}_{iK}w_K \tag{1}$$

One advantage of using the macro approach to measure food security is that the necessary data are available for the majority of the countries on an annual basis.

The Economist Intelligence Unit (EIU) has established three dimensions of food security that are divided into 28 variables. EIU provides the normalized scores and the weight for each variable. An expert consulting panel chooses the variables, the scores, and the weights. The three dimensions measured are affordability, availability, and quality.

The Food Security Indices from 2012 to 2014 for Brazil, China, Germany, Mexico, South Africa, and the United States are given in Figure 1. Three observations are compared across the countries. The scores are from 0 to 100 points, where 100 means full food security for the entire population. The highest ranked countries are the United States and Germany. Brazil and China have become leaders in availability, access, and utilization of food.

Unlike EIU, FAO uses four dimensions to measure variables: availability, access, utilization, and stability. FAO states that water availability is central to global food security. With more income, people diversify their diet to consume more meat and dairy products, both of which require more water for production. For economies based on agriculture, FAO (2013) recommends that the water availability variable be included when measuring food security.

Using national means and national aggregate data can cause problems in analyzing food security. National means data ignore inequality considerations that may play a major role in countries struggling with food insecurity. A good analogy is gross domestic product per capita

---

[1] Note that for comparative purposes, both the weight and the normalization must be the same across countries.

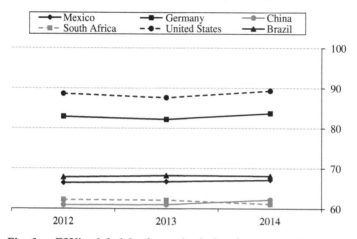

Fig. 1. EIU's global food security index. Source: *Authors' own elaboration.*

(affordability): while a good indicator of national wealth, it does not capture any inequality in the distribution of income. Likewise, national aggregates such as agricultural infrastructure (availability) do not consider heterogeneity within a country. A region of a country may possess plenty of crop storage facilities and an excellent road/port infrastructure while still having a poor agriculture infrastructure.

In addition, there are also alternative macro measurements (macro/ micro mixtures). Grünberger (2014) has proposed a methodology to improve food security measurements as derived from macro variables. He argues that the information contained in Food Balance Sheets (FBS) can be complemented by national Household Budget Surveys (HBS). An FBS is a large set of country-specific information based on production, import, export, and domestic consumption (Jacobs & Sumner, 2002). HBS identifies food purchases rather than food consumption. Grünberger (2014) has established that information obtained from both the FBS and HSB can be combined to improve the measurement of food security.

Using the macro approach toward measuring the degree of food security is relatively easy to implement and can be replicated on an annual basis and compared across countries. However, the macro approach does not provide information on vulnerable groups/regions within a country nor on the impact of a specific shock/policy (e.g., food crisis).

4. The micro approach

In the micro approach, variables used to measure food security are either at the household or individual level. Usually, those variables are collected through the use of a questionnaire.

In the mid-1990s, the US Department of Agriculture (USDA) developed the Food Security Supplement to the Current Population Survey as a direct assessment of the extent and causes of food insecurity (United States Department of Agriculture [USDA], 2000). The introduction of the FIEQ in 1995 represented a significant change in the approach to food insecurity measurement compared to traditional indirect assessment through determinants (e.g., food expenditure) or consequences (e.g., anthropometric deficiencies). FIEQ is the core of the micro approach.

FIEQ is not specific to each individual in a household. Using FIEQ, household heads are asked whether they compromise diversity, quality, and/or quantity of the food they eat due to limited money or other resources. Coates, Webb, Houser, Rogers, and Wilde (2010) have argued that FIEQ should be changed to include all individuals in the household. Food insecurity, which affects individual well-being in different ways, can have negative physical, emotional, and psychological consequences, as well as possible social aftermath issues. These outcomes are impossible to capture with any other approach. Swindale and Bilinsky (2006) state that the food security experiences approach is universally appropriate with minor adaptation.

FIEQ data obtained from the head of household is used to analyse access (financial ability to purchase food), nutrition, and food diversity. All questions are phrased in a positive way by asking household heads whether they have experienced a particular food insecurity event. Thus, a positive answer implies food insecurity.

One option for the identification of households is classifying them into four categories: food security (level 1), very low food insecurity (level 2), medium food insecurity (level 3), and severe food insecurity (level 4). This option assigns the same weight to all questions regarding food insecurity experiences. The number of questions answered positively is organized according to these four categories. This is the classification system used in the official statistics of Mexico. This procedure provides valuable information to policy makers in developing food security policies targeted to the population identified as living at level 4 (severe food insecurity).

For our purposes, this analysis is based on a binary classification: a household is food insecure if any question is answered positively. This binary classification allows us to provide a food security measurement between 0 and 100, which is very convenient to identify the level of food security and to make comparisons across countries.

FIEQ has drawbacks. Charlton and Rose (2001) argue that FIEQ is difficult to generalize for different cultures. Bashir and Schilizzi (2012) point out the absence of questions about water access and the difficulty in establishing cutoff points for the classification of different levels of food insecurity. Coates et al. (2010) argue that the responses to FIEQ vary depending on whether the interviewee is male or female (one-third of households would be assigned a different level of food security depending on the sex/gender of the interviewee).

Food security scale methodology has been successfully applied in the United States to measure household food security. It can also be applicable in other settings as long as appropriate linguistic and cultural conversions are made (USDA, 2000). In regard to developing countries, Melgar-Quiñonez (2006) concluded that the US Household Food Security Survey Module discriminates between households at different levels of food insecurity status, while González (2008) concluded that the data adapted from the questionnaire provide the basis for a valid measurement of household food insecurity.

In Latin America, there has been a movement to implement a FIEQ called Latin American and Caribbean Food Security Scale (ELCSA). Pérez-Escamilla, Paras, and Hromi-Fiedler (2008) conclude that using a food security scale such as ELCSA was a valid tool for assessing household food insecurity. Likewise, Pérez-Escamilla et al. (2004) report that food security is strongly associated with daily consumption of fruit, non-root/tuber vegetables, and meat.

While a micro approach to measuring food security implies a household questionnaire (FIEQ), there are alternative micro measurements. These include dietary intake assessment (DIA), anthropometry, household expenditures, and the FAO food deprivation method.

DIA is a measurement method based on questionnaires using different techniques such as recall (asking what was eaten on a particular day), food frequency (how often food is eaten in a day), and food diary. This method estimates daily average per capita calories consumed. Flaws include the omission of micronutrients (Bashir & Schilizzi, 2012) and the required involvement of highly trained researchers for interpreting data. The anthropometry method uses a household survey measuring human characteristics to view the impacts and consequences of food insecurity on health. Flaws in this method include high food insecurity risks in households with normal anthropometric levels (Maxwell & Frankenberger, 1992) and data inaccuracies (Bashire & Schilizzi, 2012; Dinour, Bergen, & Yeh, 2007).

In the household expenditure method, household heads are asked about food expenditures that reflect the quantity of food acquired rather than the quality of food consumed. So data reflect only the monetary value of food. Also, there are no data for intrahousehold allocation, and the available data are difficult to compare across countries (Smith, 2002).

The FAO food deprivation method (Naiken, 2002) compares the minimum energy requirements for maintaining healthy body weight through food consumption, expressed in terms of dietary energy supply (DES). The DES data refer to the sum of food acquired by households (FAO, 2002) rather than the sum of food acquired and consumed by each individual. Furthermore, the FAO method only considers the minimum calorie intake to achieve food security and not the quality of the diet (Bashir & Schilizzi, 2012).

We apply the FIEQ methodology to estimate the degree of food security in Mexico using ENIGH data from 2010 and 2012 (ENIGH is the Spanish acronym for Encuesta Nacional de Ingresos y Gastos de los Hogares (National Survey on Household Incomes and Expenses)). ENIGH is conducted on a biennial basis and contains nationally representative information for food security concerning eating habits and access to food. The questions are dichotomous, with negative responses implying food security and positive responses indicating food insecurity. The questionnaire is applied differently to households with or without children. Table 1 shows the number of households divided by their food security status. While food security increased, the change is insignificant. Table 2 translates the households from Table 1 into individuals. The number of food insecure people increased by more than three million from 2010 to 2012.

FIEQ measures the severity of food insecurity and can be used for disaggregation across different population groups (Bukusuba, Kikafunda, & Whitehead, 2007; Power, 2008). Thus, this survey identifies the food insecure people and their geographic distribution.

FAO (2002) indicates that vulnerability in urban areas is linked to access to employment and the prices of basic food commodities (e.g., insufficient income prevents the purchase of enough food to meet dietary needs), while vulnerability in rural areas is directly related to lack of production resource access, income, and access to potable water and health services. Table 3 shows the rural and urban food security estimates for the Mexican ENIGH in 2010 and 2012. The most notable change is the increase in the number of food insecure people in the urban sector, from 34 million people in 2010 to 37 million in 2012.

Table 1.   Food security at a household level, 2010 and 2012

	Food Secure, 2010	Food Secure, 2012	Food Insecure, 2010	Food Insecure, 2012
Total Households (%)	60.47	58.78	39.53	41.21
Households (millions)	17.87	18.55	11.68	13.01

Table 2.   Individuals with food security and insecurity, 2010 and 2012

	Food Secure, 2010	Food Secure, 2012	Food Insecure, 2010	Food Insecure, 2012
%	57.03	55.19	42.97	44.81
Millions	65.39	64.83	49.27	52.65

Table 3.　Total urban and rural individuals with food security and insecurity, 2010 and 2012

Individuals	Urban Secure, 2010	Rural Secure, 2010	Urban Insecure, 2010	Rural Insecure, 2010
%	46.89	10.12	29.92	13.07
Millions	53.78	11.61	34.32	14.99
Individuals	Urban Secure, 2012	Rural Secure, 2012	Urban Insecure, 2012	Rural Insecure, 2012
%	45.57	9.64	31.24	13.54
Millions	53.50	11.32	36.68	15.90

Table 4.　Food security and insecurity for children, 2010 and 2012

Individuals	Food Secure, 2010	Food Secure, 2012	Food Insecure, 2010	Food Insecure, 2012
%	51.16	48.48	48.84	51.52
Millions	13.45	12.62	12.84	13.41

Table 5.　Food security and insecurity for elderly adults aged 65 and older

Individuals	Food Secure, 2010	Food Secure, 2012	Food Insecure, 2010	Food Insecure, 2012
%	62.24	56.20	37.76	43.80
Millions	5.02	4.78	3.05	3.73

ENIGH also measures special groups such as children (18 years old and younger) and the elderly (65 years old and older). These special interest groups are shown in Tables 4 and 5. For children, food insecurity at the early life stages can increase morbidity, mortality, cognitive and psychomotor impairment, and chronic disease (USDA, 2011). The elderly are expected to possess adequate pensions to ensure food security, but this is not always the case.

5. Modeling food security

To illustrate the difficulty of approximating food security through the usual proxy variables, we test the relationships between food expenditure, poverty, and food insecurity. If our hypothesis is correct, a relatively small relationship will exist (negative between food expenditure and food insecurity; positive between poverty and food insecurity).

We use a linear projection model (Hansen, 2015) between food security (binary) and food expenditure per capita,[2] controlling for other variables (rural household and head of household education level). Then, using the Mexican ENIGH, we run the following Linear Probability Model for all households:

$$FI_i = \alpha + \beta \, food \, exp_i + \theta_1 \, rural_i + \theta_2 \, secedu_i + \varepsilon_i \qquad (2)$$

where FI_i is a food insecurity indicator for the i-th household. Food expenditure is the per capita food expenditure for the i-th household. The control variables include a dummy for rural location and a dummy if the head of household has completed secondary education. For years 2010 and 2012, heads of households who completed secondary education represent 21.44% and 22.45%, respectively. We expect that more educated heads of household suffer less food insecurity.

Tables 6 and 7 present the econometric results for 2010 and 2012. Both years show a negative and significant coefficient between food insecurity and per capita food expenses, but the coefficient magnitude is small.

Table 6. Food insecurity linear projection, 2010

Food Insecurity	Coefficient	Standard Error	t	$P > t$	95% Confidence Interval
Food Expenditure	-6.90×10^{-6}	3.22×10^{-7}	-21.43	0.00	-7.53×10^{-6} to -6.27×10^{-6}
Rural	0.084	0.014	6.02	0.00	0.057 to 0.112
Secondary Education	-0.145	0.010	-15.10	0.00	-0.163 to -0.126
Constant	0.552	0.011	52.56	0.00	0.532 to 0.573

Note: $R^2 = 0.081$.

Table 7. Food insecurity linear projection, 2012

Food Insecurity	Coefficient	Standard Error	t	$P > t$	95% Confidence Interval
Food Expenditure	-7.20×10^{-6}	5.17×10^{-7}	-13.92	0.00	-8.22×10^{-6} to -6.19×10^{-6}
Rural	0.088	0.019	4.76	0.00	0.052 to 0.125
Secondary Education	-0.172	0.015	-11.18	0.00	-0.202 to -0.142
Constant	0.604	0.017	36.24	0.00	0.572 to 0.637

Note: $R^2 = 0.107$.

---

[2] An OECD-modified scale was applied. This scale assigns a value of 1 to the household head, 0.5 to each additional adult member, and 0.3 to each child.

Table 8.   Correlation of food insecurity versus poverty, 2010 and 2012

	Food Insecurity, 2010	Poverty, 2010	Food Insecurity, 2012	Poverty, 2012
Food insecurity	1	0.3197	1	0.3249
Poverty	0.3197	1	0.3249	1

Next, we measured the relationship between poverty and food insecurity. Variable poverty was determined using the official methodology defined by the Mexican government.[3] As expected, the correlation between food insecurity and poverty for both years is positive and small (Table 8). Overall, our results suggest that although food insecurity, poverty, and food expenditures are related, an analysis using proxy variables for food insecurity is questionable.

The seminal contributions of Sen (1985) to welfare economics changed the way welfare is understood. Historically, welfare is measured through individual utility comparisons (Harsanyi, 1955) and through outcomes such as consumption or income (Slesnik, 1998). Sen argued that welfare should be based on the freedom and ability of a person to engage in activities. Sen's approach to human well-being emphasizes the importance of factors that limit the freedom of choice (e.g., health, poverty, morbidity, and social factors). We argue that another factor should be food security.

6. Conclusions

In this chapter, we examine macro and micro approaches toward measuring food security. These two approaches are very different, and we recommend the micro approach to estimate food security in a developing country. There are different methodologies for the micro approach, with FIEQ being the one that fully captures the spirit of FAO's food security definition.

Our findings are relevant for policy makers to use as a reference to set targets and to design public policies, but questions remain. Food price volatility is believed to harm vulnerable households. Can a FIEQ capture that phenomenon? Should questions be modified to better understand the effect of food price volatility on food security? Is there a relationship between food security and actual food consumption? Such questions will be interesting to study in future research on food security.

---

[3] We used capability poverty, which possesses the following indicators: average levels of education in the household, access to health services, access to social security, quality of living space, access to basic housing services, access to food, and degree of social cohesion.

Acknowledgments

The authors thank Vicente López Díaz for his helpful comments on an early version of this chapter. Thanks also go to our research assistant, Brenda I. Mejía Guerrero.

References

Anderson, S. (1990). Core indicators of nutritional state for difficult-to-sample populations. *Journal of Nutrition, 120*, 1559–1600.
Aungst, D. (2013, July 19). *Food insecurity and health impacts.* Retrieved from http://msue.anr.msu.edu/news/food_insecurity_and_health_impacts
Bashir, M. K., & Schilizzi, S. (2012). *Measuring food security: Definitional sensitivity and implications.* Retrieved from http://ageconsearch.umn. edu/bitstream/124227/2/2012AC%20Bashir,%20Khalid%20CP.pdf
Brown, J. L. (1987). Hunger in the U.S. *Scientific American, 256*, 37–41.
Bukusuba, J., Kikafunda, J. K., & Whitehead, R. G. (2007). Food security status in households of people living with HIV/AIDS (PLWHA) in a Ugandan urban setting. *British Journal of Nutrition, 98*(1), 211–217.
Charlton, K. E., & Rose, D. (2001). Nutrition among older adults in Africa: The situation at the beginning of the millennium. *Journal of Nutrition, 131*(9), 2424S–2428S.
Clay, E. (2003). Food security: Concepts and measurement. In *Trade reforms and food security: Conceptualizing the linkages.* Retrieved from http://www.fao.org/3/a-y4671e.pdf. Food and Agriculture Organization of the United Nations, Rome.
Coates, J. (2013). Build it back better: Deconstructing food security for improved measurement and action. *Global Food Security, 2*(3), 188–194.
Coates, J. C., Webb, P., Houser, R. F., Rogers, B. L., & Wilde, P. (2010). 'He said, she said': Who should speak for households about experiences of food insecurity in Bangladesh? *Food Security, 2*(1), 81–95.
Dinour, L., Bergen, D., & Yeh, M.-C. (2007). The food insecurity–obesity paradox: A review of the literature and the role food stamps may play. *Journal of the American Dietetic Association, 107*(11), 1952–1961.
Food and Agriculture Organization of the United Nations [FAO]. (1996, November). *Declaration on world food security and world food summit plan of action.* Retrieved from http://www.fao.org/docrep/003/w3613e/ w3613e00.HTM
Food and Agriculture Organization of the United Nations [FAO]. (2000). *Handbook for defining and setting up a food security information and early warning system (FSIEWS).* Retrieved from http://www.fao.org/ nr/climpag/pub/Manual%20of%20FSIEWS.pdf

Food and Agriculture Organization of the United Nations [FAO]. (2002). *The state of food insecurity in the world.* Retrieved from http://www.fao.org/docrep/003/y1500e/y1500e00.htm

Food and Agriculture Organization of the United Nations [FAO]. (2013). *Afrontar la escasez de agua.* Retrieved from www.fao.org/docrep/018/i3015s/i3015s.pdf

Food and Agriculture Organization of the United Nations, International Fund for Agricultural Development, and World Food Programme [FAO, IFAD, and WFP]. (2014). *The state of food insecurity in the world 2014. Strengthening the enabling environment for food security and nutrition.* Retrieved from http://www.fao.org/publications/sofi/2014/en/

González, W. A. (2008). Development and validation of measures of household food insecurity in urban Costa Rica confirms proposed generic questionnaire. *Journal of Nutrition, 138*(3), 587−592.

Grünberger, K. (2014). Estimating food consumption patterns by reconciling food balance sheets and household budget surveys. FAO Statistics, Working Paper Series. FAO, Rome.

Hales, S., & Blakely, T. (2002). Prediction of childhood anthropometric parameters based on a poverty index: An empirical statistical method using demographic and health survey data. In *Measurement and assessment of food deprivation and undernutrition.* Rome: FAO. Retrieved from http://www.fao.org/3/a-y4249e/y4249e0f.htm

Hamelin, A. M., Habicht, J. P., & Beaudry, M. (1999). Food insecurity: Consequences for the household and broader social implications. *Journal of Nutrition, 129,* 525S−528S.

Hansen, B. E. (2015). *Econometrics.* Retrieved from http://www.ssc.wisc.edu/~bhansen/econometrics/Econometrics.pdf

Harsanyi, J. (1955). Cardinal welfare, individualistic ethics, and interpersonal comparisons of utility. *Journal of Political Economy, 63*(4), 309−321.

Jacobs, K., & Sumner, D. A. (2002). *The food balance sheets of the Food and Agriculture Organization: A review of potential ways to broaden the appropriate uses of the data.* Retrieved from http:www.//ksph.kz/Chemistry_Food%20Safety/TotalDietStudies/FBS_Rev.pdf

Jones, A., Ngure, F., Pelto, G., & Young, S. (2013). What are we assessing when we measure food security? A compendium and review of current metrics. *Advances in Nutrition, 4,* 481−505.

Kuhnlein, H. V., Smitasiri, S., Yesudas, S., Ahmed, S., Kothari, G., Bhattacharjee, L., & Fengying, Z. (2002). Documenting traditional food systems of indigenous peoples: Process and methods with international case studies. In Measurement and assessment, *FIVIMS* proceedings, FAO, Rome.

Maxwell, S., & Frankenberger, T. (1992). *Household food security: Concepts, indicators, measurements.* A technical review, IFAD/

UNICEF. Retrieved from http://www.ifad.org/gender/tools/hfs/hfspub/

Mead, B., & Rosen, S. (2002). *Measuring access to food in developing countries: The case of Latin America.* Retrieved from http://ageconsearch.umn.edu/bitstream/19716/1/sp02me01.pdf

Melgar-Quiñonez, H. A. (2006). Household food insecurity and food expenditure in Bolivia, Burkina Faso, and the Philippines. *Journal of Nutrition, 136*(5), 1431S–1437S.

Naiken, L. (2002). *FAO methodology for estimating the prevalence of undernourishment.* Retrieved from http://www.fao.org/docrep/005/Y4249E/y4249e06.htm

Pérez-Escamilla, R., Correa-Segall, A., Kurdian, L., Sampaio, F., Marín-León, L., & Panigassi, G. (2004). An adapted version of the US Department of Agriculture food insecurity module is a valid tool for assessing household food insecurity in Campinas, Brazil. *Journal of Nutrition, 134*, 1923–1928.

Pérez-Escamilla, R., Paras, P., & Hromi-Fiedler, A. (2008). Validity of the Latin American and Caribbean household food security scale (ELCSA) in Guanajuato, México. *FASEB Journal, 22*, 871–872.

Power, E. (2008). Conceptualizing food security for aboriginal people in Canada. *Canadian Journal of Public Health, 99*(2), 95–97.

Sen, A. K. (1985). *Commodities and capabilities.* Amsterdam: North-Holland.

Slesnik, D. T. (1998). Empirical approaches to the measurement of welfare. *Journal of Economic Literature, 36*(4), 2108–2165.

Smith, L. (2002). *The use of household expenditure surveys for the assessment of food insecurity.* Retrieved from http://www.fao.org/docrep/005/Y4249E/y4249e00.htm#Contents

Swindale, A., & Bilinsky, P. (2006). Development of a universally applicable household food insecurity measurement tool: Process, current status, and outstanding issues. *Journal of Nutrition, 136*(5), 1449S–1452S.

United States Department of Agriculture [USDA]. (2000). *Guide to measuring household food security.* Retrieved from www.fns.usda.gov/sites/default/files/FSGuide_0.pdf

United States Department of Agriculture [USDA]. (2011). *Role of nutrition in learning and behavior: A resource list for professionals.* Retrieved from https://www.nal.usda.gov/fnic/pubs/learning.pdf

Ziliak, J. P. (2011). Food insecurity among older adults. *AARP.* Retrieved from http://www.aarp.org/content/dam/aarp/aarp_foundation/pdf_2011/AARPFoundation_HungerReport_2011.pdf

5

Food Security Issues: Concepts and the Role of Emerging Markets

Shida Rastegari Henneberry[a] and Claudia Diaz Carrasco[b]

[a]*Dept of Agricultural Economics, Oklahoma State University, Stillwater, 74078, OK, USA*
E-mail address: srh@okstate.edu
[b]*University of California Cooperative Extension, Riverside and San Bernardino Counties,*
Moreno Valley, 92557, CA, USA
E-mail address: cpdiaz@ucanr.edu

Abstract

Purpose − The objective of this chapter is to provide an understanding of the meaning and measurements of food security.

Methodology/approach − This chapter consolidates and examines the evolution of the many definitions of food security since 1975 and describes the four dimensions of global food security. We examine the relationship between global food crisis and food security, and the significance of Brazil, Russia, India, China, and South Africa as emerging markets.

Findings − Achieving food security will be determined by the world as a group helping developing countries in creating proper infrastructures, providing better income opportunities, and reducing financial constraints.

Practical implications − Governments, international agencies, private firms, and the world's population need to be involved in food security from seed to plate.

Keywords: Emerging markets, food security, availability, access, utilization, stability

1. Introduction

In today's globalized world, many international agencies, organizations, and governments are investing resources into the definition and design of

Frontiers of Economics and Globalization
Volume 15   ISSN: 1574-8715
DOI: 10.1108/S1574-871520150000015005

strategies in response to challenges in the twenty-first century. Global food security is one of the most important of these challenges due to its wide definition and scope, which includes issues such as poverty, hunger, and undernourishment.

In 2000, a total of 189 countries from around the world signed the Declaration of the Millennium Development Goals to eradicate extreme poverty and hunger while addressing basic human rights. Significant progress is being achieved due to the efforts of governments and international agencies. For example, in developing regions, the proportion of people living on less than US$1.25 per day has been reduced (from 47% in 1990 to 22% in 2010), and world poverty has been halved. Still, one out of eight people in the world (12.5% of the world's population) go to bed hungry and two billion people suffer from one or more micronutrient deficiencies (UN, 2013).

Food insecurity results in inadequate physical, social, and/or economic access of individuals to sufficient, safe, and nutritious food to meet their basic dietary needs for an active and healthy life (FAO, 2003). The most direct consequence of food insecurity is malnutrition, while the most indirect consequence is chronic and infectious diseases (Barrett, 2010). The Food and Agriculture Organization of the United Nations (FAO) estimates that the cost of malnutrition accounts for as much as 5% of global gross domestic product (GDP), or about US$3.5 trillion per year (FAO, 2013d). Malnutrition leads to the loss of productivity, which hampers economic growth, especially in agrarian-based societies (FAO, IFAD, & WFP, 2012).

Given that there are many definitions of food security and that ambiguity exists over its measurements, the objective of this chapter is to provide an understanding of the meaning and measurements of food security. More specifically, this chapter consolidates and examines the evolution of the many definitions of food security since 1975 and describes the four dimensions of global food security. Additionally, we analyze the relationship between global food crisis and food security. Given their significance as emerging markets, Brazil, Russia, India, China, and South Africa (BRICS) will be examined in relation to food security.

2. The definitions of global food security

Food security was first defined in 1975 by the United Nations as the "availability at all times of adequate world food supplies of basic food stuffs to sustain a steady expansion of food consumption and to offset fluctuations in production and prices" (FAO, 2003, p. 27). In other words, considering quantity and prices, the state of global food security results from the ability of the world's food producers to sustain food consumption at all times. Consequently, food security was seen as a one-dimensional issue of food availability.

Between 1983 and 1996, the definition of food security expanded to include three more dimensions in addition to availability. The expanded definition states that a food secure world depends on continuous *availability* (supplies), *access* (affordability), and appropriate *utilization* (nutritional adequacy) of foods. The *access* dimension represents the equilibrium in food supply and demand systems. In the real world where globalization and economies of scale play important economic roles in the profitability of food value chains, the equality of supply to demand might not represent efficient allocation of resources. Even without international trade and assuming a country's self-sufficiency, food may be available in some areas while being scarce in others. A decade later, the need for *sustainable* food security was emphasized, leading to the incorporation of *stability* into the concept. Thus, food security became a four-dimensional issue: availability, accessibility, utilization, and stability.

During the 1983—1996 period, researchers (Anderson, 1990; Maxwell, 1988; Staatz & Eicher, 1990) and international organizations (World Bank, 1986) helped elucidate the original generic concept of food security. The evolved definition not only encompassed the four dimensions of food security but also changed its focus from a global scope to the particular concerns of each nation.

With the approach of the twenty-first century, about 200 different interpretations of the meaning of global food security were compiled and analyzed (Smith, Pointing, & Maxwell, 1992). Table 1 demonstrates the progression of the definition of food security since 1975. Researchers such as Anderson (1990) and later FAO (1996b) incorporated the importance of *nutritional adequacy* (utilization). Other researchers (Maxwell, 1988; Staaz & Eicher, 1990) brought the *stability* dimension — food should be provided on a continuous basis to the whole global population — into the definition.

The most frequently cited definition of food security was developed in 1996 at the World Food Summit (FAO, 1996a). This definition states that "food security exists when all people, at all times, have physical and economic access to sufficient, safe, and nutritious food that meets their dietary needs and food preferences for an active and healthy life" (FAO, 1996a, web/p. 4). By using the adjectives sufficient, safe, and nutritious, this definition brings attention to the *utilization* dimension. Table 2 highlights the indicators used to measure food security.

3. The four dimensions of global food security

Food security includes four main dimensions: availability, access, utilization, and stability (FAO, 2006). These dimensions encompass the social, environmental, and political aspects of food security, with the overall

Table 1. Evolution of the definition of food security, 1975–2012

Year	Definition
1975	Availability at all times of adequate world supplies of basic food stuffs to sustain a steady expansion of food consumption, and to offset fluctuations in production and prices (FAO, 2003).
1983	Ensuring that all people at all times have both physical and economic access to the basic food that they need (FAO, 1983).
1986	Food security is access by all people at all times to enough food for an active, healthy life (World Bank, 1986).
1988	A country and people are food secure when their food system operates in such a way as to remove the fear that there will not be enough to eat (Maxwell, 1988).
1990	Food security involves assuring both an adequate supply of food (through production and trade) and access by the population to that supply (Staaz and Eicher, 1990).
1990	Food security (…) includes at a minimum: (a) the ready availability of nutritionally adequate and safe foods and (b) the assured ability to acquire acceptable foods in socially acceptable ways (e.g., without resorting to emergency food supplies, scavenging, stealing, and other coping strategies) (Anderson, 1990).
1996	Food security, at the individual, household, national, regional and global levels [is achieved] when all people, at all times, have physical and economic access to sufficient, safe, and nutritious food to meet their dietary needs and food preferences for an active and healthy life (FAO, 1996a, 2001, p. 49).
2012	Food security has come to denote the availability, access, utilization, and stability of food, universally, over time. Nutritional security is integral to this definition; beyond food being accessible, it must be nutritious and prepared and processed by the body in such a way as to support human health (Misselhorn et al., 2012).

Table 2. The suite of food security indicators

Dimension	Food Security Indicators
Availability	Average dietary energy supply adequacy
	Average value of food production
	Share of dietary energy supply derived from cereals, roots, and tubers
	Average protein supply
	Average supply of protein of animal origin
Access (physical)	Percentage of paved roads over total roads
	Road density
	Rail lines density
Access (economic)	Domestic food price index
Utilization	Access to improved water sources
	Access to improved sanitation facilities
Stability (shocks)	Political stability and absence of violence/terrorism
	Domestic food price volatility
	Per capita food production variability
	Per capita food supply variability
Stability (vulnerability)	Cereal import dependency ratio
	Percentage of arable land equipped for irrigation
	Value of food imports over total merchandise exports

Source: FAO (2013c).

goal of providing adequate food intake for the global population on a continuous basis. Each of these dimensions is described below.

3.1. Dimension 1: availability

The availability dimension addresses the supply side of food security. Consequently, trade and agricultural policies affecting imports, exports, and domestic production, as well as carryover stocks, play an important role in this dimension. This dimension is determined by the existence of "sufficient quantities of food of appropriate quality, supplied through domestic production or imports (including food aid)" (FAO, 2006, p. 1). Based solely on the availability dimension, a country will achieve food security whenever its total food supply equals its total food demand in quantitative and qualitative terms. Elements such as production, imports, exports, and changes in carryover national stocks are taken into consideration when calculating the total food supply.

To measure food availability, FAO (2013a) used a set of indicators related to the average supply of dietary energy and proteins. Kilocalories were used for energy measurement and grams were used for protein measurement to compare food supplies across countries. To calculate the adequate dietary energy supply for an individual, FAO, the World Health Organization (WHO), and the United Nations University (UNU) published a detailed methodology that considers an individual's sex, age, height, and physical activities (FAO, WHO, & UNU, 2001). By using these inputs, tables were developed in which the minimum energy requirement for adult men varied between 1,700 and 4,500 kcal (mean = 3,100) and between 1,550 and 3,850 (mean = 2,700) for adult women. It is interesting to note that the world's per capita food supply rose from about 2,200 kcal/capita/day in the early 1960s to more than 2,800 kcal/capita/day in 2009 (FAO, 2013b). This increase implies that the average food supply should be sufficient to feed everyone (adults, children, and infants) in the world.

The per capita supply represents the average supply available for the population as a whole and not what is actually consumed by each individual. An increase in food supplies does not necessarily imply a reduction in world hunger since food supplies vary by country (FAO, 2013a). The BRICS countries (Brazil, Russia, India, China, and South Africa) play an important role in determining global food supplies (Figure 1). China and India account for 19% and 18% of the world population, respectively. The capacity of these two countries to increase their food supply could be viewed as an opportunity for global food security. More specifically, global food security is expected to improve if China and India increase their domestic food production yield rather than increase their food imports.

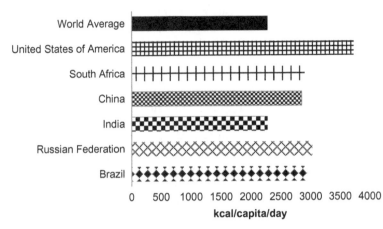

Fig. 1.   Food supply, kilocalories/person/day, BRICS, United States, and world average, 1992–2011. Source: Constructed by authors based on data from FAO (2013b).

Primarily, dependence on food imports could have an inflationary impact on global food prices that could worsen global food security.

3.2. Dimension 2: access

An adequate supply of food at the national or international level does not guarantee food security at the household level. Concerns about insufficient access to food have resulted in a greater policy focus on incomes, expenditures, markets, and prices to achieve food security (FAO, 2008). This dimension of food security refers to the availability to individuals of adequate resources and the ability to acquire appropriate foods for a nutritious diet (FAO, 2006). These opportunities are determined by two types of subdimensional resources: economic and physical. Economic access measures the affordability of food domestically, while physical access measures the infrastructure to provide access to food.

Economic access considers disposable income, food prices, and access to social economic support for individuals (FAO, IFAD, & WFP, 2013). This can be measured by an individual's purchasing power, the variability and price of food, and the availability of social protection programs that directly increase the incomes of poor families to buy food. Figure 2 shows that per capita GDP based on purchasing power parity in the BRICS countries increased between 2003 and 2013. However, this increase alone does not necessarily represent an increase in food access since a population may not always have physical access to food.

The percentage of household expenditures allocated to food is another measure of economic access. According to Engel's law, the poorer a

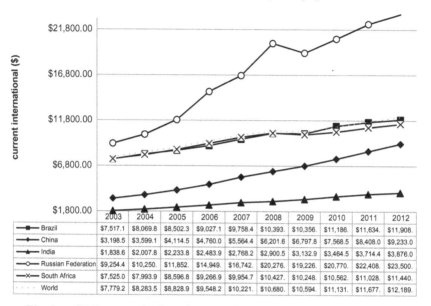

	2003	2004	2005	2006	2007	2008	2009	2010	2011	2012
■— Brazil	$7,517.1	$8,069.8	$8,502.3	$9,027.1	$9,758.4	$10,393.	$10,356.	$11,186.	$11,634.	$11,908.
◆— China	$3,198.5	$3,599.1	$4,114.5	$4,760.0	$5,564.4	$6,201.6	$6,797.8	$7,568.5	$8,408.0	$9,233.0
▲— India	$1,838.6	$2,007.8	$2,233.8	$2,483.9	$2,768.2	$2,900.5	$3,132.9	$3,464.5	$3,714.4	$3,876.0
○— Russian Federation	$9,254.4	$10,250.	$11,852.	$14,949.	$16,742.	$20,276.	$19,226.	$20,770.	$22,408.	$23,500.
✕— South Africa	$7,525.0	$7,993.9	$8,596.8	$9,266.9	$9,954.7	$10,427.	$10,248.	$10,562.	$11,028.	$11,440.
· · · World	$7,779.2	$8,283.5	$8,828.9	$9,548.2	$10,221.	$10,680.	$10,594.	$11,131.	$11,677.	$12,189.

Fig. 2.   GDP per capita based on purchasing power parity, world, and BRICS, 2003–2012. Source: *Constructed by authors based on data from World Bank (2013b).*

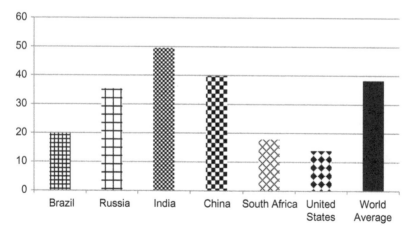

Fig. 3.   Food consumption as a share of household expenditures, 2009. Source: *Constructed by authors based on data from EIU (2013).*

household is, the larger the percentage the household will spend on food (Stigler, 1954). Figure 3 shows food consumption as shares of household expenditure in the BRICS countries and the United States in 2009. As shown in Figure 3, the average world expenditure on food is 38.3%. The

United States (13.9%) is significantly below the world average, followed by South Africa (17.8%) and Brazil (19.8). China (39.8%) and India (49.5%) are above the world average.

Physical access "is determined by the availability and quality of infrastructure, including ports, roads, railways, communications, food storage facilities, and other installations that facilitate the functioning of markets" (FAO, IFAD, & WFP, 2013, p. 20). In other words, this subdimension examines the ability to locate food close to consumers. For example, paved roads determine the impact that transportation costs have on food prices. According to Minten and Kyle (1999), the cost of food transportation on unpaved roads was twice as high as the cost of food transportation on paved roads. Ultimately, this cost is transferred to the consumer through higher food prices.

To measure the agricultural infrastructure of 107 developed and developing countries, the EIU (2013) designed an infrastructure composite indicator based on a weighted average of a series of indicators to measure the ability to store and transport crops to market. Such indicators include adequate cop storage facilities, roads, and port facilities. The composite indicator was scaled from 0 to 100, with 100 representing the most favorable infrastructure. For 2013, the average score for the 107 countries was 52.17. As expected, the developed countries scored higher because they have better transportation infrastructures (Abhijit, Duflo, & Qian, 2012).

3.3. Dimension 3: utilization

This dimension measures the adequacy of household diets and considers the importance of nonfood inputs in achieving food security. Such nonfood inputs include food preparation practices and intrahousehold distribution (FAO, 2006). The utilization dimension encompasses the manner in which food is (1) utilized inside human bodies, (2) prepared within the household, and (3) consumed by individuals.

According to FAO/WHO/UNU (2001), an adequate dietary intake varies between 1,550 and 4,500 kcal/per capita/day depending on the age, sex, and physical activity of each person. Individuals receive their energy requirements from the macronutrients (carbohydrates, protein, and fats) contained in food. Besides the quantity of food intake, the quality and variety of food are also important (FAO, 2008). From a food security perspective, food quality can be measured through the dietary availability of micronutrients (vitamins and minerals) in foods (EIU, 2013). A diversified diet from a variety of foods containing adequate macronutrients and micronutrients is important to ensure nutritional security (EIU, 2013).

One solution for an adequate diet is to increase household income (Haley, 2001). Generally, an increase in household income (especially in developing countries) is associated with an increase in the food consumption of animal-sourced protein such as meat and dairy products as well as a decrease in plant-sourced (cereal) protein (FAO, 2009b). Figure 4 illustrates this change in protein source between 2000 and 2009. Among the emerging markets, India is the only country where animal-

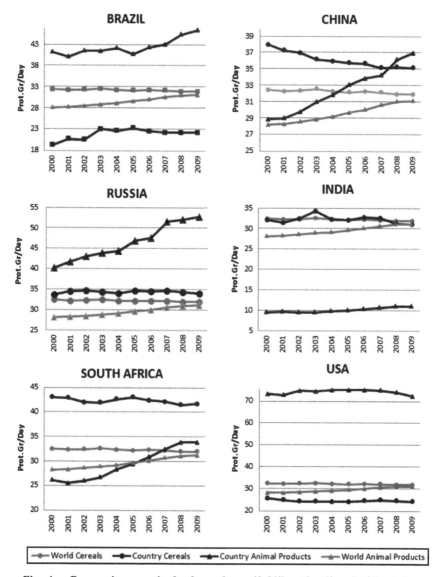

Fig. 4.   Per capita protein food supply availability (kcal/capita/day), by food source, 2000–2009. **Source: Constructed by authors based on data from FAO (2013b).**

sourced protein consumption is below the world average, primarily due to the country's large vegetarian population.

In addition to adequate food consumption, nonfood inputs such as clean water, improved sanitation facilities, and adequate healthcare services are essential for food security. Investments in nonfood inputs are increasing worldwide. According to FAO (2009b), access to clean water sources in the least developed countries has increased from 51% to 65%. China and India have increased their percentages from 67% and 70%, respectively, to 92%. This improvement is likely due to recent economic growth in these countries.

The utilization dimension considers how much, what kind, and in which form food is consumed by individuals. Effective utilization of food will create a lower percentage of undernourishment or micronutrient deficiency in a population. It is important to highlight the fact that nonfood inputs constitute an important element of utilization in food security.

3.4. Dimension 4: stability

The stability dimension involves the guarantee of sufficient, safe, and nutritious food for everyone on a continuous basis. When pursuing food security, programs should focus on providing populations the ability and infrastructure to manage risks effectively.

This dimension evaluates the permanence of the other three dimensions over time. A population, a household, or an individual must have continuous access to adequate food to ensure food security. Thus, the stability dimension considers (1) a population's access to food on a continuous basis, (2) the risks of losing access to food as a consequence of unexpected or cyclical events, and (3) external factors that have the potential to directly threaten food security.

To facilitate the measurement of this dimension, FAO has divided the stability indicators into two further subdimensions: vulnerability and risk (FAO, 2013c). Vulnerability reflects the level of exposure to risk that lessens food insecurity and is measured by four indicators that capture risks (shocks): political stability, price volatility, food production variability, and food supply variability (FAO, IFAD, & WFP, 2013).

Availability of irrigation is one of the key indicators for measuring potential risks and impacts that lead to food instability. Figure 5 shows the trend of arable land equipped for irrigation in the world and the BRICS during 1990–2011.

Another indicator for measuring stability is the share of food imports in total merchandise exports, which indicates the exposure of a country to changes in international trade conditions. Generally, an increase in food imports produces a negative impact on the stability dimension of food security. Although this ratio has declined for the world average, it has

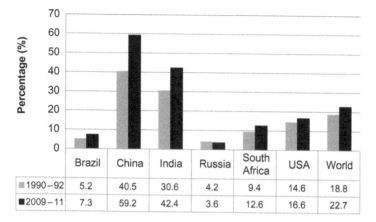

Fig. 5. Percentage of arable land equipped for irrigation, 1900−1992 and 2009−2011. Source: Constructed by authors based on data from FAO (2013b).

increased by 1% for South Africa and India (FAO, 2013c). Another measure for stability is the per capita food production variability index, which measures the variability of the net food production value divided by the population (FAO, 2013c).

4. The global food crisis and its impact on global food security

The 2007−2008 global food crisis exposed the weaknesses of households, governments, and international systems in achieving global food security (HLTF, 2008). International wheat and maize prices doubled and international rice prices tripled, impacting dramatically economic access to food (Headey, 2013). This situation prompted an immediate response from international organizations. Their first goal was to alleviate the crisis's adverse effect on the poor. Their second goal was to shift from crisis response to the pursuit of long-term agricultural and food security programs, especially in developing countries (World Bank, 2013a).

To mitigate the impact on the poor, the World Bank set out a menu of fast-track interventions in 2008 through the Global Food Crisis Response Program. These interventions totaled upward of US$1.2 billion and assisted food distribution operations and supported social safety nets and public works programs (IEG, 2012). These actions targeted all four dimensions of food security. However, further analysis is required to accurately assess the crisis response and its effectiveness. Increases in child malnutrition and general poverty were expected due to the high food prices during the global food crisis (Compton, Wiggins, & Keats, 2010). Surprisingly, there is no survey-based evidence that global food insecurity was higher in 2008 than in previous years (Headey, 2013). This may be attributed to an effective crisis response. Nevertheless, the crisis increased awareness of the need to invest in agriculture.

Timmer (2010) divides crisis-coping strategies into three categories: (1) domestic price stabilization, (2) local market availability, and (3) provision of safety nets to poor consumers. Domestic price stabilization provides more opportunities for short-term economic access to food. Local market availability facilitates quicker physical access to food. Provision of safety nets to poor consumers provides immediate response to a food crisis. Given these points, the World Bank, IFAD, and WFP have concentrated their efforts on the second and third categories.

5. Future challenges for achieving global food security

As reported by FAO (2013c), the world can produce enough food even though that food is not always available in the places where it is most needed. Thus, food insecurity is often the result of a lack of access, poor ability to utilize food, and unstable conditions (FAO, 2013a).

In the figure, population growth may become the principal threat for food availability. By 2050, the world's population is expected to reach 9.1 billion (FAO, 2009b), which includes 34% more people to feed. To achieve food security goals, total world production will need to increase by 70%. In developing countries, where the expansion of available arable land is estimated at only 20% (FAO, 2013a), achieving the 70% goal will require improving crop yield and cropping intensity (FAO, 2009b). Investment in agricultural research and development as well as agricultural technologies will be crucial for achieving the food security goals.

6. The role of emerging countries in global food security

Given that they account for a significant share of the global population (42%) and the world's arable land (30%), the BRICS countries' agricultural production policies have a significant impact on global food security (World Bank, 2013b). The BRICS countries' share of the world GDP increased from 9% to 21% between 2003 and 2013 (Figure 6). China alone tripled its share of world GDP (World Bank, 2013b).

With per capita GDP increases, the BRICS countries' share of expenditures on grains and other staple crops in total food expenditures is expected to decrease, while their share of expenditures on vegetables, fruits, meat, dairy, and fish are expected to increase. Moreover, urbanization in the BRICS countries has led to changes in lifestyle and consumption patterns. In combination with future income growth, these demand-driven changes

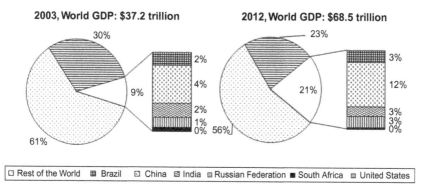

2003, World GDP: $37.2 trillion

2012, World GDP: $68.5 trillion

Rest of the World   Brazil   China   India   Russian Federation   South Africa   United States

Fig. 6. Share of emerging countries in the world's GDP, 2003 and 2012, in 2015 US dollars. Source: Constructed by authors based on data from World Bank (2013b).

are expected to directly impact the access dimension of food security (FAO, 2009a).

7. Conclusions

In the twentieth century, FAO established the globally accepted food security definition. In 2003, FAO published a set of indicators for measuring the state of food security. The acceptance of these indicators is challenged by the high variability in food preparation practices and intrahousehold distribution of food all over the world. Global food crises have motivated governments to rethink their food distribution strategies and to collaborate with various stakeholders to create sustainable programs.

The pace of the economic growth of emerging economies and its impact on their populations may be a good case study for international agencies in creating a global development model to meet the world's needs. Some emerging countries have made significant economic and infrastructure improvements in a short period of time, but these improvements do not adequately help the poorest populations. Further studies are needed to accurately measure the impact that economic growth has on health in emerging countries. This is important because dietary changes, as motivated by increasing household incomes and urbanization, may influence the rates of undernourishment (malnutrition/starvation) and overnourishment (obesity). The BRICS countries have become notable players in the global food markets through their exports and energy consumption.

The Sustainable Development Goals of the United Nations may constitute the next strategic step toward the creation of a food secure world.

Food security initiatives must address the problem of world hunger and malnutrition from a sustainable point of view. Even though ending poverty would give all populations economic access to food, this may not guarantee that the world population will receive the proper food to maintain an active, healthy live. Above all, achieving food security will be determined by the ability to help developing countries in creating proper infrastructures, providing better income opportunities, and reducing financial constraints. Finally, governments, international agencies, private firms, and the population itself need to be involved in food security from seed to plate. This is especially true since food security reaches a wide variety of disciplines, such as agriculture, nutrition, logistics, education, and marketing.

Acknowledgments

Editorial comments of Bailey Boomhower, Graduate Assistant, Master of International Agriculture Degree Program, are acknowledged.

References

Abhijit, B., Duflo, E., & Qian, N. (2012). *On the road: Access to transportation infrastructure and economic growth in China.* Washington, DC: NBER. Retrieved from http://www.nber.org/papers/w17897.pdf?new_window=1

Anderson, S. A. (1990). Core indicators of nutritional state for difficult-to-sample populations. *Journal of Nutrition, 120*(Suppl. 11), 1560.

Barrett, C. B. (2010). Measuring food insecurity. *American Association for the Advancement of Science, 327*, 825. doi:10.1126/science.1182768

Compton, J., Wiggings, S., & Keats, S. (2010). *Impact of the global food crisis on the poor: What is the evidence?* Retrieved from http://www.odi.org.uk/sites/odi.org.uk/files/odi-assets/publications-opinion-files/6371.pdf

Economist Intelligence Unit [EIU]. (2013). *Global food security index 2013: An annual measure of the state of global food security.* Retrieved from http://www.foodsecurityindex.eiu.com/Index

Food and Agriculture Organization of the United Nations [FAO]. (1983). *World food security: A reappraisal of the concepts and approaches.* Rome: FAO.

Food and Agriculture Organization of the United Nations [FAO]. (1996a). *Declaration on world food security and world food summit plan of action.* Retrieved from http://www.fao.org/docrep/003/w3613e/w3613e00.htm

Food and Agriculture Organization of the United Nations [FAO]. (1996b). *Food for all: World food summit report*. Retrieved from www. fao.org/docrep/x0262e/x0262e00.htm#TopOfPage

Food and Agriculture Organization of the United Nations [FAO]. (2001). *The state of food insecurity in the world, 2001*. Retrieved from http:// www.ftp.fao.org/docrep/fao/003/y1500e/y1500E04.pdf

Food and Agriculture Organization of the United Nations [FAO]. (2003). *Trade reforms and food security: Conceptualizing the linkages*. Retrieved from http://www.ftp.fao.org/docrep/fao/005/y4671e/y4671 e00.pdf

Food and Agriculture Organization of the United Nations [FAO]. (2006). *Food security* (Policy Brief 2). Retrieved from http://www.ftp.fao.org/ es/ESA/policybriefs/pb_02.pdf

Food and Agriculture Organization of the United Nations [FAO]. (2008). *An introduction to the basic concepts of food security. Practical guides*. Retrieved from http://www.fao.org/docrep/013/al936e/al936e00.pdf

Food and Agriculture Organization of the United Nations [FAO]. (2009a). *Global agriculture towards 2050*. Retrieved from http://www. fao.org/fileadmin/templates/wsfs/docs/Issues_papers/HLEF2050_ Global_Agriculture.pdf

Food and Agriculture Organization of the United Nations [FAO]. (2009b). *How to feed the world, 2050*. Retrieved from http://www.fao. org/fileadmin/templates/wsfs/docs/expert_paper/How_to_Feed_the_ World_in_2050.pdf

Food and Agriculture Organization of the United Nations [FAO]. (2013a). *FAO statistical yearbook, 2013*. Retrieved from http://www. fao.org/docrep/018/i3107e/i3107e.PDF

Food and Agriculture Organization of the United Nations Statistics [FAO]. (2013b). *FAOSTAT database*. Retrieved from http://faostat. fao.org/

Food and Agriculture Organization of the United Nations Statistics [FAO]. (2013c). *Food security indicators*. Retrieved from http://www. fao.org/economic/ess/ess-fs/ess-fadata/en/#.U0Rp6_ldWSp

Food and Agriculture Organization of the United Nations Statistics [FAO]. (2013d). *The state of food and agriculture*. Retrieved from http://www.fao.org/docrep/018/i3300e/i3300e.pdf

Food and Agriculture Organization of the United Nations, International Fund for Agricultural Development, & World Food Program [FAO, IFAD, & WFP]. (2012). *The state of food insecurity in the world, 2012*. Retrieved from http://www.fao.org/docrep/018/i3434e/i3434e.pdf

Food and Agriculture Organization of the United Nations, International Fund for Agricultural Development, & World Food Program [FAO, IFAD, & WFP]. (2013). *The state of food insecurity in the world, 2013. The multiple dimensions of food security*. Retrieved from http://www. fao.org/docrep/018/i3434e/i3434e00.htm

Food and Agriculture Organization of the United Nations, World Health Organization, & United Nations University [FAO, WHO, & UNU]. (2001). *Human energy requirements.* Retrieved from http://ftp.fao.org/docrep/fao/007/y5686e/y5686e00.pdf

Haley, M. (2001). Changing consumer demand for meat: The US example, 1970–2000. In A. Regmi (Ed.), *Changing structure of global food consumption and trade* (pp. 41–48). Washington, DC: USDA/ERS. Retrieved from http://www.ers.usda.gov/media/293645/wrs011_1_.pdf

Headey, D. (2013). *The impact of the global food crisis on self-assessed food security.* Retrieved from http://www-wds.worldbank.org/external/default/WDSContentServer/WDSP/IB/2013/01/22/00015834.9_20130122134535/Rendered/PDF/wps6329.pdf

High Level Task Force [HLTF]. (2008). *Outcomes and actions for global food security.* Retrieved from http://www.un.org/en/issues/food/taskforce/pdf/OutcomesAndActionsBooklet_v9.pdf

Independent Evaluation Group [IEG]. (2012). *The World Bank: Response to the global economic crisis − Phase II.* Retrieved from http://www.oecd.org/derec/49755570.pdf

Maxwell, S. (1988). *National food security planning: First thoughts from Sudan.* IDS Workshop. University of Sussex, Brighton, United Kingdom.

Minten, B., & Kyle, S. (1999). The effect of distance and road quality on food collection, marketing margins, and traders' wages: Evidence from the former Zaire. *Journal of Development Economics, 60,* 467–495.

Misselhorn, A., Aggarwal, P., Ericksen, P., Gregory, P., Horn-Phathanothai, L., Ingram, J., & Wiebe, K. (2012). A vision for attaining food security. *Current Opinion in Environmental Sustainability, 4,* 7–17. doi:10.1016/j.cosust.2012.01.008

Smith, M., Pointing, J., & Maxwell, S. (1992). *Household food security: Concepts and definitions.* Retrieved from http://web.ifad.org/gender/tools/hfs/hfspub/hfs_3.pdf

Staatz, J., & Eicher, C. (1990). Agricultural development ideas in historical perspective. In C. Eicher & J. Staatz (Eds.), *Agricultural development in the third world* (pp. 8–38). Baltimore, MD: John Hopkins University Press.

Stigler, G. J. (1954). The early history of empirical studies of consumer behavior. *Journal of Political Economy, 62*(2), 95–113.

Timmer, C. P. (2010). Reflections on food crises past. *Food Policy, 35,* 1–11.

United Nations [UN]. (2013). *The millennium development goals report 2013.* Retrieved from http://www.un.org/millenniumgoals/pdf/report-2013/mdg-report-2013-english.pdf

World Bank. (1986). *Poverty and hunger: Issues and options for food security in developing countries*. Washington, DC: World Bank.

World Bank. (2013a). *What do we do?* Retrieved from http://www.world bank.org/en/about/what-we-do

World Bank. (2013b). *World development indicators*. Retrieved from http://databank.worldbank.org/data/home.aspx

6

An Income-based Food Security Indicator for Agricultural Technology Impact Assessment

John Antle, Roshan Adhikari and Stephanie Price

Department of Applied Economics, Oregon State University, Corvallis, 97330, OR, USA;
E-mail address: John.antle@oregonstate.edu, roshanadhikari778@gmail.com and
pricest@oregonstate.edu

Abstract

Purpose – A food security indicator for technology impact assessment is needed that can be constructed with available data, is comparable over time and space, and represents the multiple dimensions of food security.

Methodology/approach – In this chapter, we review some commonly used food security indicators, analyze the extent to which these indicators satisfy key criteria, and introduce a food security indicator constructed for use in an economic impact assessment and that exhibits a number of desirable properties.

Findings – This income-based indicator is similar to a consumption-based poverty indicator, utilizing an estimate of the income required to purchase a food "basket" that meets nutritional requirements and comparing the food security income requirement to a household's per capita income.

Social implications – The applicability of the indicator is illustrated with an analysis of the impacts of legume inoculation technology developed for smallholder farms in Tanzania and other parts of Africa. We conclude with a discussion of suggested improvements for food security indicators used for technology impact assessment.

Keywords: Food security, indicator, technology adoption, Tanzania, soil nutrients

Frontiers of Economics and Globalization
Volume 15   ISSN: 1574-8715
DOI: 10.1108/S1574-871520150000015006

1. Introduction

The 1996 World Food Summit developed the concept that food security exists when everyone has continuous access to safe, nutritious food for a healthy life (Pinstrup-Andersen, 2009). At the 2009 World Summit of Food Security, this concept was extended by adding availability, access, utilization, and stability to the definition of food security (Ecker & Breisinger, 2012). Given its multidimensional nature, food security must be assessed by a suite of indicators and methods (Wineman, 2014). Moreover, many economic models exist that in principle could be used to assess food security impacts of technology, policy, and climate change. Yet, thus far most researchers have not incorporated food security effectively due to data and other model limitations (van Wijk et al., 2014).

The ultimate goal of food security measurement is the utilization of a single measure that is valid and reliable, comparable over time and space, and able to capture different elements of food security (Maxwell, Coates, & Vaitla, 2013). In spite of the development of many different indicators, no single one meets these criteria. While demand for a better food security indicator is apparent, how food security measurement should be improved remains less clear (Headey & Ecker, 2012).

In this chapter, we review the main food security indicators that can be used for technology impact assessment and introduce an income-based food security indicator (IBFS) that addresses many of the issues in measuring food security. This income-based indicator is attractive because it can be incorporated into many of the economic farm household models for technology, policy, and climate impact assessment. We demonstrate the advantages of this indicator using a model of farm technology impact assessment (Tradeoff Analysis Model for Multi-dimensional Impact Assessment (TOA-MD)) to evaluate the potential impacts of legume inoculation technology, which is being developed to improve soil productivity in smallholder farms in a number of regions of Africa. We illustrate our approach using data from the World Bank's Living Standards Measurement Survey to assess the potential of this technology in Tanzanian maize–legume systems.

This chapter reviews several existing food security indicators and the need for an alternative indicator, and briefly describes the proposed food security indicator and how it can be used to assess food security outcomes. This chapter also describes the Tanzania case study as well as its data and results.

2. Farm household food security indicators and agricultural technology

Agricultural technologies and related innovations have been found to improve crop productivity, lower food prices, and increase the ability of households to withstand risk. All of these results directly contribute to sustainable food and nutrition security (Asfaw, Shiferaw, Simtowe, & Lipper, 2012; Minten & Barrett, 2008). While a number of studies have analyzed productivity, income, and the poverty effects of different agricultural technologies, relatively little research had directly linked technologies to household food security outcomes (Kabunga, Dubois, & Qaim, 2014). To the degree that analysts have estimated the impact of technology adoption on food security, very few have explored all four dimensions (availability, access, utilization, and stability) of food security.

Most researchers assessing the impact of technology adoption on food security use one (or a combination) of four types of food security indicators (Headey & Ecker, 2012): calorie deprivation or availability (Mulugeta & Hundie, 2012), monetary poverty (Bezu, Kassie, Shiferaw, & Ricker-Gilbert, 2014; Smale & Mason, 2013), dietary diversity (Tasciotti & Wagner, 2014), and subjective/experiential indicators (Kabunga et al., 2014; Kassie, Jaleta, Shiferaw, Mmbando, & De Groote, 2012). These studies share the drawback of limiting analysis to a single dimension – mainly access or availability – while disregarding the multidimensional nature of food security. We briefly review each of these approaches.

Food supply and utilization data are useful for estimating food shortages and surpluses, developing projections of future demand, and setting targets for agricultural production (FAO, 2001). But caloric availability indicators are unsatisfactory in three ways. First, these indicators rely on the problematic assumption that the mean distribution of calorie consumption in the population equals the average dietary supply (Svedberg, 2000). Second, the nutritional relevance of caloric indicators is limited: many countries possess a very weak or nonexistent correlation between calorie deprivation and anthropometric indicators of malnutrition (Headey & Ecker, 2012). Third, calorie deprivation is not a reliable indicator of trends, shock impacts, or seasonality (Maxwell et al., 2013).

Monetary Poverty Indicators (MPIs) link access to food to monetary proxy (income, consumption, wealth, or expenditure) under the premise that higher incomes imply higher food security. The majority of the work in this field (e.g., Subramanian & Deaton, 1996) has found a positive relationship between calorie consumption and a monetary proxy. However, several other researchers draw opposite conclusions. For example, Deaton and Drèze (2009) show that calorie consumption in India has decreased despite increases in real income, while Bouis, Haddad, and Kennedy (1992) demonstrate that calorie consumption depends on the income elasticity of each food item rather than income alone. MPIs have been criticized for their lack of cross-sectional and intertemporal validity. These types of indicators are difficult to compare across countries (due to exchange rates) and within countries (due to rural–urban differences).

Dietary Diversity Indicators (DDIs) use information on the number of different foods or food groups consumed by an individual or a household over a given reference period. Nutritionists have acknowledged dietary diversity as both a proxy for food access and a key indicator of good nutrition (Ruel, 2003). Despite their cost-effectiveness and positive associations with other proxy indicators of household food security, DDIs are limited by the amount of available data. Specifically, in order to carry out an ex ante analysis, studies can only predict the effects of economic shocks if data are available on past shock effects on dietary diversity. Furthermore, DDIs are not always comparable across countries because preferences and diets across countries vary markedly.

Generally, subjective indicators are calculated using data from surveys in which respondents rate the severity of their food insecurity. These indicators possess an advantage over other indicators discussed previously in this section because the former gauge expectations of respondents (e.g., inflation rates) and contain a relatively low cost of subjective data. However, survey design (e.g., order of questions) can affect responses regarding food insecurity, thereby generating unreliable results. Moreover, due to the nature of the survey questions, the changes in these indicators may not be comparable to changes in other indicators (Headey & Ecker, 2012).

Thus, extant research mainly disregards the multidimensional and complex nature of food security. The most common suggestions for improving food security relate to data collection and the ability to assess food security over time. Barrett (2010) and Headey and Ecker (2012) suggest standardization of data collection to allow for better cross-sectional validity. In addition, increasing the frequency and efficiency of surveys helps capture the temporal aspects of food security and the ability of households to adapt to shocks (Headey & Ecker, 2012). Moreover, the predictive accuracy of food security indicators in forecasting future food security states is important to cost-effectively concentrate data collection on measures with the best targetable actions (Barrett, 2010).

3. An IBFS

Many economic models are used for technology impact assessment and other policy analysis, but few have incorporated food security indicators into their analytical framework (van Wijk et al., 2014). We propose an IBFS that addresses several highlighted issues. This indicator can be used in any technology assessment that predicts changes in per capita income (such as the TOA-MD model in the application presented below) and can be used with the various other household-level or farm population models that generate farm household income predictions. Our indicator is similar to the Foster–Greer–Thorbecke (1984) poverty indicators, but instead of comparing income to a poverty line, the IBFS estimates the income required to purchase a food basket that meets nutritional requirements and then compares this food security income requirement to the household's per capita income. Given the availability of sufficiently disaggregated data, our indicator could be extended to assess the food security of individuals within a household.

The IBFS is calculated in three steps. First, the share of income devoted to food purchases is either estimated from observational data or specified as a parameter, S_f; second, the cost (C_f) of a nutritionally adequate food basket is estimated using data on per capita nutritional requirements (macronutrients and micronutrients), typical food consumption patterns, and the nutritional content of foods; and third, the IBFS threshold is defined as $\tau_f = C_f / S_f$, which indicates the amount of income needed per person for the purchase of a nutritionally adequate diet. If a household's per capita income is less than τ_f, then the household cannot afford a nutritionally adequate food basket. Dividing τ_f by per capita income and multiplying by 100 produces a food security index in which a household with an index value of 100 is food secure, while a household with a value less than 100 is food insecure.

When combined with the TOA-MD model (presented below), this indicator addresses several problems with the current suite of food security indicators. First, the TOA-MD model can be used to predict the impacts of technology adoption as well as price, income, and agricultural production shocks on per capita income. Thus, these effects can be translated into impacts on food insecurity using the IBFS. Second, any nutrient outcomes (micro or macro) associated with the food basket can be assessed. The food basket can also be designed to include only micronutrients or macronutrients to evaluate population-specific nutrition outcomes.

Furthermore, the IBFS inherits the desirable aggregation properties of the Foster–Greer–Thorbecke poverty indicator and is thus unit-free so that it can be compared across space and time. However, the indicator is based on the cost of a food basket that reflects consumer preferences. Thus, the indicator relies strongly on a correct accounting for differences regarding share of income allocated to food purchases across populations. Given projected changes in income and other socioeconomic variables (e.g., in studies of climate change impacts), the IBFS may also be useful in forecasting future food security states.

In principle, the IBFS can also assess the stability of food security if it is possible to model the stability (or variation) in income and costs of food. In most cases, and as in the case study presented below, the stability dimension cannot be represented due to data limitations.

4. An application of the IBFS

We illustrate the use of the IBFS in an assessment of the adoption and impact of a legume inoculant technology in Tanzania. This technology is designed to increase legume, maize, and livestock by-product yields. Farmers apply the inoculant to legume seeds, which increases nitrogen fixation and increases yields of crops grown with the legume or in a rotation. Legume cultivation is functionally important in settings where many smallholders cultivate maize without applying sufficient nutrients to maintain soil fertility. Inoculating legumes – whether intercropped or rotated with maize – substitutes for purchased nitrogen fertilizer or organic amendments such as manure.

Additionally, farmers may also need to utilize a number of complimentary practices and inputs to achieve the maximum potential of the technology. Farmers must use a variety of legumes that matches the available strain of inoculant; thus, they may need to purchase seed. To fully access the benefits from the increased nitrogen in the soil, farmers may also need to apply other nutrients, notably phosphorous. Soil quality and maize yields will increase with increased N and P levels and organic matter from legume crop residue. Improved soils may attract invasive plants and increased crop yields may attract pests; thus, pesticides or herbicides may be necessary. Although additional costs and labor will be required to implement the technology, the yield benefits are expected to result in higher productivity and farm incomes.

4.1. The TOA-MD model

The TOA-MD uses a statistical characterization of a farming population to assess adoption potential of a new technology (such as legume inoculant) and its impacts on farm household income (Antle, 2011; Antle, Stoorvogel, & Valdivia, 2014). Documentation of the model, including the data used in this analysis, are available at tradeoffs.oregonstate.edu. In addition to economic impacts, other quantifiable outcomes associated with a change in production system (such as environmental or social outcomes) can be included through appropriate indicators. In this analysis, we include several food security indicators, including the income-based food security indicator discussed above. This model is based on the logical structure of the "Roy model" from the econometric policy evaluation literature (Heckman & Vytlacil, 2007). This model posits a farmer's choice between two systems according to the expected value received from each system according to $max_h v(h), h = 1, 2$, where $v(h)$ is an expected economic return under a set of farming practices in system h. Let System 1 be a baseline system currently in use, and let System 2 be a new or modified system (e.g., the use of legume inoculant). We define the expected opportunity cost of changing from System 1 to System 2 as $\omega = v(1) - v(2)$.

In a farming population, there are various observable and unobservable factors that influence expected returns. Such factors include the physical environment, weather, farmer abilities, and resources. To account for this variability, in the TOA-MD model, the expected opportunity cost ω is assumed to be distributed in the farm household population with normal probability density $\varphi(\omega|\mathbf{p})$, where $\mathbf{p}$ represents exogenous price and other variables that define this distribution. Farmers choose their farming system based on the expected opportunity cost of adoption: if $\omega < 0$, a farmer expects a higher economic outcome from adopting System 2, and vice versa if $\omega > 0$. Using this distribution $\varphi(\omega|\mathbf{p})$, the TOA-MD model calculates a predicted adoption rate $r(p)$ as the proportion of farms that could benefit economically from adoption. When a new technology is introduced, there is a process of learning about the new technology and a resulting diffusing process that are not represented in the TOA-MD model. There may be factors that actually constrain adoption by farmers: lack of information, limited access to the technology, or lack of financial resources to acquire it. Thus, it is important to interpret the predicted adoption rates from this model as indicating the *potential* rate of adoption that can be achieved once the technology has been disseminated, and becomes available, at the cost assumed in the setup of the TOA-MD model.

The expected opportunity cost ω in the TOA-MD model is equivalent to the (negative of) the marginal treatment effect, which is the fundamental concept in the analysis of exogenous effects or treatment effects in the econometric policy evaluation literature (Heckman & Vytlacil, 2007). In the context of technology adoption, the treatment is the new technology represented by System 2. The average treatment effect (ATE) is the difference in mean outcomes between the two systems for the entire population. The treatment effect on the treated (TT) is the mean effect on adopters of the new technology, and the treatment effect on the untreated (TU) is the mean effect on non-adopters (Antle et al., 2014).

The TOA-MD model is parameterized by using economic and technological information to estimate mean and variance of the distribution $\varphi(\omega|\mathbf{p})$. The mean and variance of ω in turn are determined by the means, variances, and covariance parameters of $v(1)$ and $v(2)$ because $\omega = v(1) - v(2)$. Thus, the model parameterization involves estimating these parameters of the distributions of expected returns for each system. To calculate farm household income, the TOA-MD model also utilizes statistics for the distributions of nonagricultural income and farm household size.

In the Tanzanian farming systems studied here, System 1 consists of households producing crops and livestock that do not currently employ the legume inoculant technology. System 1 is parameterized using the distribution of farm characteristics observed in a subset of the population represented in the World Bank's Living Standards Measurement Survey TZA NPS 2010–2011 (Tanzania National Bureau of Statistics [NBS] and Ministry of Finance, 2012). These parameters include area, household size, off-farm income, and net returns from crop and livestock activities. To characterize System 2, we assume the legume inoculation technology causes a proportional increase in net returns for activities that directly and indirectly benefit from the technology. As the technology will vary in effectiveness across the population, we assume the proportional increase of net returns is a random variable with a coefficient of variation of 1, implying the standard deviation of this productivity increase equals the mean impact. This assumption can be interpreted as a mid-range value for the heterogeneity of the technology impact and is justified by data from other studies that show a similar degree of heterogeneity in technology impacts (Antle, Diagana, Stoorvogel, & Valdivia, 2010). This assumption can be subjected to sensitivity analysis to investigate its effect. In the TOA-MD model, adoption rates are not highly sensitive to this assumption except in cases of extremely low or high adoption rates (the adoption rates predicted are not in those ranges). The other parameters in the model are correlations between the economic returns to the activities within each system and the correlation between the returns of the base system and the alternative system. To estimate these correlations, we use the observed System 1 information and the assumptions used to form System 2, as discussed in the TOA-MD model documentation available at tradeoffs.oregonstate.edu.

The average proportional increase of net returns and the technology cost are estimates based on information contained in progress and monitoring reports published as part of the N2Africa project (Woomer, Huising, & Giller, 2014; Woomer, Kadenge, Wanza, & Rose, 2011). N2Africa is a project led by Wageningen University, the International Institute of Tropical Agriculture (IITA), and International Center for Tropical Agriculture – Tropical Soil Biology and Fertility (CIA-TBSF) to implement nitrogen-fixing technologies in Africa. The project has compiled data sourced from the FAO, an N2Africa baseline survey on farm trials, and an N2Africa scientific review to characterize baseline conditions and project future impacts of their technology. This analysis combines existing survey datasets along with technical estimates of yield increases and costs to estimate projected adoption and other outcome indicators in the TOA-MD framework.

For this analysis, we consider smallholder farmers who cultivate legumes and maize. Farmers in this population typically cultivate multiple crops (monocropped, intercropped, and rotational-cropped), integrate livestock and aquaculture into crop activities, and do not invest much in productive inputs. Households in this population have a strong preference for maize and are possibly food insecure. To accurately characterize a population's response to the availability of this technology in the marketplace, the model must consider the population of farmers actually being served. This point seems simple, but a farming population will have a distinct distribution of characteristics such as size, income, and crop activities. The TOA-MD model uses a population's heterogeneity as a fundamental driver of its projections; thus, the target population must be accurately identified for a correct estimate of the first and second moments of these drivers. Observable or unobservable characteristics of farming households may necessitate disaggregation into subpopulations (strata) or exclusion from the analysis. Using the Living Standards Measurement Survey TZA NPS covering agricultural production and household data, we identify smallholder households that produce both maize and legumes. We then disaggregate these into strata of different farming systems (crop only, mixed crop and livestock, or majority permanent crops) and productivity level (high or low maize or legume yields per hectare). The subset population in this analysis comprises the poorest, smallest, and least productive farms that cultivate both maize and legumes during the two growing seasons covered by the survey. Table 1 displays summary statistics of TOA-MD model parameters by strata for farms within the target population.

4.2. Adoption analysis

Table 2 summarizes the adoption rates predicted by the TOA-MD model for each stratum of the population and for the population in its entirety. The TOA-MD model projects adoption rates that range from about 35% to 52% and average about 43%. The adoption analysis also shows a modest positive impact of the technology on poverty rates in most strata due to the high baseline poverty rate. These results suggest that strata with low productivity will adopt with less success than their high productivity system counterparts. Additionally, mixed production system populations will see a slightly higher level of adoption than crop-only systems due to the benefits that accrue from integrating crop residues into livestock activities. The model predicts the least amount of adoption for populations that produce primarily permanent crops such as fruit or tree nuts. Given the adoption projections, the projected outcomes of net returns (income), income per capita, and poverty rate of strata are calculated. Roughly, adopters of the technology have higher net returns and income per capita, as well as lower poverty rates, than non-adopters. Whether these improvements are due to the adoption of technology is unclear.

Table 1. Food security sample summary statistics, low off-farm income farms

	High Productivity			Low Productivity			All households
	Crop only	Mixed	Majority permanent crops	Crop only	Mixed	Majority permanent crops	
Household count	108	43	32	259	48	176	666
Household size							
Mean	5.0	6.8	5.8	4.9	6.9	5.4	5.3
Standard deviation	2.0	2.9	2.5	2.6	3.0	2.9	2.7
Farm size							
Mean	1.9	2.0	1.8	1.7	1.9	1.5	1.7
Standard deviation	1.3	1.2	1.2	1.2	1.1	1.2	1.2
Agriculture net returns (US$)							
Mean	387	721	819	247	625	413	399
Standard deviation	368	568	593	314	539	400	433
Off-farm income (US$)							
Mean	351	289	309	306	185	339	312
Standard deviation	541	570	469	556	486	570	549
Income per capita (US$)							
Mean	186	175	225	137	129	168	159
Standard deviation	271	169	243	216	159	198	217
Poverty rate (%)							
HHs below $1 per day	90%	86%	84%	92%	94%	90%	90%
Persons below $1 per day	94%	92%	89%	94%	97%	95%	94%

Table 2. *TOA-MD adoption analysis results, low off-farm income households*

	High Productivity			Low Productivity			All Households
	Crop only	Mixed	Majority permanent crops	Crop only	Mixed	Majority permanent crops	
Adoption rate (%, at ω = 0)							
Households	49.2	51.6	42.4	44.4	49.1	34.9	43.9
Net returns (US$)							
Adopters	$674	$1,297	$1,040	$481	$1,143	$579	$666
Non-adopters	$349	$689	$757	$202	$614	$370	$358
Total	$509	$1,003	$877	$326	$874	$443	$496
Treatment effects on net returns (% of US$)							
ATE	2.8	10.2	-4.3	3.7	8.9	-12.2	-0.3
TT	58.2	73.2	15.0	58.8	79.5	17.8	46.4
TU	-65.6	-73.8	-19.7	-83.7	-82.8	-30.1	-58.5
Income per capita (US$)							
Adopters	$237	$273	$280	$209	$228	$220	$227
Non-adopters	$162	$168	$222	$135	$137	$170	$156
Total	$199	$222	$246	$167	$182	$187	$188
Treatment effects on income per capita (% of US$)							
ATE	1.4	7.3	-3.2	1.7	6.9	-6.7	-0.3
TT	31.9	52.8	11.1	29.3	61.6	10.5	27.1
TU	-34.3	-52.6	-14.3	-37.0	-63.8	-16.5	-32.4
Poverty rate (%)							
Adopters	79	71	69	83	82	82	80
Non-adopters	92.1	93.2	82.7	94.6	97.1	90.9	92.7
Total	85.4	81.8	77.1	89.6	89.8	87.8	87.2
Treatment effects on poverty rate (% of counterfactual)							
ATE	-2.9	-7.2	0.7	-1.7	-4.4	1.3	-1.7
TT	-12.5	-22.5	-8.9	-9.0	-15.1	-4.8	-10.2
TU	4.9	5.5	7.1	3.5	2.4	3.9	4.0

4.3. Impacts on food security

Given the adoption projections, an income-based threshold, and projected outcomes of income per capita, we can implement the food security indicator in TOA-MD by using the above data to calculate the appropriate income threshold for food security. To calculate the income-based threshold for IBFS, we first use a nutritionally adequate food basket defined for the poorest households by the Tanzania National Bureau of Statistics (Tanzania NBS and Ministry of Finance, 2012). The food basket is obtained as the average food consumption of the bottom 50% of the population, ranked in terms of real per adult equivalent consumption and representing the preferences of the smallholder farmers in our analysis. We can then calculate the cost of a food basket for individuals based on their calorie requirements; the average annual per capita cost of the basket is US$147 for the target population. The share of income spent on food (S_f) (i.e., the ratio of per capita food expenditure and per capita income) is then used to calculate the income-based threshold for the food security indicator: $\tau_f =$ (cost of food basket per capita $[C_f]$/share of income spent on food per capita $[S_f]$). The average share of income spent on food for the smallholder farmers is 0.73, and the income-based threshold is US$196.

The results from the TOA-MD simulation (presented in Table 3) indicate that technology adoption generates a positive impact on food security and that the impact varies by level of adoption. We find that the likely adoption rates of the legume inoculant technology are in the range of 35%−52% depending on the type of farming system and the productivity level of the household. The likely impact of the technology on agricultural incomes of the adopting households ranges from 18% to 73%, with an overall impact of about 46%. The likely impact of the technology on the food insecurity status among the adopting population is a decrease in the range of 11%−42%, with an average of 23% for all adopters.

As expected, we also found that the IBFS produces qualitative impacts similar to the income-based poverty indicator. This is because adoption raises per capita incomes and reduces poverty and food insecurity. However, the magnitude of baseline values of poverty and food insecurity are quantitatively very different, and quantitative impacts of the technology differ substantially between poverty and food insecurity reductions. The adoption analysis results show that decreases in poverty rates for adopters are in the range of 4%−22% across the various strata, whereas decreases in food insecurity rates range from 11% to 42%.

Several extensions of the IBFS are possible. First, we can use the IBFS to quantify the intensity of food insecurity, similar to the concept of the poverty gap introduced by Foster, Greer, and Thorbecke. A measure of food insecurity intensity can be calculated as $100 \, (FS - E[PCI \mid \tau_f \geq PCI]/\tau_f)$, where $E[PCI \mid \tau_f \geq PCI]$ is the mean of PCI for

Table 3. Impacts of legume inoculant technology adoption on food insecurity using the income-based indicator in the TOA-MD model analysis

	High Productivity			Low Productivity			All Households
	Crop only	Mixed	Majority permanent crops	Crop only	Mixed	Majority permanent crops	
Adoption rate (%)							
Households	49.2	51.6	42.4	44.4	49.1	34.9	43.9
Food insecure (%)							
Base	57	56.9	40.2	63.6	68.3	54.3	58.8
Adopters	39.8	32.2	30.7	46.9	41.5	44	42.5
Non-adopters	59.3	58.3	43.3	66.6	68.8	57.1	61.3
Total	49.7	44.8	38	57.8	55.4	52.5	52.9
Counterfactual (%)							
Adopters	54.4	55.2	36.1	59.2	67.5	49.2	55.1
Non-adopters	74	80.7	52.1	79.3	88.2	65.3	74.3
Treatment effects (%)							
ATE	−1.3	−4.4	2.1	−1.4	−5.7	3.1	−0.7
TT	−14.5	−23.1	−5.5	−12.4	−26	−5.2	−12.6
TU	14.7	22.4	8.8	12.8	19.4	8.2	13.1
Treatment effects (% of counterfactual)							
ATE	−2.2	−7.7	5.2	−2.3	−8.3	5.7	−1.1
TT	−26.7	−41.8	−15.2	−20.8	−38.5	−10.6	−22.9
TU	25.8	39.4	21.9	20.1	28.4	15.2	22.2

food insecure households. Second, it would be possible to compute an IBFS for each household member by accounting for differences by age and gender, intrahousehold income allocation, and food allocation. Third, it would be possible to account for instability of food availability and income were data available by subannual time periods such as growing seasons.

5. Conclusions

In this chapter, we introduce an IBFS that addresses several limitations of currently and commonly used food security indicators. The IBFS estimates the income required to purchase a food basket that meets nutritional requirements and then compares this food security income requirement to the household's per capita income. Were sufficiently disaggregated data available, the indicator could be extended to assess the food security of individuals within a household. Given the availability of basic food consumption data to estimate the cost of the food basket, the IBFS can be used with any economic modeling framework that predicts per capita incomes. The IBFS can also be used in assessments of the impacts on food security of any type of exogenous change, including technological innovations, changes in prices or policy, or climate change. Given a definition of a nutritionally adequate diet, the IBFS can be used consistently over space and time and can be aggregated across subpopulations to obtain an aggregate indicator for a population.

Using the TOA-MD economic impact assessment model and data from the World Bank's Living Standards Measurement Survey, we illustrated the use of the IBFS in an ex ante analysis of the impacts of a technology developed to improve soil fertility and increase yields of maize, legumes, and livestock in smallholder farmers in Tanzania and other parts of Africa. Our analysis predicted a moderate rate of adoption of this technology, and showed that adopters of the technology have higher net returns, higher income per capita, and improved food insecurity. We concluded that the IBFS provided a potentially useful tool for multidimensional impact assessments that can be implemented with the kinds of data increasingly available in many regions of the developing world. Future research should compare the IBFS with other commonly used indicators such as calorie and nutrient deficiencies and coping strategies while extending the IBFS to account for intensity of food insecurity, intrahousehold distribution, and instability of food availability and incomes.

Acknowledgments

This research was supported in part by a grant from the United Kingdom Agency for International Development. The material is based on work supported by the National Institute of Food and Agriculture, United States Department of Agriculture, under award number 2011-68002-30191.

References

Antle, J. M. (2011). Parsimonious multi-dimensional impact assessment. *American Journal of Agricultural Economics*, *93*(5), 1292–1311.

Antle, J. M., Diagana, B., Stoorvogel, J., & Valdivia, R. (2010). Minimum-data analysis of ecosystem service supply in semi-subsistence agricultural systems: Evidence from Kenya and Senegal. *Australian Journal of Agricultural and Resource Economics*, *54*, 601–617.

Antle, J. M., Stoorvogel, J., & Valdivia, R. (2014). New parsimonious simulation methods and tools to assess future food and environmental security of farm populations. *Philosophical Transactions of the Royal Society B*, *369*. doi:10.1098/rstb.2012.0280.

Asfaw, S., Shiferaw, B., Simtowe, F., & Lipper, L. (2012). Impact of modern agricultural technologies on smallholder welfare: Evidence from Tanzania and Ethiopia. *Food Policy*, *37*(3), 283–295.

Barrett, C. B. (2010). Measuring food insecurity. *Science, 327*(5967), 825–828.

Bezu, S., Kassie, G. T., Shiferaw, B., & Ricker-Gilbert, J. (2014). Impact of improved maize adoption on welfare of farm households in Malawi: A panel data analysis. *World Development, 59,* 120–131.

Bouis, H., Haddad, L., & Kennedy, E. (1992). Does it matter how we survey demand for food? Evidence from Kenya and the Philippines. *Food Policy, 17*(5), 349–360.

Deaton, A., & Drèze, J. (2009). Food and nutrition in India: Facts and interpretations. *Economic and Political Weekly, 44*(7), 42–65.

Ecker, O., & Breisinger, C. (2012). *The food security system: A new conceptual framework.* IFPRI Discussion Paper no. 01166. IFPRI, Washington, DC. Retrieved from http://afrim.org.ph/IDLS/files/original/23d29eb544d63a37e297e6e6deb57d47.pdf

Food and Agricultural Organization of the United Nations [FAO]. (2001). *Food balance sheets: A handbook.* Rome: FAO. Retrieved from http://www.fao.org/docrep/003/X9892E/X9892E00.HTM

Foster, J., Greer, J., & Thorbecke, E. (1984). A class of decomposable poverty measures. *Econometrica, 52*(3), 761–766.

Headey, D., & Ecker, O. (2012). *Improving the measurement of food security.* IFPRI Discussion Paper no. 01225. IFPRI, Washington, DC. Retrieved from http://www.ifpri.org/sites/default/files/publications/ifpridp01225.pdf

Heckman, J. J., & Vytlacil, E. J. (2007). Econometric evaluation of social programs. Part I: Causal models, structural models, and econometric policy evaluation. In J. J. Heckman & E. E. Leamer (Eds.), *Handbook of econometrics* (pp. 4779–4874). Amsterdam: North-Holland.

Kabunga, N. S., Dubois, T., & Qaim, M. (2014). Impact of tissue culture banana technology on farm household income and food security in Kenya. *Food Policy, 45,* 25–34.

Kassie, M., Jaleta, M., Shiferaw, B. A., Mmbando, F., & De Groote, H. (2012). *Improved maize technologies and welfare outcomes in smallholder systems: Evidence from application of parametric and non-parametric approaches.* Retrieved from https://ideas.repec.org/p/ags/iaae12/128004.html

Maxwell, D., Coates, J., & Vaitla, B. (2013). *How do different indicators of household food security compare? Empirical evidence from Tigray.* Medford, MA: Tufts University. Retrieved from http://www.alnap.org/pool/files/different-indicators-of-hfs.pdf

Minten, B., & Barrett, C. B. (2008). Agricultural technology, productivity, and poverty in Madagascar. *World Development, 36,* 797–822.

Mulugeta, T., & Hundie, B. (2012). *Impacts of adoption of improved wheat technologies on households' food consumption in Southeastern Ethiopia.* Retrieved from http://ageconsearch.umn.edu/bitstream/126766/2/Mulugeta.pdf

Pinstrup-Andersen, P. (2009). Food security: Definition and measurement. *Food Security, 1*(1), 5–7. Retrieved from http://doi.org/10.1007/s12571-008-0002-y

Ruel, M. T. (2003). Operationalizing dietary diversity: A review of measurement issues and research priorities. *Journal of Nutrition, 133*(11), 3911S–3926S.

Smale, M., & Mason, N. M. (2013). *Hybrid seed, income, and inequality among smallholder maize farmers in Zambia.* IAPRA Working Paper no. 72. Indaba Agricultural Policy Research Institute, Lusaka, Zambia. Retrieved from http://www.saipar.org:8080/eprc/handle/1234 56789/26

Subramanian, S., & Deaton, A. (1996). The demand for food and calories. *Journal of Political Economy, 104*(1), 133–162.

Svedberg, P. (2000). *Poverty and undernutrition: Theory, measurement, and policy.* Oxford: Oxford University Press. Retrieved from https://ideas.repec.org/b/oxp/obooks/9780198292685.html

Tanzania National Bureau of Statistics (NBS) and Ministry of Finance. (2012). *Tanzania national panel survey, wave 2, 2010–2011.* Dar es Salaam, Tanzania: NBS.

Tasciotti, L., & Wagner, N. (2014). Urban agriculture and dietary diversity: Empirical evidence from Tanzania. *European Journal of Development Research.* Retrieved from http://doi.org/10.1057/ejdr.2014.38.

van Wijk, M., Rufino, M., Enahoro, D., Parsons, D., Silvestri, S., Valdivia, R., & Herrero, M. (2014). Farm household models to analyze food security in a changing climate: A review. *Global Food Security, 3*(2), 77–84.

Wineman, A. (2014). *Multidimensional household food security measurement in rural Zambia.* Retrieved from http://ageconsearch.umn.edu/bit stream/169819/2/Wineman%202014%20-%20Multidimensional%20 Food%20Security%20Measurement%20in%20Zambia.pdf

Woomer, P., Kadenge, E., Wanza, J., & Rose, P. (2011). *N2Africa podcaster no. 9. (Podcaster).* Retrieved from http://www.iita.org/c/document_library/get_file?uuid = 079ddc75-08f4-45a6-8225-456c0926df 2f&groupId = 25357

Woomer, P., Huising, J., & Giller, K. (2014). *N2Africa final report of the first phase 2009–2013.* Retrieved from http://www.N2africa.org

7

Dual Nature and the Human Face of Food (In)security

Dragan Miljkovic

Department of Agribusiness & Applied Economics, North Dakota State University, Fargo, ND, 58108-6050, USA
E-mail address: Dragan.Miljkovic@ndsu.edu

Abstract

Purpose – This chapter proposes a novel nonnormative approach to evaluating quality, effectiveness, and efficiency of food security.

Methodology/approach – On the demand side, we consider the quality, effectiveness, and efficiency of the food security system, whose mechanisms should be evaluated by their impact on the quality of life of an endangered population. On the supply side, the motives of food aid donors and food security providers (directly and via policy mechanisms) are discussed in the context of the deservingness heuristic.

Findings – The model illustrates three problems with measuring food security-related quality of life: peoples' different expectations, the different points at which people stand on their food security trajectory, and the potential for an evolving reference value of peoples' expectations. The deservingness heuristic is the mechanism behind the domestic and international food security aid that occurs via evolutionary forces, or cultural, institutional, and ideological forces.

Social implications – Food security is a problem that requires a humanistic approach rooted in the evolutionary process/development of the human race. Food security can be misused by the food aid/welfare recipients for their own purposes. Likewise, food security programs by food aid/welfare donors can be targeted unethically when used to achieve the ideological, institutional, and political goals of the donors. Differentiating between the behavioral causes of providing food security may be helpful in predicting whether aid/welfare will be provided to the needy at all.

Frontiers of Economics and Globalization
Volume 15 ISSN: 1574-8715
DOI: 10.1108/S1574-871520150000015007

Keywords: Deservingness heuristic, environmental and evolutionary causes, food security, quality of life

1. Introduction

The prevailing definition of food security is the one agreed upon at the 1996 World Food Summit: "A situation that exists when all people, at all times, have physical, social and economic access to sufficient, safe and nutritious food that meets their dietary needs and food preferences for an active and healthy life" (Barrett, 2010, p. 825). Its expansive scope has made reaching this ambitious definition elusive. The definition has three major supports: availability, access, and utilization. So far, most food security efforts have centered on availability, which is the supply side of the issue. Although major progress has been made in that area, the insistence on using new technologies to make affected regions food self-sufficient seems to ignore a basic tenet of economic efficiency: that one can be productively but not economically efficient. Moreover, the lack of institutions and the seemingly inevitable tragedy of the commons (Hardin, 1968) in agriculture resource use undermine these economically counterintuitive strategies which have been pursued for decades by international agriculture organizations.

Access and utilization represent the demand side of the food security problem. But sometimes a different problem occurs. Be it domestic governments or international organizations, multiple intermediaries often exclude other similarly relevant players when it comes to the access and distribution of food aid. These strategic behaviors and cognitive biases of participants may, and often, lead to the tragedy of anticommons (Heller, 1998), which denies the endangered population any access to existing world food surpluses.

Economics is a primarily normative science based on well-defined theories of individual and organizational behavior such as the theory of rational choice. Rational choice theory and its axioms rely on the theory of expected utility, demand analysis, and other important concepts in modern economics. When measuring poverty and the related issue of food security, relying on normative economic measures and their resulting corrective policies may be insufficient. This is a humanistic problem as much as an economic problem, and one pointed out by many prominent economists and humanists (Hicks, 1997; Sen, 1983, 1985, 1999; Stiglitz, Sen, & Fitoussi, 2009). Ignoring the human side of food security while using economic theory — which was developed to fit a different framework — provides only a partial understanding and short-term solution to this problem. A better way to understand the existing dynamics of food security is through a positive approach based on the behavioral heuristics of both recipients and donors of food aid and transfers. Given that economic rationality can be synonymous with flawless intelligence

(Miljkovic, 2005), an approach deviating from a rational choice paradigm can come under criticism by those who base their reasoning on traditional institutional economics. We think it is a risk worth taking.

A novel approach to food security is proposed here. On the demand side, we consider that the quality, effectiveness, and efficiency of food security systems should be evaluated by their impact on the quality of life of endangered populations. While there is no consensus on the definition of quality of life, we assume quality of life to constitute those aspects of an individual's subjective experience that relate both directly and indirectly to leading an active and healthy life. On the supply side, the motives of food aid donors and food security providers (as enacted directly and via policy mechanisms) are discussed in the context of the deservingness heuristic. Our approach reconciles the supply and demand sides of food security. The implications of this approach are discussed in the conclusions of this chapter.

2. Demand for food security

A central proposition in this chapter is that food security is not an autonomous societal goal. Rather, it is a means to achieve a minimum acceptable level of quality of life, (i.e., an opportunity to lead an active and healthy life). Agreeing on and measuring the minimum acceptable level of quality of life is a difficult task since there exists a tendency to regard quality of life as a constant. We contend that the meaning and perception of an active and healthy lifestyle vary over time. People assess their quality of life by comparing their expectations with their experience. We propose a model of the relationship between expectations and experience and use it to illustrate problems in measuring the quality of life.

In the context of food security, quality of life is measured by whether the availability of and access to food limits people's ability to fulfill their normal roles (e.g., working, attending school). Understanding the mechanisms through which food security interventions influence the quality of life and the determinants of quality of life may help to maximize global food security.

A primary aim of food security policy measures is enhancing the quality of life by reducing the impact of the unavailability/lack of food. Yet, people experiencing an inadequate food supply (measured by availability or access) may not report a poor quality of life. Therefore, the relationship between symptoms (lack of food) and quality of life is neither simple nor direct. Considering quality of life as the discrepancy between our expectations and our experience provides a way of explaining the manner in which we evaluate it.

The everyday lives of human beings are complex. However, when examining a human life, researchers need to simplify their analyses. We do this by using sets of stable assumptions (i.e., expectations) to inform our observations. In the case of food security and quality of life, people may have expectations about the availability of food, the variety of food, the accessibility of food, the level of satisfaction derived from eating food, the physical discomfort experienced from an inadequate food supply, and the activities they will or will not be able to pursue due to their food intake.

2.1. A model of quality of life

A model of quality of life is used to show a number of possible trajectories in food insecurity (Figure 1). Figure 1(a) illustrates a model of an acute episode of severe yet short-term food insecurity for a relatively young person (A—D). This first scenario represents the relationship between the child's quality of life expectations and actual experience. When expectations are matched by current experience, there is no

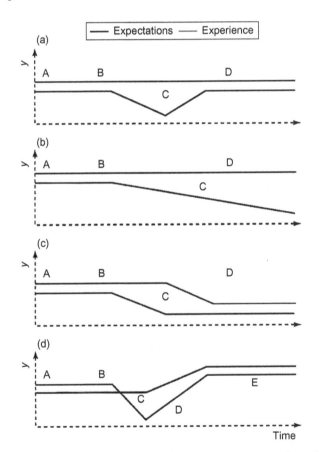

Fig. 1. (a—d) Quality of life model (top line = expectations, lower line = experience).

quantifiable impact on quality of life (period A, before the onset of the food insecurity episode). Whenever the experience of food security falls short of expectations (period B, after the onset of symptoms), there is an impact (i.e., period C).

The second scenario is a chronic episode of food insecurity in which the person may believe that at his/her age, he/she should not be experiencing any food insecurity or hunger (Figure 1b). Because his/her expectations remain unchanged, he/she may have difficulties operating in a normal fashion as well as performing even simple tasks. Thus, the gap between expectations and experience persists during period C.

In the third scenario (Figure 1(c)), the initial expectation of the person that his/her food insecurity situation will be resolved is replaced by the acceptance that he/she will have to function within the constraints of the present situation. Thus, the discrepancy in period C is reduced when the person revises his/her expectations. In period D, homeostasis is reestablished.

The fourth scenario (Figure 1(d)) considers a person who has lived under the circumstances of food insecurity for a longer period of time and has experienced some functional limitations during that same period. However, this person's expectations match his/her experience (period A) because he/she has adapted to the change in the food security situation. If he/she is then exposed to a food security program but has low expectations of its efficacy, shortly after exposure he/she will feel more positive about the future. Hence his/her experience is better than his/her expectations (period C). If this person then revises his/her expectations in light of his/her experience (period D), then homeostasis is reached at a higher level than before the introduction of the food security program.

2.2. Implications for measuring quality of life

The model illustrates three problems with measuring food security as related to quality of life: (1) people have different expectations; (2) people may be at different points on their food security trajectory; and (3) the reference value of people's expectations may change over time.

The first problem occurs because expectations are learned from experiences and are therefore highly specific to, and vary among, individuals. Furthermore, expectations are subject to differences in socioeconomic, demographic, psychological, and cultural factors. Expectations concerning quality of life are closely related to people's relationships with their social and physical environments. This may lead to structural variations in evaluations of the impact of food security programs/measures on the quality of life. These variations can be incorporated into the model on the y axis and would be represented by something that classifies people on the basis of their expectations and experiences, such as food/health needs. People's evaluations of quality of life are made within horizons of possibilities that comprise a fundamental component of their identity. These horizons are determined by factors such as age, gender, ethnic group, social class, disability, or personal biography. Existing measures of quality of life do not account for the expectations related to food insecurity; that is, they do not incorporate the boundaries within which levels of expectation and experience are measured. The result is that someone with low expectations while experiencing inadequate food security may not evaluate a more severe food insecurity experience as having an impact on his/her quality of life. Conversely, someone with high expectations who has never experienced food insecurity may evaluate a minor food insecurity experience as possessing a significant impact on his/her quality of life. This problem may have profound implications if food aid and other food security programs are prioritized and planned according to quality of life measurements.

The second problem highlighted by the model is the dependence of the magnitude of impact on the time of measurement. With existing measurements, it is impossible to ascertain the point at which the individual's food insecurity trajectory was measured. Moreover, responses to food insecurity are highly personal: individuals follow no standardized pattern. This means that even in a strictly monitored program in which quality of life is measured at equal intervals (and after the same duration following the implementation of a food security program) for all individuals, these individuals may nonetheless stand at different points on their food insecurity trajectories (e.g., at points A, C, or D in the model).

The third problem highlighted by the model arises because experience constantly changes expectations: people constantly move toward an ever changing point of equilibrium. Both psychological and sociological research provide evidence that quality of life is a dynamic construct – that is, the mechanisms by which people evaluate or quantify their quality of life change over time and in response to many factors (Carr, Gibson, & Robinson, 2001; Chamberlain & Zika, 1992; Diener, 2000; Headey, Holmström, & Wearing, 1984). The result is inherent instability. Response shifts can become problematic. For example, in Figure 1(c), no change would be detected if the person's quality of life were measured during period A and again during period D using existing measures. This is because the period during which the impact occurred, and during which his/her expectations changed, has been overlooked. Thus, someone may have experienced an impact on his/her quality of life (period C), but since this person adapted to the change in his/her food insecurity circumstances by altering his/her expectations, he/she may still be considered to possess a poorer quality of life during period D than before the introduction of a food security program (period A).

3. Food security supply: the deservingness heuristic

Heuristics in scientific research are often perceived as signs of weakness of certain theories and disciplines; that is, theories and disciplines are considered nonscientific if heuristics are used for explanation and justification. Some researchers define heuristics as judgmental shortcuts (Kahneman, 2003; Simon, 1982; Sniderman, Brody, & Tetlock, 1991). In psychology, heuristics is defined as combining (1) a fast-information processing mode and (2) a frugal decision rule in which particular judgments follow from a narrowly defined and limited set of cues (Gigerenzer, Todd, & the ABC Research Group, 2001).

The theories of bounded rationality constitute perhaps the best-known cases of heuristic prominence in economics (Kahneman, 1994; Kahneman & Tversky, 1979; Simon, 1955, 1982, 1996, 1997). From a positive point of view, heuristics are acceptable because they help to describe the world in terms of the way it is rather than in terms of how it should be. Therefore, this section addresses the issue of food security from a positive rather than a normative point of view.

Welfare spending (domestic and international) constitutes a major part of the federal budget of developed democracies. Voters in developed democracies consider domestic welfare spending (which includes education, health care, and elder care) as a core responsibility of the welfare state. Food security is also considered important in this regard (Gilens, 2000). Given the political and economic/fiscal importance of welfare, people form opinions on welfare policies through an examination of the context and economic effectiveness of these policies. However, people often use a simple heuristic in determining the success of a welfare program: do the recipients deserve the benefits or not? (Gilens, 2000; Petersen, 2012; Petersen, Slothuus, Stubager, & Togeby, 2011; van Oorschot, 2000, 2006). Known as the deservingness heuristic, this heuristic prompts people to categorize recipients as deserving or undeserving based on personal judgments. People strongly oppose welfare spending that benefits individuals regarded as lazy (i.e., recipients expend little effort to help themselves), while people support benefits to individuals regarded as unlucky (i.e., recipients who have failed due to circumstances beyond their control). These judgments do not apply in international cases, where deservingness is based on a different set of criteria such as cultural, institutional, and/or ideological societal characteristics (Barrett, 2002; Barrett & Maxwell, 2007; Clay, Molla, & Habtewold, 1999).

In studying heuristics, it is important to distinguish the heuristic mechanism itself from the input on which the mechanism operates. Many sources contribute to the deservingness heuristic in the form of perceptions of recipient effort (Gilens, 2000; Larsen, 2006). Such sources include cultural settings or institutional arrangements. Moreover, based on Chaiken, Liberman, and Eagly (1989), learning in this manner persists for many years. Understanding the perceptions of recipient effort influenced the way scientists explain their interest in recipient deservingness in the context of social welfare. However, while the deservingness information may be acquired from the environment, some experts do not accept that such information is in itself a product of learning (Gigerenzer, Todd, & the ABC Research Group, 2001; Petersen, 2012; Tooby & Cosmides, 1992). These experts assert that some heuristics are ingrained in human nature rather than representing the product of a specific cultural, ideological, or institutional environment. Petersen (2012) in particular has pursued the analysis of the deservingness heuristic in the context of its evolutionary roots. From an evolutionary fitness standpoint, providing help is a potentially risky strategy since it may present nontrivial adaptive problems to the helper. Assuming the presence of a free-rider problem (Olson, 1971), providing help is only adaptive to the extent it is reciprocal. In other words, those who receive help should also give help (Axelrod, 1984). The challenge here is that adaptive help-giving requires one to avoid helping cheaters who strategically receive more than they give. Instead, help must be channeled to reciprocators (those who will return the favor). Considering the deservingness heuristic in this context, a basic necessity for the evolution of adaptive help-giving has been the evolution of cognitive categories enabling individuals to represent and discriminate between cheaters and reciprocators in exchange situations (Cosmides & Tooby, 2005). Some psychological experiments have confirmed how individuals possess such specialized abilities for categorizing others as cheaters or reciprocators (Cosmides & Tooby, 2006). In our case, to research the roots of the deservingness heuristic in a food security context is not as important as testing for its actual presence in both domestic social welfare and international food aid contexts. Thus, we propose that the deservingness heuristic is the mechanism behind both domestic and international food security aid, and that this heuristic can be motivated by its evolutionary roots or via cultural, institutional, and/or ideological forces.

4. Deservingness in the modern welfare state

Modern societies consist of millions of people. Most of these people do not know and will never meet each other. Mass society is a fairly recent cultural phenomenon, being no older than a few thousand years. Our ancestors were likely to spend most of their lives in relatively confined areas and thus were unlikely to encounter many strangers throughout the course of their lives. Based on the evolutionary hypothesis, a few thousand years is not enough time for natural selection to formulate complex cognitive categories. Hence, reasoning about mass society and its macro dynamics is likely to rest on explicit and learned categories (Cosmides & Tooby, 2006). The concept of help-giving has also evolved over time and has been adapted based on life in small-scale social groups characterized by familiar face-to-face interactions (Dunbar, 1998; Kelly, 1995). Thus, the cheater and reciprocator categories should presume a small-scale context and direct attention away from irrelevant factors.

In the context of the modern welfare society and economy, one of these irrelevant factors is the large-scale nature of the welfare state itself. It is suggested that people should think of large-scale welfare in the same terms as small-scale help-giving. In other words, while the problems of large-scale government-sponsored welfare are different from small-scale help-giving in communities, the operation of these two systems should be the same while their differences should be irrelevant. Specifically, people should be able to differentiate between the two systems in the absence of cheater-relevant information (i.e., people should not regard national policies and mass politics as something removed from their everyday lives) (Delli Carpini & Keeter, 1996).

According to the evolutionary hypothesis, the cognitive categories of cheater and reciprocator constitute parts of our universal species-typical psychology. In contrast, learning-oriented explanations suggest that the tendency to differentiate between unlucky and lazy welfare (food aid) recipients and to treat the two groups differently arises from specific welfare institutions, ideologies, and political cultures. This differentiating tendency predicts variation among individuals in terms of how welfare recipients are categorized according to their respective efforts. It is thus critical to test the evolutionary explanation against previous arguments by investigating whether people categorize food aid and welfare recipients according to significant cultural factors. Building on the evolutionary perspective, our prediction is that all people – including those living in collectivistic cultures, universal welfare states, and politically liberal communities – categorize food aid and welfare recipients on the basis of effort cues as readily as citizens in individualistic cultures, residual welfare states, and politically conservative communities.

A final factor to consider is political sophistication and awareness. General literature on public opinion has focused on political sophistication as the basis of political learning (Zaller, 1992). Political sophistication regulates the extent to which we learn information from political elites. If categorization on the basis of effort cues is learned from political elites, categorization should be most prominent among the politically sophisticated.

Providing food security, nationally or internationally, via state welfare systems or nonprofit organizations can thus be construed as motivated by very different factors. The stability and longevity of food security programs may be dependent on the very causes of their existence. Future empirical/experimental studies should focus on a comparative analysis of the most dissimilar systems (Anckar, 2008; Przeworski & Tenne, 1970). For instance, in looking at the difference between universal welfare and residual welfare, we can compare Scandinavian countries (universal welfare states with a collectivist culture) with the United States (residual welfare state with an individualistic culture). If statistical testing using representative samples from these two different systems confirms uniform responses regarding food security (food aid and welfare) across these two populations, then one can conclude that the responses emerge from evolved, species-typical psychological categories. If not, then the learned and environmental components would be the determining factors. The duration and nature of food security programs will likely vary over time as these environmental components change over time.

5. Reconciling quality of life and deservingness heuristics

When should welfare or food aid recipients be content with their situation? Just because their quality of life has improved, does that guarantee that people are content with their marginally improved quality of life? For instance, does delivery of food aid to a poor country following a disaster (drought, flood, earthquake, war) solve the problems of those directly impacted? Does welfare disbursement to those considered unlucky in life solve their problems? Is further aid and welfare distribution warranted? Should donors continue providing aid to those in need? Is the perception of recipients about their own quality of life relevant to donors? These questions lead economists to consider food security an economics problem only rather than a socioeconomic—psychological—development problem since the former simplifies decision making. Yet, the effectiveness of such an approach can only be measured relative to achieving the goals set out by donors and by assuming fully rational behavioral—economic agents, including the recipients of welfare and food aid.

Food security is much more than an economic issue, and dealing with it only as such ultimately leads to short-term solutions that can further destabilize food security for endangered populations. Rational outcomes imply rational agents, and rationality, as understood in economic terms, does not necessarily motivate behaviors exhibited in food security contexts. If food security programs are motivated by institutional, political, or ideological mechanisms rather than evolution-oriented mechanisms, then such programs are likely to be determined by the interests of food security donors rather than the quality of life of endangered populations. Too often, stick-and-carrot policies condition changes to welfare programs that would otherwise help recipient populations. Stick-and-carrot policies may work in the short term, but in the long term they only perpetuate food insecurity.

Food security is a problem that requires a humanistic approach rooted in an understanding of the evolutionary process of the human race. While food security can be misused by recipients for political or other purposes, and by donors to achieve their own ideological, institutional, or political goals, saving human lives should remain a primary goal of all ideologies or political systems, even at the cost of rewarding so-called cheaters. Within the framework of food security, deservingness heuristics studies can help us better understand behaviors and attitudes toward the needy segments of populations.

References

Anckar, C. (2008). On the applicability of the most similar systems design and the most different systems design in comparative research. *International Journal of Social Research Methodology, 11*(5), 389–401.

Axelrod, R. (1984). *The evolution of cooperation*. New York, NY: Basic Books.

Barrett, C. B. (2002). Food security and food assistance programs. *Handbook of Agricultural Economics, 2*, 2103–2190.

Barrett, C. B. (2010). Measuring food insecurity. *Science, 327*(5967), 825–828.

Barrett, C. B., & Maxwell, D. (2007). *Food aid after fifty years: Recasting its role*. New York, NY: Routledge.

Carr, A. J., Gibson, B., & Robinson, P. G. (2001). Is quality of life determined by expectations or experience? *British Medical Journal, 322*(7296), 1240–1243.

Chaiken, S., Liberman, A., & Eagly, A. (1989). Heuristic and systematic processing within and beyond the persuasion context. In J. Uleman & J. Bargh (Eds.), *Unintended thought* (pp. 212–251). New York, NY: Guilford Press.

Chamberlain, K., & Zika, S. (1992). Stability and change in subjective well-being over short-term periods. *Social Indicators Research, 26*(2), 101–117.

Clay, D. C., Molla, D., & Habtewold, D. (1999). Food aid targeting in Ethiopia: A study of who needs it and who gets it. *Food Policy, 24*(4), 391–409.

Cosmides, L., & Tooby, J. (2005). Neurocognitive adaptations designed for social exchange. In D. Bass (Ed.), *Handbook of evolutionary psychology* (pp. 584–627). Hoboken, NJ: Wiley.

Cosmides, L., & Tooby, J. (2006). Evolutionary psychology, moral heuristics, and the law. In G. Gigerenzer & C. Engel (Eds.), *Heuristics and the law* (pp. 182–212). Cambridge, MA: MIT Press.

Delli Carpini, M. X., & Keeter, S. (1996). *What Americans know about politics and why it matters*. New Haven, CT: Yale University Press.

Diener, E. (2000). Subjective well-being: The science of happiness and a proposal for a national index. *American Psychologist, 55*(1), 34–43.

Dunbar, R. I. M. (1998). The social brain hypothesis. *Evolutionary Anthropology*, 6(5), 178–190.

Gigerenzer, G., Todd, P. M., & the ABC Research Group. (2001). *Simple heuristics that make us smart.* New York, NY: Oxford University Press.

Gilens, M. (2000). *Why Americans hate welfare: Race, media, and the politics of antipoverty policy.* Chicago, IL: University of Chicago Press.

Hardin, G. (1968). The tragedy of the commons. *Science, 162,* 124–142.

Headey, B., Holmström, E., & Wearing, A. (1984). The impact of life events and changes in domain satisfactions on well-being. *Social Indicators Research, 15*(3), 203–227.

Heller, M. A. (1998). The tragedy of the anticommons: Property in the transition from Marx to markets. *Harvard Law Review, 111,* 621–688.

Hicks, A. (1997). *Power and food security.* Rome: FAO.

Kahneman, D. (1994). New challenges to the rationality assumption. *Journal of Institutional and Theoretical Economics, 150*(1), 18–36.

Kahneman, D. (2003). A perspective on judgment and choice: Mapping bounded rationality. *American Psychologist, 58*(9), 697.

Kahneman, D., & Tversky, A. (1979). Prospect theory: An analysis of decision under risk. *Econometrica, 47*(2), 263–291.

Kelly, R. L. (1995). *The foraging spectrum. Diversity in hunter-gatherer lifeways.* Washington, DC: Smithsonian Institution Press.

Larsen, C. A. (2006). *The institutional logic of welfare attitudes.* Burlington, VT: Ashgate.

Miljkovic, D. (2005). Rational choice and irrational individuals or simply an irrational theory: A critical review of the hypothesis of perfect rationality. *Journal of Socio-Economics, 34*(5), 621–634.

Olson, M. (1971). *The logic of collective action.* Cambridge, MA: Harvard University Press.

Petersen, M. B. (2012). Social welfare as small-scale help: Evolutionary psychology and the deservingness heuristic. *American Journal of Political Science, 56*(1), 1–16.

Petersen, M. B., Slothuus, R., Stubager, R., & Togeby, L. (2011). Deservingness versus values in public opinion on welfare: The automaticity of the deservingness heuristic. *European Journal of Political Research, 50*(1), 25–52.

Przeworski, A., & Tenne, H. (1970). *The logic of comparative social inquiry.* New York, NY: Wiley.

Sen, A. (1983). *Poverty and famines: An essay on entitlement and deprivation.* Oxford: Oxford University Press.

Sen, A. (1985). A sociological approach to the measurement of poverty: A reply to professor Peter Townsend. *Oxford Economic Papers, 37*(4), 669–676.

Sen, A. (1999). *Development as freedom.* Oxford: Oxford University Press.

Simon, H. A. (1955). A behavioral model of rational choice. *Quarterly Journal of Economics, 69*(1), 99–118.

Simon, H. A. (1982). *Models of bounded rationality* (Vol. 2). Cambridge, MA: MIT Press.

Simon, H. A. (1996). *Sciences of the artificial* (3rd ed.). Cambridge, MA: MIT Press.

Simon, H. A. (1997). A letter to Ariel Rubinstein. In A. Rubinstein (Ed.), *Modeling bounded rationality* (pp. 187–194). Cambridge, MA: MIT Press.

Sniderman, P., Brody, R. A., & Tetlock, P. E. (1991). *Reasoning and choice: Explorations in political psychology.* Cambridge: Cambridge University Press.

Stiglitz, J., Sen, A., & Fitoussi, J.-P. (2009). *The measurement of economic performance and social progress revisited: Reflections and overview.* Paris: Commission on the Measurement of Economic Performance and Social Progress.

Tooby, J., & Cosmides, L. (1992). The psychological foundations of culture. In J. Barkow, L. Cosmides, & J. Tooby (Eds.), *The adapted mind: Evolutionary psychology and the generation of culture* (pp. 19–136). New York, NY: Oxford University Press.

van Oorschot, W. (2000). Who should get what, and why? On deservingness criteria and the conditionality of solidarity among the public. *Policy and Politics, 28*(1), 33–48.

van Oorschot, W. (2006). Making the difference in social Europe: Deservingness perceptions among citizens of European welfare states. *Journal of European Social Policy, 16*(1), 23–42.

Zaller, J. R. (1992). *The nature and origins of mass opinion.* New York, NY: Cambridge University Press.

8

Innovations in International Food Assistance Strategies and Therapeutic Food Supply Chains

Lisa F. Clark and Jill E. Hobbs

Department of Bioresource Policy, Business & Economics, University of Saskatchewan, Saskatoon, S7N 5A8, SK, Canada
E-mail address: lisa.clark@usask.ca and jill.hobbs@usask.ca

Abstract

Purpose — Discusses how changes in institutional objectives for international food assistance have influenced the organization of supply chains for innovative therapeutic foods designed to address problems of malnutrition and undernutrition.

Methodology/approach — Draws upon insights from donor and international organization reports, policy documents, and academic publications to reveal the structure, goals, and objectives of international organizations involved in food assistance strategies. Explores how innovations in Ready-to-Use Therapeutic Foods and Ready-to-Use Supplementary Foods fit into food assistance strategies and broader humanitarian goals.

Findings — Informed by the United Nations Millennium Development Goals, international food assistance strategies have broadened beyond acute malnutrition to include chronic undernutrition. Food assistance strategies have shifted toward a focus on local and regional procurement (LRP) over transoceanic aid, with Public Private Partnerships (P3s) playing a facilitating role.

Originality/value — This chapter raises important considerations to factor into the design and execution of international food assistance strategies using LRP/P3 modes of organization. It contributes to an understanding of the challenges of organizing international food assistance strategies that include socioeconomic goals of sustainability and nutrition objectives.

Frontiers of Economics and Globalization
Volume 15   ISSN: 1574-8715
DOI: 10.1108/S1574-871520150000015016

Keywords: International food assistance, therapeutic food products, local and regional procurement, Public Private Partnerships, Millennium Development Goals

1. Introduction

International food assistance strategies conventionally attempt to identify the best ways to get the necessary calories to people in emergency situations as quickly, safely, and efficiently as possible. As policy, infrastructure, and patterns of development shift over time, however, the aims of food assistance strategies have expanded. The current challenges of the global food assistance regime are no longer just about securing enough calories for every person but have come to include securing nutritious, micronutrient-rich foods in a sustainable and usually localized way.

Discussions surrounding food assistance have also broadened beyond addressing malnutrition to include *under*nutrition as part of the food security agenda. Byiers and Seravesi (2013) view undernutrition as not only an issue of access to nutritious food, but they also broaden the definition to include socioeconomic factors. They claim that undernutrition is also "about awareness of the importance of nutritional choices, storage and cooking choices, and general health and hygiene—all within the scope of personal food preferences" (p. vii). This inclusive description of what constitutes undernutrition places "ready-to-use" therapeutic foods within broader socioeconomic considerations beyond the immediate nutritional needs of individuals. The focus on addressing undernutrition is also reflective of the shift in goals of food assistance strategies since 2000.

Although innovative therapeutic foods (which include Ready-to-Use Therapeutic Foods (RUTFs) and Ready-to-Use Supplementary Foods (RUSFs))[1] are designed to treat severe malnutrition and chronic undernutrition, they are themselves not novel; however, the way supply chains for these products are organized has experienced a significant change. The goals of organizations such as the Food and Agriculture Organization (FAO) and the World Food Program (WFP) have evolved to include sustainable economic development initiatives alongside the goals of fighting malnutrition and undernutrition under the rubric of food security. To implement those goals, international organizations have mandated Local and Regional Procurement (LRP) strategies and the

---

[1] RUTFs are designed to tackle malnutrition through addressing micronutrient deficiencies and are usually part of an emergency aid scenario; in contrast, RUSFs are designed to be consumed on an ongoing basis to address undernutrition related to micronutrient deficiencies. These concepts are discussed in more detail in the next section.

Public Private Partnership (P3) model to organize supply chains for innovative therapeutic foods to not only meet immediate nutritional needs for the undernourished but also invest in long-term socioeconomic development to address poverty which is a major contributing factor to food insecurity.

Drawing on insights from academic studies, policy documents, and research institute and nongovernmental organization reports, this chapter discusses how changes in institutional objectives for food assistance have influenced the organization of supply chains for innovative therapeutic foods. It begins by examining the structure, goals, and objectives of international organizations and how they incorporate food security and sustainable development goals into food assistance strategies. It also discusses how innovations in RUTFs and RUSFs fit into food assistance strategies. This chapter then examines the challenges and benefits of two approaches that are increasingly utilized to organize supply chains and decision making within food assistance strategies: P3s and LRP. It concludes by addressing some future research questions relevant to the design and execution of food assistance strategies for therapeutic foods.

2. The international food assistance regime

2.1. Structure, goals, and objectives

The literature on innovative therapeutic food products designed to treat acute malnutrition and chronic undernutrition in at-risk populations is diverse, spanning the natural and social sciences, including nutrition, agricultural economics, and policy studies. It is a difficult task to find a broad, common theme that links these bodies of research beyond the general focus on the effectiveness of products at addressing nutritional deficiencies and the effectiveness of various strategies in meeting food security objectives. The central link that connects all these issues is the institutional structure that serves to bring stakeholders together to set goals, objectives, and standards to guide international food security initiatives.

The institutional framework for enhancing food security comprises stakeholders that include food assistance as part of their mandate. Programs of the United Nations, such as FAO, WFP, and UNICEF, collaborate within institutional frameworks to develop humanitarian and food assistance goals to be met through technological, social, and economic interventions in parts of the world that are in need of assistance. International organizations like the FAO contribute to institutional guidelines for food security that are used to develop food assistance strategies. The FAO identifies four dimensions of food security that it argues should be considered when developing strategic plans for food assistance:

food availability, economic and physical access to food, food utilization, and price stability over time (Levy, 2013).

The WFP has its own set of strategic objectives, as does UNICEF. This trio of United Nations-affiliated organizations is central to decision making and procurement of innovative food products designed to alleviate acute or chronic malnutrition in emergency situations which are part of the bigger food assistance picture. UNICEF's conceptual framework not only factors in underlying causes of undernutrition in terms of micronutrient deficiencies but also considers other issues related to the consumption of foods such as clean water, hygiene, maternal education, and economic development (de Pee, van den Briel, van Hees, & Bloem, 2010). These three agencies coordinate with stakeholders, including nongovernmental organizations such as Médecins Sans Frontières (Doctors Without Borders), state-level international development departments or agencies like USAID, private businesses such as Nutriset, and philanthropic donor groups such as the Gates Foundation, to organize and allocate resources and decision-making structures for food assistance.

The overarching set of goals guiding the FAO, WFP, and UNICEF in their efforts to address food insecurity is included in the United Nations Millennium Development Goals established in 2000. Built upon the concept of sustainable development established in 1987,[2] the Millennium Development Goals provide a more nuanced interpretation of sustainable development to include a focus on poverty reduction, food access, education, gender equality, health, and environmental sustainability. Goal 1 is to eradicate extreme poverty and hunger in the world by 2015. Reducing child mortality is Goal 4, and improving maternal health is Goal 5. The latter two goals are closely related to Goal 1. Principles of sustainable development are incorporated into Millennium Development Goals-based policy platforms designed to address food insecurity. There are two central foci to the food security and sustainable development mandates of the Millennium Development Goals: addressing the long-term socioeconomic impacts of micronutrient deficiencies and reducing poverty. They involve both technological and economic interventions. The first intervention involves technical transfer related to agricultural production that serves to scale-up local supply chains, and the second involves approaches to improve upon how ready-to-use food products are produced and

---

[2] The definition of sustainable development used by the United Nations is found in the 1987 document "Our Common Future: Towards Sustainable Development." Adopted by the United Nations in 1992, the concept of "sustainable development" is defined as "development that meets the needs of the present without compromising the ability of future generations to meet their own needs." This definition calls for a convergence between three pillars of progress: economic development, social equity, and environmental protection (Drexhage & Murphy, 2010).

distributed (Guimon & Guimon, 2010, p. 4). These interventions are components of other stakeholder mandates related to food security and sustainable development. For example, the objectives of the G8 2012 New Alliance for Food Security and Nutrition (NAFSN) are to generate greater private investment in agricultural development in the developing world while scaling up innovation to achieve sustainable food security outcomes, reduce poverty, and end hunger. The G8 NAFSN is committed to facilitating growth in finance, science, technology, and risk management in developing countries (G8, 2012).

Millennium Development Goals 4 and 5 can be included in what Byiers and Seravesi (2013, p. viii) label as Phase 2 of the nutrition agenda, which they view as the evolving focus of global efforts to address hunger and nutritional deficiencies since the ratification of the Millennium Development Goals. Also included in the second phase of the nutrition agenda is an emphasis on addressing undernutrition in the first 1,000 days of a child's life, where lack of micronutrients such as zinc, vitamin A, and iron can have irreversible lifelong health consequences for children from conception to 2 years of age, including stunting and wasting (Arimond et al., 2013; Victoria et al., 2008).[3] Stunting and wasting in childhood have serious long-term implications for the health of those affected, including higher susceptibility to infectious and chronic diseases and impaired intellectual development, which can further exacerbate poverty (Caulfield, Richard, Rivera, Musgrove, & Black, 2006, p. 551). Hawkes and Ruel's (2011) criteria for therapeutic products designed to treat undernutrition as part of food security and sustainable development include a number of socioeconomic goals. From their perspective, effective therapeutic foods must be safe and nutrient-rich to aid in fighting micronutrient deficiencies. To be effective, the therapeutic food must also be accessible to key populations and eaten by those affected by undernutrition. The food must be affordable to at-risk populations and available in places accessible by these groups. The food must also be commercially viable. For the local agricultural producers and agro-processors, proponents argue that the therapeutic food must be produced in a way that makes it commercially viable and sustainable for those along the supply chain (Nweneli, Robinson, Humphrey, & Henderson, 2014, p. 3). Focusing on the nutritional needs of particular demographics is an approach that has changed how food assistance strategies are designed

---

[3] UNICEF does not market or encourage the use of emergency food assistance products (RUTFs) for infants younger than 6 months of age. It "adheres to the established international norms and guidelines for infant and young child feeding, including exclusive breastfeeding for the first six months of life. [It] does not view RUTF as a substitute for best nutritional practices or normal household food" (UNICEF, 2013, p. 1).

and how therapeutic food products are produced and delivered to those in need.

2.2. Ready-to-use therapeutic and supplementary foods

Although RUTFs and RUSFs have different objectives, they are both food products that help to address the very complex problems of malnutrition and undernutrition in at-risk populations. First-generation RUTFs consisted of a corn–soy blend of ingredients to address micronutrient deficiencies. These products were meant to address severe malnutrition, but studies of their effectiveness show that innovative lipid-based nutrient supplements using groundnuts or pulses as a lipid source have been somewhat more successful than corn–soy blends in preventing and treating wasting in children (Puett et al., 2013, p. 2), although researchers continue to experiment with ingredient combinations to improve upon existing formulations. RUTFs are also innovative in their delivery system. RUTFs are a form of home-based treatment, as opposed to the feeding center model that was previously used to distribute food when food crisis situations arose (Paul et al., 2012, p. 225). RUTFs are designed to be consumed intensively as part of a short-term emergency treatment and are exclusively distributed through food assistance agencies like the WFP, UNICEF, and Doctors Without Borders.

RUSFs, unlike RUTFs, are designed to be consumed daily for longer periods of time to make up for lack of micronutrients and essential fatty acids in an individual's diet. RUSFs are not designed to provide 100% of daily calories (as with RUTFs) but are designed to combine with other complementary home-based foods. Many lipid-based nutrient supplement RUTFs and RUSFs being produced contain similar ingredients (pulses or groundnuts [usually peanuts], sugar, oil, dried milk, and mineral–vitamin complex). The French food company Nutriset developed and produces lipid-based RUTFs and RUSFs for international food assistance.

Nutriset's RUTF *Plumpy'Nut*, developed in 1996 and commercialized in 2001 as a short-term emergency treatment for malnutrition (Maestre et al., 2014), is one of the most widely used RUTF procured by UNICEF and WFP. With this product, the ingredients are combined to create a paste or bar that does not require refrigeration or any additional preparation before it is eaten. Nutriset also produces a number of brand-name RUSFs, including *Evol'Nutributter*, *Plumpy'Doz*, and *Plumpy'Sup*. In some of the newer RUSF formulations, lipids are also sourced from foods other than groundnuts, like chickpea. The goal of newer formulations of RUSFs is to develop therapeutic food products that help to treat micronutrient deficiencies and prevent stunting and wasting using as the lipid source pulses and chickpeas that are grown closer to the point of distribution of the final product.

Despite the promise that RUSFs hold for addressing undernutrition and meeting food security goals, there are some challenges to using this approach. Even with the provision of information, education, and free or highly subsidized distribution of preventative health products like RUSFs, adoption and usage rates over the long-term remain low (Thurber et al., 2013). Willingness to pay for preventative health products is also a challenge, as it is difficult to attribute long-term health gains to lipid-based nutrient supplement products, especially when other health habits such as improved hygiene practices are implemented (Lybbert, 2013). A combination of limited spending power and low levels of awareness of nutritional needs are ongoing barriers to use (Maestre et al., 2014, p. 11). There is also an ongoing concern regarding the long-term financial sustainability of companies manufacturing RUTFs and RUSFs that rely on funding from agencies and donors to produce food assistance products.

3. Policy instruments for food assistance

In addition to orienting food assistance strategies toward achieving broader, long-term socioeconomic development goals, the institutional framework for food security has encouraged the use of policy instruments that have achieved a degree of success in other contexts. In general, policy instruments can be understood as tools used by decision makers within institutional frameworks to implement mandates and meet goals. Policy instruments in the food assistance context include the application of specific models of organization to existing socioeconomic structures to meet the established goals, such as specific approaches to the sourcing of ingredients for RUTFs or the structure of supply chain relationships to deliver RUSFs. Efforts to address malnutrition and undernutrition in the context of sustainable development goals have focused on nurturing partnerships between stakeholders and scaling up the capacity of local and regional supply chains. A number of food assistance initiatives use LRP strategies and P3s that involve multiple stakeholders to meet their objectives of addressing malnutrition and undernutrition, as well as to meet the sustainable development objectives encompassed in the Millennium Development Goals.

3.1. LRP strategies

LRP strategies, more broadly referred to as innovative international food assistance instruments, are defined as the "purchase of food within a country where it is to be distributed or in a nearby country—and the use of cash and voucher transfers in place of direct distribution of food and commodities" (Lentz, Barrett, Gómez, & Maxwell, 2013, p. 2). One of the most significant policy changes in the way international food assistance strategies are organized has been the shift from transoceanic food aid to LRP strategies. This policy shift is based on the humanitarian disaster that emerged in the aftermath of the 2004 Indian Ocean tsunami. The devastation to roads, ports, and other types of infrastructure caused by the tsunami reveals the vulnerability of a system of food assistance to logistical disruptions in transportation routes which depend upon functional transoceanic and on-land transportation networks to distribute emergency food aid. The destruction of that transportation infrastructure, which greatly compromised the ability of donors to deliver food aid efficiently and effectively, reveals the weaknesses in food assistance production chains that are single-sourced (i.e., all stages of production are within donor countries) (So, Vickery, Swaminathan, & Gilland, 2009). Because the way food assistance supply chains were organized before the tsunami compromised the efforts of international organizations to provide emergency food aid and medical care, reforms have occurred in the food assistance policies of the European Union, Canada, and the United States. These jurisdictions have shifted their frameworks from focusing on single-sourced transoceanic in-kind food aid to incorporating cash-based and voucher programs to reduce exclusive dependency on single-sourced products.

Several studies conclude that locally and regionally based RUTF supply chains are more efficient and cost-effective than those heavily reliant on transoceanic transportation networks (Haggblade & Tschirley, 2007; Hanrahan, 2010; OECD, 2005; USGAO, 2009; WFP, 2006, 2010). It is also argued that LRP chains have the potential to bolster local marketing channels, support farmers, and improve food quality and safety, which may contribute to several Millennium Development Goals (Lentz, Barrett, & Gomez, 2012). It is further argued that local production reduces the inherent risk of single sourcing which helps to decrease the time necessary to transport products and foster economic self-sufficiency (So et al., 2009). The WFP, UNICEF, and others have policies promoting LRP as the preferred method of sourcing raw materials for RUTFs. As a result, 45% of total RUTFs purchased by UNICEF are produced in Africa for distribution in African countries (UNICEF, 2013).

The policy shift towards more diversified approaches to supply chain organization for the provision of RUTFs and RUSFs has not been a problem-free transition. Lentz et al. (2013) note that the enforcement of procurement contracts for emergency food aid products in new markets is difficult and that these policies have received criticism for distorting trade behavior. Some scholars caution against the assumption that LRP is the most efficient and effective way to organize supply chains for RUTFs and RUSFs. Others reason that LRP should not be viewed as a panacea for all food assistance challenges, and unreasonable expectations can lead to oversight. As Lentz et al. (2012, p. 2) caution, "LRP may often outperform transoceanic food assistance on some counts, it is unlikely to advance all objectives in all contexts." Concerns over investment in production capacity, patent controls, and quality control have also been raised regarding LRP strategies (So et al., 2009). Efforts to use LRP to produce RUTFs are being evaluated for their effectiveness and are being assessed on whether they are able to deliver available, affordable, acceptable, and nutritionally appropriate food products (Hawkes & Ruel, 2011).

There are several demonstrative examples of LRP strategies for therapeutic food supply chains in African countries. Dala Foods in Nigeria is an example of a local agro-processor partnered with international food assistance donors and private enterprises to produce therapeutic food products for domestic markets. The company produces several therapeutic food product lines alongside its regular product lines (teas, millet, and couscous), which have become household brand names in Nigeria (Gambo & Safiyanu, 2014). Dala Foods produces low-cost therapeutic food products from traditional grains and a powdered juice drink (*Instant Zobo*) made from hibiscus. The motivation behind the company's production of these products is to get affordable, nutritionally dense supplementary foods to Nigerians who have limited spending power and may suffer from micronutrient deficiencies (Business Innovation Facility, 2014). As Gambo and Safiyanu (2014) note, contracts with global relief organizations have increased sales and revenue for Dala Foods in this ready-made niche market, giving the company access to international markets through donor organizations.

Dala Foods has three development impact areas that it seeks to address through the production and sales of its therapeutic food product lines: engage smallholder farmers in the supply chain as suppliers; engage low-income people as distributors; improve the lives of consumers by giving them access to nutritious, safe, affordable, and accessible products (Business Innovation Facility, 2014). The company uses traditional foods and packaging so the products are easily recognizable to consumers. The products are packaged in small units to make them more affordable. In this endeavor, the company faces competition with other food manufacturers that offer similar products in the domestic market (Nweneli et al., 2014).

In Tanzania, agro-processor Power Foods Industries Limited produces RUTFs for local populations. Established in 1993, it is a mid-sized, locally owned and operated business sourcing its raw materials (millet, sorghum, cassava, maize, and soybean) from local producers. The company specializes in producing packages and convenient versions of cereal-based foods traditionally prepared in the home. It produces *Power Flour* for two markets: (1) institutional buyers like the WFP as an RUSF and (2) domestic markets targeted to women and children (Maestre et al., 2014). Power Foods is also licensed to produce Nutriset's *Plumpy'Nut* for regional distribution. Nutriset participates in knowledge exchange through the sharing of technical expertise and know-how in production and marketing of its products via on-the-job training activities with the employees of Power Foods (Kway, 2014, p. 73). This has made private investments in the production capacity of Power Foods vital to its ability to produce and distribute RUTFs. The company indicates that it is committed to producing nutritious food products to distribute to those in need, but faces challenges in making the business economically sustainable. The company is further challenged by the lack of familiarity consumers have with its fortified flour product *Power Flour* (Maestre et al., 2014, p. 12). Expanding educational programs to include consumers of RUSFs can help to increase familiarity with new brands and address challenges concerning consumers' willingness to pay for health attributes with credence properties (Anim-Somuah, Henson, Humphrey, & Robinson, 2013; Paul et al., 2012).

In summary, LRP strategies used in food assistance programs in African countries such as Nigeria and Tanzania require significant investment and involvement of multiple stakeholders, including local farmer organizations and agro-processors. This is particularly important when producing therapeutic food products designed to address micronutrient deficiencies for consumers with limited spending power, who may not have the necessary information regarding the long-term health benefits of RUSFs.

3.2. Public Private Partnerships

An economic intervention implemented alongside LRP strategies for food assistance is the organization of stakeholders and resources into P3s. P3s are defined by Spielmann and von Grebmer (2004, p. 3) as "any collaborative effort between the public and private sectors in which each sector contributes to the planning, resources, and activities needed to accomplish a mutual objective." Kaan and Liese (2011, p. 386) define transnational P3s as "institutionalized transboundary interactions between public and private actors which aim at the provision of collective goods." Every stakeholder in P3 arrangements takes on a degree of risk (financial, technical, and/or organizational) and responsibility in the partnership and in all activities related to the product. Ideally, long-term, beneficial progress can be achieved by applying the P3 model to organize stakeholder resources and responsibilities, including utilizing the core competencies and complementary expertise of the stakeholders. As Kraak, Swinburn, Lawrence, and Harrison (2013, p. 11) posit, "a well-designed and executed partnership can develop good governance structures to support transformative systems change that is more likely to improve nutrition and health outcomes. An incompatible and poorly executed partnership can damage public trust, credibility, and all partners' brand reputations."

P3s are viewed by some as a promising way of organizing business relations for the supply of RUSFs/RUTFs because they can help to scale-up existing supply chain networks by bringing together the business expertise of industry, the humanitarian objectives of nongovernmental organizations, and the fiduciary responsibility of governmental organizations to protect and promote the health of its their citizens. Formal linkages with public and private sector stakeholders are crucial to establishing and maintaining LRP strategies for products designed to address malnutrition and micronutrient deficiencies among at-risk populations. In food assistance strategies, the traditional business model is modified to foster cooperative information exchanges between the holders of knowledge and technological know-how and ready-to-use food companies in the local context. The emphasis in these partnerships is typically on keeping the value-added stages of the supply chain as local and disaggregated among producers as possible, while investors' purpose for involvement prioritizes technical transfer and humanitarian assistance over solely profit-driven motives. Private sector motivations for participation may also be part of a company's broader Corporate Social Responsibility platform.

The P3s described in this section take the form of an international organization partnering with private agro-processors to manufacture RUTFs, while working with international food companies and donors to develop and promote technological transfers to be incorporated into the supply chains. In the case of P3s for therapeutic food products, food assistance agencies work with various levels of government, private foundations, private businesses, and local food producers and processors to produce the ready-to-use foods for local markets. This is largely out of necessity, as the cost pass-through to consumers typically covers less than half of the production costs of RUSFs (Lybbert, 2013). RUSFs would likely be impossible to produce without the cooperative involvement of nonprofit agencies and companies willing and able to accept the risk of financial loss and engage in technical transfer initiatives.

An example of an agro-processor involved in a P3 is the Ethiopian company Hilina Enriched Foods (HEF). It produces RUSFs using locally sourced chickpeas produced by cooperative farmer unions. Established in 1998, HEF specializes in manufacturing and processing foods specifically designed to address malnutrition and other micronutrient deficiencies among Ethiopians. Its purpose is to supply enriched products to various agencies of the United Nations like UNICEF; it is set to expand its operations to ramp up production. HEF has produced Nutriset's *Plumpy'Nut* since its establishment, sourcing 70% of the ingredients locally (HEF, 2010). It is part of the "PlumpyField Network," which is organized as a P3 using an LRP strategy designed to link local producers in a network of information, expertise, and technical sharing with Nutriset. This network, established in 2005, has nine members in a number of developing countries. It supplies 35% of RUTFs used by UNICEF and other humanitarian agencies (Plumpyfield.com, 2014). It has increased the number of its agreements with small landholders and has developed information exchange relations with universities to improve the agricultural technologies on which it depends. The network is also involved in the National Agrofood Laboratory that is designed to address a research and development gap at the local level (Grow Africa Secretariat, 2014, p. 63).

Guts Agro Industry is another agro-processor located in Ethiopia that produces a chickpea-based RUSF for the domestic market. Guts Agro produces a brand of Shiro (a dal-like food product) called *Yanet Shiro* that includes chickpea flour and spices. Between 2009 and 2013, the company was contracted by the WFP to produce RUSFs. USAID assisted Guts Agro with an expansion of production facilities (grain separator, mill, roaster, mixer, and packer) to process 4,000 metric tons of chickpeas sourced from 52,000 small landholders in three cooperative producer unions (Grow Africa Secretariat, 2014, p. 63; Merhatsidk, 2014; USAID, 2014). Because *Yanet Shiro* is a relatively new product, there is no long-term assessment data of the commercial success of the company's involvement in producing RUSFs. However, progress updates indicate that the company is sourcing its raw materials from 10,000 small landholders through three cooperative farmer unions. It has also signed a memorandum of understanding with the WFP to produce a chickpea-based RUSF for a project that includes the government of Ethiopia and USAID (Grow Africa Secretariat, 2014).

There are many cases of P3 arrangements establishing localized supply chains that attempt to address sustainable development and food security objectives of the Millennium Development Goals. But there is some skepticism regarding the motivation behind industry investment in products that have uncertain or unpredictable demand patterns and little opportunity for generating profit. Nevertheless, strained public resources and a lack of financial resources to access beneficial technologies have made partnerships between public and private stakeholders a virtual necessity for many food assistance projects that include the objectives of encouraging socioeconomic sustainability and reducing poverty. It is difficult to speculate at this point as to whether P3s will allow businesses to develop models that can offer nutrient-rich foods to poor consumers on a commercially sustainable basis (Maestre et al., 2014).

4. Further questions and considerations

Further questions and considerations need to be addressed with respect to the effectiveness of food assistance strategies that incorporate therapeutic foods. One suggestion to make P3s more effective is the expansion of mandates to include nutrition awareness campaigns and invest in "institutional mechanisms that signal nutritional quality to consumers" (Maestre et al., 2014, p. 2). Understanding the contours of consumer markets is fundamental to product design, especially anticipated costs per unit, marketing strategies, distribution channels, and consumer preferences. These are important factors to consider with regard to therapeutic foods to ensure they reach, and are responsive to the needs of, their intended recipients or consumers. In the case of areas where poverty is widespread and poor harvests are an ongoing reality, individuals may not have access to financial resources to purchase nutritionally dense foods and may lack the dietary knowledge necessary to choose more nutritious products when given the opportunity. A person cannot choose a nutritionally superior product if he or she does not have the means, access, or knowledge to do so. Education and affordability play particularly important roles in these circumstances. Beyond health and nutritional impact, it will be important to assess and understand underlying user preferences, the constraints of local supply chains, and the opportunity costs of adjusting dietary choices in the design and delivery of RUTFs/RUSFs. Health motivations, or nutritional education, alone may be insufficient to influence purchasing patterns, but the presence and degree of influence of these factors on consumer choices must be determined, which will require information gathering at the grassroots level (Thurber et al., 2013, p. 1739).

More broadly, a clearer understanding of the roles, capacities, and interests of stakeholders at the local level is important to understand how food assistance strategies meet their intended objectives and the challenges that may prevent them from doing so. This includes analyzing how multilevel governmental agencies, educational institutions, small- or medium-scale agro-processors, cooperative farmer groups, and consumers interact and communicate with each other. Research that assesses the qualities of interactions among stakeholders and the frequency and types of information they exchange can be useful to future food assistance strategies. This includes consumer research (surveys, economic experiments, interviews) that can help identify information gaps, such as the level of nutritional awareness, and the willingness and ability to adopt new foods among at-risk populations, which may be a crucial factor in the adoption of RUSFs. For example, a study investigating Ethiopian food security revealed that there is variation in the understandings of the words "nutrition" and "healthy" by urban and rural Ethiopians (Levy, 2013, pp. 5–11).

Research that examines the structure and challenges of existing domestic food supply chains and the opportunities to integrate RUSFs into these supply chains on a sustainable basis could be particularly important in educating researchers, policy makers, and donors about the motivations and interests of consumers, farmers, farmer organizations, and local agro-food processors. This information could lead to more informed food assistance strategies that are responsive to stakeholder needs and cognizant of local constraints.

Despite the massive efforts attempting to address the chronic problem of undernutrition since the establishment of the Millennium Development Goals, progress has been slow in terms of reducing levels of undernutrition (Maestre et al., 2014). Efforts continue and those initiatives that have made progress appear to be the ones that consider the design and development of a nutritionally appropriate product, the broader socioeconomic contexts, the organization of supply chain relationships, and the commercial and cultural realities of the local marketplace.

Acknowledgments

This research was conducted under the *Development of Innovative Therapeutic Food Products for Treating Malnutrition and Responding to Emergencies within High Risk Communities* project funded by the Global Institute for Food Security (GIFS), University of Saskatchewan, Saskatchewan Agriculture Development Fund and Growing Forward 2. Thank you to Neil A. Hibbert for his helpful comments on an earlier draft of this chapter.

References

Anim-Somuah, H., Henson, S., Humphrey, J., & Robinson, E. (2013). Strengthening agri-food value chains for nutrition: Mapping value chains for nutrient-dense foods in Ghana. IDS Evidence Report no. 2. Institute of Development Studies, Brighton, United Kingdom.

Arimond, M., Zeilani, M., Jungjohann, S., Brown, K. H., Ashorn, P., Allen, L. H., & Dewey, K. G. (2013). Considerations in developing lipid-based nutrient supplements for prevention of undernutrition: Experience from the international lipid-based nutrient supplements (iLiNS) project. *Maternal & Child Nutrition.* doi:10.1111/mcn.12049

Business Innovation Facility. (2014). *Dala Foods Nigeria Limited: Developing soluble juice drinks for the BoP.* Retrieved from http://businessinnovationfacility.org/page/project-profile-dala-foods-nigeria-limited-soluble-juice-drinks

Byiers, B., & Seravesi, S. (2013). *The enriching business of nutrition: Market-based partnerships and regional approaches to nutrition: What role for CAADP?* ECDPM Discussion Paper no. 149. Retrieved from http://ecdpm.org/wp-content/uploads/2013/10/DP-149-Partnerships-Regional-Approaches-Nutrition-Role-CAADP-2013.pdf

Caulfield, L. E., Richard, S. A., Rivera, J. A., Musgrove, P., & Black, R. E. (2006). Stunting, wasting, and micronutrient deficiency disorders. In D. T. Jamison, J. G. Breman, A. R. Measham, G. Alleyne, M. Claeson, D. B. Evans, … P. Musgrove (Eds.), *Disease control priorities in developing countries* (2nd ed., pp. 551–568). Washington, DC: World Bank. Retrieved from http://www.ncbi.nlm.nih.gov/books/NBK11761/

de Pee, S., van den Briel, T., van Hees, J., & Bloem, M. W. (2010). Introducing new and improved food products for better nutrition. In S. Omano, U. Gentilinl, & S. Sandstrom (Eds.), *Revolution: From food aid to food assistance: Innovation and overcoming hunger* (pp. 157–177). Rome: World Food Program.

Drexhage, J., & Murphy, D. (2010). *Sustainable development: From Bruntland to Rio 2012.* New York, NY: International Institute of Sustainable Development. Retrieved from http://www.un.org/wcm/webdav/site/climatechange/shared/gsp/docs/GSP1-6_Background%20on%20Sustainable%20Devt.pdf

G8, Camp David. (2012). *G8 cooperation framework to support: The 'New Alliance For Food Security And Nutrition' in* Ethiopia. Retrieved from http://www.usaid.gov/sites/default/files/documents/1868/EthiopiaCooperationFramework.pdf

Gambo, M. K., & Safiyanu, A. M. (2014). Dala Foods Nigeria Limited: Effective product development and management in Nigeria. *International Food and Agribusiness Management Review, 17*(B), 125–129.

Grow Africa Secretariat. (2014, May). *Grow Africa 2013-2014, Agricultural partnerships take root across Africa: Second annual report on private-sector investment in support of country-led transformations in African agriculture.* Retrieved from http://www3.weforum.org/docs/IP/2014/GA/WEF_GrowAfrica_AnnualReport2014.pdf

Guimon, J., & Guimon, P. (2010). *Innovation to fight hunger: The case of Plumpy'Nut.* UAM-Accenture Working Papers #2010/01. Retrieved from http://www.uam.es/docencia/degin/catedra/documentos/1_guimon_guimon.pdf

Haggblade, S., & Tschirley, D. (2007). *Local and regional food aid procurement in Zambia.* Food Security Country Working Papers 28. USAID, Washington, DC.

Hanrahan, C. E. (2010, January 26). *Local and regional procurement for US international emergency food aid.* CRS Report for Congress, Congressional Research Service, 7-5700, R40759. Retrieved from http://nationalaglawcenter.org/wp-content/uploads/assets/crs/R40759.pdf

Hawkes, C., & Ruel, M. T. (2011, February). *Value chains for nutrition.* Retrieved from http://www.ifpri.org/sites/default/files/publications/2020anhconfpaper04.pdf

Hilina Enriched Food Processing Center P.L.C. (HEF). (2010). *Company profile – Country profile – Nutrition information – Links. PlumpyField Network*. Retrieved from http://www.hilinafoods.com/about_hilina.php

Kaan, C., & Liese, A. (2011). Public private partnership in global food governance: Business engagement and legitimacy in the global fight against hunger and malnutrition. *Agriculture and Human Values, 28,* 385–399.

Kraak, V. I., Swinburn, B., Lawrence, M., & Harrison, P. (2013). The accountability of public private partnerships with food, beverage, and quick-serve restaurant companies to address global hunger and the double burden of malnutrition. United Nations System: Standing Committee on Nutrition. *SCN News, 39,* 11–24.

Kway, E. E. (2014). Backward linkages of firms under export processing zone authority in Tanzania. *International Journal of Education and Research, 2*(7), 63–76.

Lentz, E. C., Barrett, C. B., & Gómez, M. I. (2012). *The impacts of local and regional procurement of US Food Aid: Learning alliance synthesis report*. Retrieved from http://dyson.cornell.edu/faculty_sites/cbb2/files/papers/LRPCh1Lentzetal11Jan2012Update.pdf

Lentz, E. C., Barrett, C. B., Gómez, M. I., & Maxwell, D. G. (2013). On the choice and impacts of international food assistance instruments. *World Development, 49,* 1–8.

Levy, J. (2013). *Gallup: Ethiopia food security scale focus group report and recommendations*. Retrieved from http://www.fao.org/fileadmin/templates/ess/voh/Gallup_FAO_Food_Security_in_Ethiopia_Focus_Group_Report_FINAL__08_28_13_.pdf

Lybbert, T. J. (2013). Hybrid public-private delivery of preventative lipid-based nutrient supplement products: Key challenges, opportunities, and players in an emerging product space. United Nations System: Standing committee on nutrition. *SCN News, 39,* 32–39. Retrieved from http://www.cmamforum.org/Pool/Resources/Hybrid-public-private-delivery-LNS-2011.pdf

Maestre, M., Robinson, E., Humphrey, J., & Henson, S. (2014). *The role of businesses in providing nutrient-rich foods for the poor: A case study in Tanzania. Reducing Hunger and Undernutrition*. IDS Evidence Report no. 52. Retrieved from http://mobile.opendocs.ids.ac.uk/opendocs/bitstream/handle/123456789/3518/ER52.pdf?sequence=1

Merhatsidk, M. (2014). Ethiopia's chickpea industry sees boost by large-scale initiative. *Addis Fortune, 14,* 728. Retrieved from http://addisfortune.net/articles/ethiopias-chickpea-industry-sees-boost-by-large-scale-initiative/

Nweneli, N., Robinson, E., Humphrey, J., & Henderson, S. (2014). *The role of businesses in providing nutrient-rich foods for the poor: Two case studies in Nigeria*. IDS Evidence Report no. 64. Retrieved from http://opendocs.ids.ac.uk/opendocs/bitstream/handle/123456789/3648/ER64

%20The%20Role%20of%20Businesses%20in%20Providing%20Nutri
ent-rich%20Foods%20for%20the%20Poor%20Two%20Case%20Stu
dies%20in%20Nigeria.pdf?sequence=1

Organisation for Economic Co-operation and Development (OECD).
(2005). *The development effectiveness of food aid and the effects of its
tying status.* Paris: OECD.

Paul, K. H., Muti, M., Chasekwa, B., Mbuya, M. N. N., Madzima, R.
C., Humphrey, J. H., & Stoltzfus, R. J. (2012). Complementary feeding
messages that target cultural barriers enhance both the use of lipid-
based nutrient supplements and underlying feeding practices to
improve infant diets in rural Zimbabwe. *Maternal & Child Nutrition, 8,*
225–238.

Plumpyfield.com. (2014). *PlumpyField's mission and vision.* Retrieved
from http://www.nutriset.fr/en/plumpyfield/plumpyfield-mission-and-
vision.html

Puett, C., Salpéteur, C., Lacroix, E., Houngbé, F., Aït-Aïssa, M., &
Israël, A. D. (2013). Protecting child health and nutrition status with
ready-to-use food in addition in urban Chad: A cost-effectiveness analysis. *Cost Effectiveness and Resource Allocation, 11*(27). doi:10.1186/
1478-7547-11-27. Retrieved from http://www.resource-allocation.com/
content/pdf/1478-7547-11-27.pdf

So, A., Vickery, C. M., Swaminathan, J., & Gilland, W. (2009).
Supplying ready-to-use therapeutic foods to the Horn of Africa. In *A
nutrition articulation project: A supply chain analysis — Background and
overview of the project.* Retrieved from http://www.unicef.org/supply/
files/8._RUTF_supply_chain_evaluation_and_forecasting_1.pdf

Spielmann, D. J., & von Grebmer, K. (2004, January). *Public private partnerships in agricultural research: An analysis of challenges facing industry and the consultative group on international agricultural research.*
EPTD Discussion Paper no. 113. Retrieved from http://www.ifpri.org/
sites/default/files/publications/eptdp113.pdf

Thurber, M. C., Warner, C., Platt, L., Slaski, A., Gupta, R., & Miller, G.
(2013). To promote adoption of household health technologies, think
beyond health. *American Journal of Public Health, 103,* 1736–1740.

UNICEF. (2013, June 1). Ready-to-use therapeutic food for children with
severe acute malnutrition. Position Paper No. 1 (pp. 1–4). UNICEF.
Retrieved from http://www.unicef.org/media/files/Position_Paper_
Ready-to-use_therapeutic_food_for_children_with_severe_acute_mal
nutrition__June_2013.pdf

United States Government Accountability Office [USGAO]. (2009).
*International food assistance: Local and regional procurement can
enhance the efficiency of US food aid, but challenges may constrain its
implementation* (GAO-09-570). Retrieved from http://www.gao.gov/
products/GAO-09-570

USAID. (2014, April 10). New chickpea products launched by New Alliance For Food Security And Nutrition partner guts agro industry. *USAID News.* Retrieved from http://www.usaid.gov/ethiopia/news/new-chickpea-products-launched-g-8-new-alliance-food-security-and-nutrition

Victoria, C. G., Adair, L., Fall, C., Hallal, P. C., Martorell, R., Richter, L., & Sachdev, H. S. (2008). Maternal and child undernutrition consequences for adult health and human capital. *Lancet, 371,* 340–357.

World Food Program (WFP). (2006, February). *Food procurement in developing countries. Policy issues* (Agenda item 5, Executive Board First Regular Session, 1/2006/5-C). Retrieved from http://www.wfp.org/eb

World Food Program (WFP). (2010). Annual food procurement report 2010. Rome: WFP.

9

Managing High and Volatile Food Prices in Developing Countries Since 2000

Maros Ivanic[a] and Will Martin[b]

[a]*Results Measurement Unit, Office of the Chief Economist, International Finance Corporation, 2121 Pennsylvania Avenue, NW Washington, DC 20433 USA*
E-mail address: mivanic@ifc.org
[b]*International Food Policy Research Institute (IFPRI), Washington, DC, USA*
E-mail address: w.martin@cgiar.org

Abstract

Purpose – This chapter examines the long-run behavior of real food prices and the impact of food prices on poor and vulnerable households. It also examines the price policy responses of governments to high and volatile food prices, and the impact of food prices and policies on the poorest in the society.

Methodology/approach – We focus on the impacts of food price changes on individual households, particularly on those living near the poverty line using the standard World Bank measure of poverty at US$1.25 per day in purchasing power.

Findings – We found that the effect of an exogenous increase in food prices typically raises poverty in the short run when many poor households are net buyers of grain and wage rates do not have time to fully adjust. In the long run, higher food prices increase food output and raise the wage rates of poor households from unskilled off-farm labor. The end result is that higher food prices can contribute to long-run poverty reduction.

Practical implications – Combining the impact of the price changes and government policy responses allows an assessment of the overall impact of higher world food prices on poverty.

Keywords: Food security, rice, shocks, volatile food prices

Frontiers of Economics and Globalization
Volume 15   ISSN: 1574-8715
DOI: 10.1108/S1574-871520150000015017

1. Introduction

Since 2000, world prices of key staple foods such as rice and wheat have tended to increase in real terms. This marked a dramatic change from the previous century, in which the dominant feature of food prices was their secular decline. Food prices have also been highly volatile which has raised serious concerns about vulnerable, low-income households. Policy makers in developing countries have responded to these developments by insulating their markets from price shocks in the short run, but have subsequently transmitted these price increases into domestic markets. This combination of measures appears consistent with recent findings about the impact of higher food prices on the poor and about problems associated with price insulation.

We begin this chapter by examining the long-run behavior of real food prices. To illustrate the nature of the challenge, we look at the real price of rice dating back to 1900. This analysis shows the strong decline in real prices until 2000, followed by a possible reversal in this trend. It also highlights the continuing importance of volatility in real prices of this staple food.

We then turn to the price policy responses of governments to the high and volatile prices since the turn of the millennium. This analysis reveals that governments typically resist the initial, rapid increases in prices by using measures such as export taxes and import tariff reductions. Subsequently, however, they often transmit these price increases into their domestic markets so that the increases in prices are transmitted almost entirely in this manner.

Following this, we consider the impact of food prices on poor and vulnerable households. Although some households benefit from higher food prices, others are adversely affected in the short run, depending on their status as net producers or consumers of food and the extent to which their incomes adjust to food price changes. Low-income households tend to spend a large share of their incomes on staple foods, making them potentially vulnerable to increases in prices.

Our primary concern in this chapter is with the impact of food prices and policies on the poorest in society. We focus on the impacts of food price changes on individual households, particularly on those living near the poverty line using the standard World Bank measure of poverty at US$1.25 per day in purchasing power. One very simple indicator of the effect at the household level is the change in the poverty headcount – the number of people living below the poverty line. An economic shock that increases the number of people below the poverty line is clearly adverse. We found that the effect of an exogenous increase in food prices typically raises poverty in the short run, when many poor households are net buyers of grain, and wage rates do not have time to fully adjust. In the long run, higher food prices increase food output and raise the wage rates of poor households from unskilled off-farm labor. The end result is that higher food prices can contribute to poverty reduction. Combining the impact of the price changes and government policy responses allows an assessment of the overall impact of higher world food prices on poverty.

2. The behavior of real rice prices

Rice is a key staple food for a large proportion of the world's poorest consumers, so the price of rice influences consumer welfare through its impact on the cost of living, and on consumer income. Figure 1 shows the behavior of the real price of rice based on the 1976 level of one. A striking feature of the graph is the trend decline in real prices from 2 in 1990 to under 0.6 in 2014. This enormous decline in the real price of this key staple took place despite a 350% increase in the world population, from around 1.6 billion in 1990 to 7.2 billion in 2014 (http://www.census.gov). This remarkable achievement of declining food prices occurred despite substantial reductions in the area of arable land per person since 1950 (Bruinisma, 2009).

After the real price of rice reached its lowest recorded level of 0.35 in 2001, it subsequently rose to much higher levels, peaking at almost three times as high in 2008. While it is far from clear whether there is a new normal of higher food prices, higher prices have been an unusual feature, especially since the price series for storable commodities such as rice are characterized by short, sharp peaks and sustained troughs such as the ones from 1931 to 1946 or from 1982 to 2000. Prices for other key staple

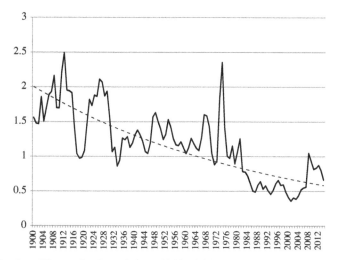

Fig. 1. The real price of rice: 1900–2014. Sources: *Pfaffenzeller, Newbold, and Rayner (2007), World Bank Pink Sheet (2015).*

foods such as wheat have exhibited broadly similar behaviors as the price of rice, with an apparent reversal of the price trend, and high and volatile prices since the turn of the millennium in 2000.

3. Policy responses

A widely observed policy response to fluctuations in world prices of food is for developing countries and historically industrial countries to insulate their markets from these changes. When prices surged in 2007–2008, many exporters from developing countries used export restrictions to lower their domestic prices relative to world prices. Even more countries lowered either their import taxes or their consumption taxes on food (Wodon & Zaman, 2010). But these responses are not confined only to situations involving sharp price increases. Countries frequently increase protection when food prices fall, seemingly to protect the interests of net sellers of food.

Examining the responses, key commodities yield more interesting patterns. Developing countries tend to employ extremely strong levels of insulation against rapid changes in food prices and to transfer sustained food prices to the domestic markets. This pattern is shown in Figure 2 for average domestic and international prices of rice, wheat, maize, edible oils, and sugar. Insulating policies seem to be motived by the management of adverse impacts of higher food prices on the poor. Later, after producers are able to respond to by increasing supply, policy makers allow domestic prices to rise more or less in line with world prices.

For individual countries, this policy approach effectively stabilizes its own prices. Use of trade policy measures is likely to be less costly than stabilization using storage measure policies alone. The fact that this approach to stabilization is so widely used, however, creates a serious

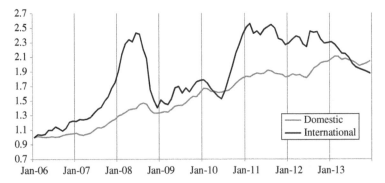

Fig. 2.   Domestic and world price index of rice, wheat, maize, oil, and sugar: developing countries. Source: Ivanic and Martin (2014b).

collective action problem. One can demonstrate that if every country seeks to reduce its price by the same amount, the domestic price remains unaffected (Martin & Anderson, 2012). The mechanism is simple – export restrictions in exporting countries increase world prices, as do import duty reductions in importing countries. So while the policy appears effective for each individual country, it is collectively ineffective since the reduction in domestic prices relative to world prices is offset by the resulting rise in world prices. The analysis by Martin and Anderson (2012) suggests that almost half of the increase in world rice prices between 2006 and 2008 was the result of countries insulating their markets against the increases in world prices. This creates a problem since countries that would prefer not to use export controls or import barrier reductions in response to a rise in prices may feel compelled to do so because of the actions of others, which further reinforces the increase in world prices.

In reality, countries insulate to varying degrees, but there is no guarantee that insulation will reduce global poverty. Historically, some of the most enthusiastic users of price insulation have been relatively wealthy countries such as members of the European Community, with its pre-Uruguay Round system of variable import levies.

To learn whether the pattern of interventions during the 2006–2008 price surge actually reduced poverty, Anderson, Ivanic, and Martin (2013) examined the actual interventions and assessed their effects on global poverty, taking into account the effects of the interventions on the world price. They concluded that the interventions appeared to reduce poverty by 80 million people as long as the effects of these trade interventions on world prices were not taken into account. Once these interventions were considered, the effect generated a small but not statistically significant increase in world prices.

Many countries use combinations of trade policy measures and storage policy measures to reduce the volatility of their domestic prices. In principle, the combination of these two policy measures has the potential to be more effective than using either trade policy measures or storage policy measures alone (Gouel & Jean, 2014). In reality, the combination of trade and storage policy measures does not eliminate the adverse effects of a country's food price volatility policies on the rest of the world (Gautam, Gouel, & Martin, 2014). In addition, using the combined policy measures tends to be extremely expensive and includes limitations that frequently cause prices to collapse (Knudsen & Nash, 1990).

The central role of the World Trade Organization (WTO) is to deal with collective action problems that affect the level of world prices and/or their volatility. The use of bindings on import tariffs reduces the extent to which importing countries can depress world prices by discouraging imports. The Uruguay Round introduced important measures to discourage the insulation of domestic prices against world price changes, which exacerbates volatility. These reforms include banning variable import levies and subjecting administered prices to disciplines under both the market access and domestic support pillars.

Because of its mercantilist focus, the WTO has done very little to discourage the use of export restrictions – from the point of view of another exporter, a competitor's export restrictions create export opportunities. While quantitative export restrictions are subject to the general proscription under Article XI of GATT, export taxes are not constrained except in limited instances such as restrictions negotiated under WTO accession agreements. However, unless all are disciplined, export restrictions are likely to contribute to upward pressure on food prices in times of crisis, making it difficult for other exporters not to follow suit and for importers to refrain from lowering domestic prices through duty and tax reductions.

4. Effective food price changes on poverty

One widely accepted measure of the short-run effect of a small change in a commodity price on household welfare is given by the household's net trade share for that good, as defined by Deaton (1989). A household that is a net seller of a good will benefit when the price of that good rises. Conversely, a household that is a net buyer will lose when the price rises. This is only an approximation since demand can respond quickly. However, given the magnitude of the relevant demand elasticities, the associated second-order impact is generally quite small, leaving the first-order measure as a good approximation. Essentially, this is the same measure that is used here for determining the effect of a change in prices on national income (Martin, 1997). The concept of the short run used in this analysis is the length of time in which other effects such as output adjustment or effects on wages do not arise. Some analyses, such as that by Ravallion (1990), suggest that much of the long-run impact is felt after 3 years.

At the household level, there are some important stylized facts that influence the likely effect of this measure, such as that poor households spend a large share of their incomes on food. This might suggest that the poor always lose when food prices rise. However, this need not always be the case. On the one hand, most of the world's poor live in rural areas and the majority earn their living from agriculture. On the other hand, many farmers in developing countries are also net buyers of food. Thus, the short-run effect of food prices on poverty becomes an empirical question that can be resolved only by using detailed data on the income sources and expenditure patterns of households.

A great deal of evidence shows that short-run increases in food prices raise poverty in most developing countries (de Hoyos & Medvedev, 2011; Ivanic & Martin, 2008; Ivanic, Martin, & Zaman, 2012; Jacoby, 2013;

Wodon & Zaman, 2010). This is often the case, even in countries, such as Brazil, that are net food exporters and therefore benefit from the terms-of-trade effect of the shock (Ferreira, Fruttero, Leite, & Lucchetti, 2013). In countries, such as Vietnam, where agricultural resources are relatively evenly distributed, higher prices of key products such as rice may lower poverty (Ivanic & Martin, 2008). Similarly, higher prices for milk appear to lower poverty in Peru, where the milk producers are much poorer than their customers. The net increase in poverty associated with a food price rise does not mean that all people are adversely affected. For example, Ivanic et al. (2012) found that although higher prices in 2010 resulted in a net increase in the extreme poverty of 44 million people, 68 million dropped below the poverty line and 24 million rose above it.

As more time is allowed for markets to adjust to changes, two additional factors need to be considered. First, changes in food prices may result in changes in factor returns. Second, changes in the output patterns of poor households may occur. The factor return most likely to affect poor households is the wage rate they receive for their unskilled off-farm labor (Lasco, Myers, & Bernsten, 2008; Ravallion, 1990). The effect on wage rates is likely to be much more important when the product considered is very labor intensive and the production of the good involves a large share of the intermediate inputs.

5. Short-run effects

Available evidence suggests that the full effect of food price changes on wage rates and output volume takes time to materialize. A useful measure of the short-run effects of higher food prices on poverty can consider only the direct impact on incomes due to the initial net trade position of the households. This measure is an important building block in understanding long-run measures that add wage rate and output change effects. These measures are potentially vulnerable to mismeasurement of the initial production or consumption levels of the households, an issue for which further research seems required (Carletto, 2012; Headey & Fan, 2010). They also take into account a small second-order impact − the ability of consumers to adjust the quantities they consume in response to price changes. Given the low value of compensated demand elasticities for small countries, this refinement makes very little difference in the estimated impacts.

Table 1 presents results from a simulation analysis of these short-run effects based on survey data for 31 countries (Ivanic & Martin, 2014a). Two key features of this analysis need to be taken into account. First, these results are based on a broad food price index rather than on changes in prices of particular foods. Second, they are based on a specific type of price change − one that results from shocks outside the target developing countries. This is a realistic approach for an event such as the food price shock of 2006–2008, which appears to have arisen primarily from external factors such as the sharply increasing demand for food-stuffs from the biofuel sector in industrial countries (Wright, 2014). The short-run poverty effects presented in Table 1 appear to adversely affect the poor in most countries (with the exception of Albania, Cambodia, China, and Vietnam) for which 10% increases in food prices reduce poverty. Strikingly, the poverty effects are frequently highly non-linear in food price changes. For most countries, the effects are mono-tonic but frequently far from linear in the price change. This effect rises to very high levels in countries such as India, Indonesia, and Pakistan.

Table 1.   Short-run poverty effects of food price increases, US$1.25 per day

Country	Survey Year	10%	50%	100%
Albania	2005	−0.1	0.7	4.8
Armenia	2004	0	1.3	4.9
Bangladesh	2005	1.4	9.7	18.1
Belize	2009	0.5	3.2	8.6
Cambodia	2003	−3.0	−10.1	−14.9
China	2002	−1.3	−4.0	−3.2
Côte d'Ivoire	2002	1.1	7.2	17.6
Ecuador	2006	0.3	2.3	7.2
Guatemala	2006	1.4	9.7	27.2
India	2005	2.6	14.2	25.8
Indonesia	2007	1.7	10.2	25.2
Malawi	2004	0.7	3.1	5.7
Moldova	2009	0	1.1	7.9
Mongolia	2002	1.4	8.7	21.6
Nepal	2002	0.5	3.2	6.8
Nicaragua	2005	1.1	5.8	17.4
Niger	2007	0.6	6.9	17.1
Nigeria	2003	1.0	5.6	9.8
Pakistan	2005	2.7	14.0	27.5
Panama	2003	0.3	2.5	8.0
Peru	2007	0.2	1.5	6.9
Rwanda	2005	1.1	4.4	8.5
Sierra Leone	2011	2.4	12.5	22.1
Sri Lanka	2007	1.8	11.6	29.1
Tajikistan	2007	0.8	8.7	28.1
Tanzania	2008	1.9	8.2	14.5
Timor-Leste	2007	1.9	10.0	20.1
Uganda	2005	0.7	3.8	8.7
Vietnam	2010	−0.4	2.1	12.8
Yemen, Rep.	2006	2.0	13.4	33.2
Zambia	2010	1.1	6.0	12.5
World		0.8	5.8	13.0

Source: Based on data and models collected by the authors

The results for the 31 countries presented in Table 1 are used as a sample to infer the global effects on poverty, following the sampling methodology outlined in Ivanic et al. (2012). They provide a useful summary of the effects, with global poverty rising despite declines in poverty in important countries such as China and Vietnam.

6. Long-run effects

As noted above, the long-run effects of a change in food prices differ from the short-run effects for two major reasons: the effects of food price changes on wages and the change in the volume of output resulting from the food price increase (i.e., the supply response). While our earlier work on the effects of food prices on poverty focused on the short-run effects, with an allowance for potential short-run wage changes (Ivanic & Martin, 2008), our more recent work examines the long-run effects, allowing for both changes in wage rates and changes in the quantities of output supplied (Ivanic & Martin, 2014a). In the long-run effect analysis, we assess the implications of changes in food prices for the wage rate received for unskilled off-farm labor. Given our desire to capture the impact of price changes on a range of commodities, we cannot use the type of econometric model used in Ravallion (1990). Instead, we develop for each country a model like the production module of the Global Trade Analysis Project (GTAP) model. These country models are similar in structure to the variable-coefficient model of international trade (Caves & Jones, 1973, pp. 182–185) in that output in each sector is determined by the level of a composite factor input. This substitution between factors in forming the composite factor input follows a constant elasticity of substitution technology. The version we use adds the real-world phenomenon of intermediate inputs that magnify the impact of output price changes on factor returns.

In medium-run analyses, all factors, except labor, are fixed in each sector, and the changes in output occur through intersectoral labor movements. In the long-run analyses, we allow movements of labor and capital in a manner consistent with the Heckscher–Ohlin trade model, modified to allow for the real-world imperfect mobility of land between sectors. The resulting elasticities of wage rates, with respect to the prices of agricultural goods, vary by country but are typically around unity for increases in all agricultural prices. For consistency with the economy-wide analysis used to estimate the wage effects of food price changes, we use the structure of the GTAP general equilibrium model to represent household response.

The long-run impacts of commodity prices on wages used in this analysis are drawn from simulation models of each economy rather than from direct estimation of statistical relationships. While we would prefer to have direct econometric estimates of these relationships, this is simply not feasible given constraints on the availability of data for many countries and the number of commodities involved. Despite the constraints, the relationships between food price changes and wage rates received for unskilled off-farm labor are broadly consistent with those obtained by Headey (2014) using econometric techniques applied to data for 68 countries. They are also broadly consistent with the findings by Jacoby (2013) for India using cross-sectional data and by Ravallion (1990) and Lasco et al. (2008) in country studies for Bangladesh and the Philippines, respectively. The recent experience of wages in Ethiopia (Headey, Nisrane, Worku, Dessa, & Seyoum Taffesse, 2012) also seems to suggest that these impacts can be relatively large. By contrast, Nicita, Olarreaga, and Porto (2014) using an ingenious symmetry relationship found impacts of food prices on wages that are much smaller, leaving the long-run relationship between food prices and poverty essentially the same as that of the short-run relationship.

Considering the global estimates shown in the first column of Table 2, we found that global poverty rises in the short run with increases in food prices. For a 10% price increase, global poverty is estimated to rise by 0.8 percentage points. The rate of increase appears to be increasing in the observed price range. When the food price shock increases fivefold to 50%, poverty is predicted to rise by 5.8 percentage points. Furthermore, doubling the shock to 100% more than doubles the global poverty increase to 13 percentage points. The positive relationship between food prices and poverty reflects the fact that most poor people are net food buyers. Because food production or wages respond to higher prices in the short-run scenario, poverty necessarily increases in this situation.

One important question involves the source of the differences between the short-run and long-run results in Table 2. The second column shows the results when the impact of wage changes is added to the direct impact of higher food prices. Since unskilled off-farm labor is a very important source of income for many poor households, and the impacts of higher food prices on wages for unskilled off-farm labor are found to be important for many countries, it is not surprising that the impact of higher wages has important, favorable impacts on poverty. Moving to the

Table 2.   Global poverty effects of general food price increases, US$1.25 per day

Scenario	Household Group	Short Run	Short Run + Wages	Medium Run	Long Run
10%	All	0.8	−1.1	−1.2	−1.4
50%	All	5.8	−3.9	−4.8	−5.8
100%	All	13	−5.7	−7.6	−8.7

Source: Ivanic and Martin (2014a)

medium-run scenario, in which farmers are able to change their outputs of food commodities, is quite similar to the second column. This implies that the ability to adjust food output and transfer labor between agriculture and other sectors has a much smaller impact than the wage-change impact emphasized by Jacoby (2013). Moving to the long-run scenario, in which all factors are mobile, increases the importance of adjustment responses, but these still remain quite small relative to the impacts of higher wages resulting from the food price impacts.

7. Poverty reduction

One initially puzzling feature of the food crisis associated with higher food prices was the seemingly sharp decline in poverty during the 2006–2012 period, where food prices rose substantially. Headey and Fan (2010) and Headey (2011) raised the key question of how this could be reconciled with the adverse short-run impacts of higher prices estimated in studies such as Ivanic and Martin (2008). Recent results on the difference between short-run and long-run impacts of food price changes and the pattern of transmission of food price increases offer a potential explanation for this puzzle.

A study by Ivanic and Martin (2014b) found that price transmission was very low in the initial phase of the food price increases. This reduced the adverse impacts of higher food prices on poverty, while at the same time exacerbating the increase in world food prices. With the sustained increase in world food prices, domestic prices rose when the wage responses took effect. When world food price changes, food price transmission, and food price impacts on poverty were combined, the food price increases over the 2006–2012 period contributed substantially to the large reductions in poverty observed during this period.

In Figure 3, while poverty reduction was more rapid without food price increases in the early stages of the food crisis, starting from around 2010, when international food prices declined from their 2008 peaks and domestic prices caught up with international prices, it appears that the higher food prices likely contributed to the reduction in global poverty. Extrapolating these differences to 2015 suggests that higher food prices contributed to the overall poverty reduction. Of the 8% decline in poverty between 2006 and the projection for 2015, it appears that food price increases may have been responsible for five of these percentage points.

This result does not mean that increases in food price are desirable. A better outcome would be increased crop productivity in developing country agriculture that raises the incomes of farmers at any given price and reduces poverty by lowering the cost of living for consumers. For this reason, Ivanic and Martin (2015) found that increased productivity growth in developing country agriculture is more beneficial for poverty reduction

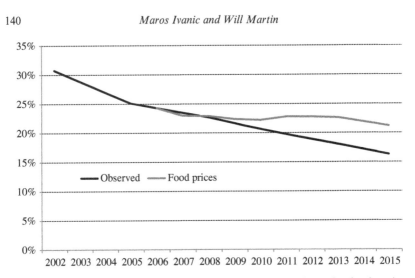

Fig. 3.   Global poverty headcount: observed versus without food price rises.

than is increased productivity in other sectors. To the extent that the increase in prices since 2000 was not exogenous to developing countries and may have reflected a deceleration in productivity growth, the effect of this productivity deceleration would be expected to have adverse impacts for global poverty. Continuing investment in improving agricultural productivity in developing countries remains extremely important for global poverty reduction.

8. Conclusions

This chapter began by examining the long-run behavior of rice, one of the world's most important staple food. This investigation revealed the large sustained and cumulative decrease in the world price of rice since 1900. Starting from 2000, there was evidence of the possibility of a reversal in this trend. This examination also illustrated the high volatility of this series over the entire period, including the post-2000 period.

We then examined the key policy response of developing countries in dealing with the problem of food price volatility. This included price insulation in the short-run and long-run transmissions of the price of rice into world markets. The response of short-run price insulation makes sense for individual countries but introduces a collective action problem that appears to render the response ineffective in stabilizing most prices and in mitigating the adverse poverty effects of price surges. Augmenting trade policy measures with storage measures reduces the collective action problem but does not appear to overcome it and raises serious challenges involving management, cost, and sustainability. There appears to be a strong case for first-best policies based on social safety nets at the national level, as well as efforts to diminish the collective action problem through agreements that restrain beggar-thy-neighbor policy responses.

Next, we turned to the question of the short-run and long-run impacts of food price changes on poverty. This analysis focused on the effects of food price changes on individuals and households. As Ferreira et al. (2013) showed in regard to Brazil, some people were adversely affected by food price changes even when their country benefited from the change. The evidence surveyed pointed strongly to increased food prices resulting in net increases in poverty in the short run. Invariably, only the net sellers of food rose out of poverty.

This chapter also examined the emerging evidence of the long-run effects of food price changes on poverty. In the long-run, there would be two important differences in the first-round impacts: wages would have time to fully adjust to the change in prices and producers would have the opportunity to adjust their output levels to the change in prices. In the long run, evidence suggested that higher food prices tended to lower poverty in most countries, frequently by substantial margins. Results would be more adverse for developing countries in which an increase in prices was due to a decrease in productivity.

We considered whether the increase in food prices since 2000 had unanticipated favorable impacts on poverty reduction. The impact was probably substantial after the initial adverse impact based on the assumption that the food price rise was exogenous to developing countries. However, if the impact reflected a deceleration in productivity in developing country agriculture, then the effect of that shock would have been unfavorable for poverty reduction.

References

Anderson, K., Ivanic, M., & Martin, W. (2013). *Food price spikes, price insulation, and poverty.* Policy Research Working Paper No. 6535. World Bank, Washington, DC.

Bruinisma, J. (2009). *Resource outlook to 2050: By how much do land, water, and crop yields need to increase by 2050?* Rome: FOA.

Caves, R., Jones, R. (1973). World Trade and Payments: An Introduction. Boston: Brown and Co.

Carletto, C. (2012, September 19). *Presumed poorer until proven net-seller: Measuring who wins and who loses from high food prices.* Washington, DC: World Bank.

de Hoyos, R., & Medvedev, D. (2011). Poverty effects of higher food prices: A global perspective. *Review of Development Economics, 15*(3), 387–402.

Deaton, A. (1989). Rice prices and income distribution in Thailand: A non-parametric analysis. *The Economic Journal, 99*(395), 1–37.

Ferreira, F., Fruttero, A., Leite, P., & Lucchetti, L. (2013). Rising food prices and household welfare: Evidence from Brazil in 2008. *Journal of Agricultural Economics, 64*(1), 151–176.

Gautam, M., Gouel, C., & Martin, W. (2014). *Managing wheat price volatility in India*. Unpublished draft. World Bank: Washington, DC.

Gouel, C., & Jean, S. (2014). *Optimal food price stabilization in a small open developing country*. Policy Research Working Paper no. 5943. World Bank, Washington, DC.

Headey, D. (2011). *Was the global food crisis really a crisis? Simulations versus self-reporting*. Discussion Paper no. 01087.International Food Policy Research Institute, Washington, DC.

Headey, D. (2014). *Food prices and poverty reduction in the long run.* Washington, DC: IFPRI.

Headey, D., & Fan, S. (2010). Reflections on the global food crisis. Research Monograph 165. IFPRI, Washington, DC.

Headey, D., Nisrane, F., Worku, I., Dessa, M., & Seyoum Taffesse, A. (2012). *Urban wage behavior during food price hikes: The Case of Ethiopia*. ESSP-II Working Paper no. 41. IFPRI, Washington, DC.

Ivanic, M., & Martin, W. (2008). Implications of higher global food prices for poverty in low-income countries. *Agricultural Economics, 39*, 405–416.

Ivanic, M., & Martin, W. (2014a). *Short-run and long-run impacts of food price changes on poverty*. Policy Research Working Paper no. 7011. World Bank, Washington, DC.

Ivanic, M., & Martin, W. (2014b). *World food price rises and the poor 2006–2012: A slow food price crisis?* Unpublished mimeograph. World Bank, Washington, DC.

Ivanic, M., & Martin, W. (2015). *Sectoral productivity growth and poverty reduction: National and global impacts*. Unpublished mimeograph. World Bank, Washington, DC.

Ivanic, M., Martin, W., & Zaman, H. (2012). Estimating the short-run poverty impacts of the 2010 surge in food prices. *World Development, 40*(11), 2302–2317.

Jacoby, H. G. (2013). *Food prices, wages, and welfare in rural India.* Policy Research Working Paper no. 6412. World Bank, Washington, DC.

Knudsen, O., & Nash, J. (1990). Domestic price stabilization schemes in developing countries. *Economic Development and Cultural Change, 38*(3), 539–558.

Lasco, C., Myers, R., & Bernsten, R. (2008). Dynamics of rice prices and agricultural wages in the Philippines. *Agricultural Economics, 38*, 339–348.

Martin, W. (1997). Measuring welfare changes with distortions. In J. Francois & K. K. Reinert (Eds.), *Applied methods for trade policy analysis: A handbook*. Cambridge: Cambridge University Press.

Martin, W., & Anderson, K. (2012). Export restrictions and price insulation during commodity price booms. *American Journal of Agricultural Economics, 94*(2), 422−427.

Nicita, A., Olarreaga, M., & Porto, G. (2014). Pro-poor trade policy in sub-Saharan Africa. *Journal of International Economics, 92*(2), 252−265.

Pfaffenzeller, S., Newbold, P., & Rayner, A. (2007). A short note on updating the Grilli and Yang commodity price index. *World Bank Economic Review, 21*(1), 151−163.

Ravallion, M. (1990). Rural welfare effects of food price changes under induced wage rate responses: Theory and evidence for Bangladesh. *Oxford Economic Papers, 42*(3), 574−585.

Wodon, Q., & Zaman, H. (2010). Higher food prices in sub-Saharan Africa: Poverty impact and policy responses. *World Bank Research Observer, 25*(1), 157−176.

World Bank. (2015). World Bank Commodities Price Data (The Pink Sheet). http://www.worldbank.org/en/research/commodity-markets. print.

Wright, B. (2014). Global biofuels: Key to the puzzle of grain market behavior. *Journal of Economic Perspectives, 28*(1), 73−98.

10

Food Security and Anti-Piracy Strategies: The Economics of Protecting World Food Program Shipments

William A. Kerr

University of Saskatchewan, Saskatoon, S7N 5A8, SK, Canada
E-mail address: william.kerr@usask.ca

Abstract

Purpose – The World Food Program provides food aid to areas of the world where food security is poor or non-existent – often failed states. Food can be a weapon in such places and food aid shipments a target for capture. This paper investigates the cost-effectiveness of international efforts to protect World Food Program aid shipments destined for Somalia from seaborne pirates off the Horn of Africa.

Findings – The lessons of history were ignored by those attempting to prevent food aid shipments from falling into the hands of pirates. The international community initially used very expensive naval assets to protect shipments. Over time, in an effort to reduce costs, the strategy and assets used to secure shipments evolved. This slow, cost-reduction-driven evolution of the international community's anti-piracy efforts off the Horn of Africa has distinct parallels with the evolution of anti-piracy efforts in the eighteenth and nineteenth centuries. One difference between the historic and current anti-piracy strategies is that there does not appear to be an exit strategy for the latter.

Practical implications – Future anti-piracy initiatives might look to previous strategies to avoid the costly experience associated with Somalia-bound food aid shipments.

Social implications – Achieving food security objectives can be a resource-intensive activity in failed states. This paper provides insights into how the resource cost of providing food security can be reduced.

Keywords: Food aid, food security, naval assets, piracy, World Food Program

Frontiers of Economics and Globalization
Volume 15   ISSN: 1574-8715
DOI: 10.1108/S1574-871520150000015018

JEL classifications: F 55; Q 18

1. Introduction

The most food insecure societies are typically found in areas of military conflict or in failed states. Making individuals more food secure in such areas often requires direct shipments of food aid. The World Food Program (WFP) is an important provider of food shipments to areas of the world where personal security is tenuous or does not exist at all. When lawlessness dominates a society, food can become a valuable weapon in intimidating groups of non-supporters and rewarding supporters and allies. Preventing food from reaching unsympathetic groups weakens them while supplying food to members of one's own group – including those doing the fighting – is central to ensuring their loyalty. One source of food available for capture is international food aid shipments. Thus, protecting food aid shipments is, at times, an important aspect of food security efforts. Somalia is a failed state characterized by contending local warlords, armed conflict, and disruptions to local food production. The WFP has provided shipments of food aid to Somalia for more than a decade. One facet of the failed Somali state has been the rise of seaborne piracy off the Horn of Africa. One desirable target for pirates is ships carrying WFP food aid cargos. In response to this seaborne threat, a major international military effort is being mounted by the European Union (EU), among others, to provide anti-piracy services to protect these shipments. Initially, very costly (and unsustainable) naval assets were used in this effort. Over time, in attempts to reduce the cost of anti-piracy activities, less expensive strategies have been developed.

This paper traces the evolution of anti-piracy strategies to protect WFP shipments and their efficacy from their inception until their current configuration. Some interesting parallels to the development of anti-piracy strategies in the eighteenth and nineteenth century are drawn which suggest that an exit strategy for current anti-piracy activities does not yet exist.

2. Food security

From the point of view of an individual, food security has three central pillars. First, global agricultural productivity advances must keep pace with global population growth (Kerr, 2011). Otherwise, there will be increasingly scarcer food. In this situation, food security will deteriorate for a subset of the population. Once the growth rate in global food production exceeds the rate at which population is increasing, then food security will become a function of distribution. In particular, individual food security depends on accessing food on a daily basis. It does not matter if food is available if one does not have access (resources to purchase food). Without access, a person is food insecure. For example, while food is generally available in modern market economies, there are individuals in society who do not have the resources to access the food. Hence, there is a role for food banks (places where food stocks are supplied free of charge to people in need). Food banks play a redistributive role by providing a channel for accessing food that is not based on individual resources. They extend a measure of food security to an additional segment of society.

Feeling food secure is tenuous in even the most advanced societies. All one has to do is observe the behavior of individuals when a natural disaster, such as a hurricane, is imminent. Food store shelves are quickly depleted. In all likelihood, the shortage of food is temporary, for a few days at most, yet the lack of perceived food security spurs extraordinary behavior.

Beyond the reduction in the short-term availability of food supplies brought about by a natural disaster, the deterioration in the availability of food arises from three sources. First, a disruption in local food production can reduce availability. Since most of the food consumed in the world is produced locally, crop failures (or livestock losses) can lead to a decline in the number of individuals who are food secure, especially in areas where there are prolonged local disruptions in production. Local crop failures happen all the time in modern market economies but go virtually unnoticed due to the well-functioning supply chains of food retailers who easily switch to alternative sources of food supplies. When crops fail, prices rise, providing the incentive for food to move from other areas where supplies are more abundant. Only if this arbitrage cannot take place due to inadequate transportation infrastructures, poorly developed supply chains, or trade barriers will food availability become a problem (Kerr, 2011). When food is unavailable due to a local disruption in production combined with a failure to move food from alternative sources of supply, food security no longer exists. In the worst cases famines arise. People either starve or they move to where food is available. Examples include the Irish famine of the 1840s, Chinese famines in the twentieth century, and the ongoing tragedies in Africa – all have entailed starvation and populations fleeing famine areas (Kerr, 2011).

There is another facet of food security in the case of famines that deserves examination. This relates to the dynamic aspects of a famine's evolution. Famines usually start with a local food production failure. The immediate effect is a rapid rise in the price of food. If this does not bring forth supplies from other locations, food price increases will not be moderated. The rising prices are exacerbated by those with resources acquiring and hoarding food (holding food for future personal or family consumption) or purchasing food for speculative purposes (holding food with the expectation that prices will be higher in the future). As prices rise, the poor quickly exhaust their resources acquiring what food they can. When their resources are fully depleted, they starve. It is important to remember that in a famine, the poor have no resources to purchase food. Thus, even if food eventually flows into famine areas, the population cannot purchase it. This was the case in the Irish famine – the *an Gorta Mór* – in the nineteenth century where food was actually available but the Irish peasants had no money to purchase food. The British government finally relented and restored a modicum of food security by instituting a system of food distribution, primarily soup kitchens (Bloy, 2002). Thus, for effective food security in cases of famine, there needs to be an adequate system in place to distribute food directly to those lacking the resources to purchase it.

Disruptions to local food production can arise for a number of reasons beyond crop failures due to adverse agronomic conditions. Armed conflict can lead to crops being burnt or livestock slaughtered. Furthermore, crops and livestock can often be appropriated by one or both of the contending factions, leaving civilian populations without access to food. Subsequently, stocks of seed normally retained from harvests may not exist, leading to a failure to plant. If conflict leads to lawlessness and, in particular, no property rights enforcement, farmers may feel it is too risky to sow their crops. Armed conflict can also mean that populations have shifted location to escape violence, meaning they have no access to arable land for farming.

In addition, armed conflict may deter those outside the area affected by disruptions to agricultural production from shipping food into the area to take advantage of the arbitrage opportunities that exist. Their shipments may be subject to the same threats of destruction or expropriation as local production. Furthermore, even if food could be delivered, local populations may not have any resources to purchase it. It is in these situations where emergency food aid systems are required. Such systems must have (1) the resources to acquire food in unaffected areas, (2) the ability to securely transport food to where it is needed, and (3) the means to distribute the food to those in need and who lack resources.

In areas where food is scarce and there are contending factions or a collapse in the rule of law, food aid shipments come to have strategic value if they can be appropriated from those supplying them. When food is scarce, stocks of food can become valuable weapons for those contending for societal control. Once a food aid shipment can be appropriated by a local faction, it can be used to deny access to those who support contending factions or fail to support the faction controlling the food with sufficient enthusiasm. Food scarcity, particularly when there has been a failure to plant, can directly affect those fighting for contending factions. Captured food aid shipments can be used to feed combatants and to reward loyalty among supporters. They can also be sold to finance operations. Hence, food aid shipments become desirable targets. This means that those supplying food aid, or those who support their efforts, must expend resources to ensure that food aid shipments reach the desired recipients.

3. The world food program in Somalia

In 2008, Josette Sheeran, Executive Director of the UN World Food Program, complained that pirates attacking UN ships off the coast of southern Somalia were decimating the lifeline for more than 1.2 million people (Sheeran, 2008). While the WFP's efforts in Somalia fluctuate depending on drought or civil strife in the country, even in times of relatively bountiful harvests and relative calm, its activities are substantial (WFP, Somalia, n.d.-a). This is because, after decades of turmoil, there are very large numbers of displaced persons, many living in camps with no income-generating activities that could be used to purchase food. On average, the WFP transports 2 million tonnes of food per year which translates into 30 ships at sea on any given day (WFP, Logistics, n.d.-b). At the height of the 2008 food crisis, there was a stream of ships moving to ports in Somalia. Given the narrow margins of food security at the ends of the WFP supply chains, disruptions to supplies could lead to widespread hunger for refugee camps and other communities dependent on the WFP for food. Given the difficulties associated with the post-port logistics in Somalia, it is very difficult for the WFP to stockpile food at the distribution points for local populations. Furthermore, stockpiles of food often become inviting targets for local militias or bandits. Operations by looters put WFP employees at risk, as well as the populations in the refugee camps. Hence, it is prudent to have a flow-based distribution system rather than one based on replenishment of stockholdings. Of course, that means that flows must be secure and disruptions kept to a minimum. The capture of ships – given the large size of their individual cargoes – by pirates has disrupted WTP supply chains to the extent that flow-based logistics strategies become unsustainable.

The capture of ships containing large quantities of food has also altered Somalia's domestic political landscape, as those who control food distribution can use food to enhance their power and control over the population. As outlined above, in a food-depleted country, distribution of food can buy the loyalty of one's fighters, or free up resources that would have been used to purchase food for one's militias for other purposes such as buying weapons and munitions, fuel, or vehicles. In addition, distribution of food at low prices can be used to gain/retain the loyalty of the local populations. Withholding food can be used to punish those whose loyalty is questionable (Kraska & Pedroso, 2013). The distribution of WFP food acted to reduce the potency of food as a local political weapon. Thus, reducing the incidence of piracy against WTP ships has wider ramifications.

The WFP operation in Somalia provides food to significant populations of people displaced by conflict or by drought. These displaced individuals often end up in refugee camps operated by the United Nations (UN) with food supplied by the WFP (World Food Program, 2012). Failure of the WFP flow-based food supply system may also disrupt the broader UN operation by reducing both the reality and perception of UN-operated refugee camps as safe havens where the necessities of life can be obtained and a degree of security can be provided. If food is unavailable in the refugee camps, individuals may choose to seek out alternatives and leave the camps for better access to food. The dispersion of displaced persons makes the job of the UN agencies responsible for their well-being much more difficult. Maintaining the flow of WFP food has wider importance in failed states such as Somalia, so a means to reduce the impact of sea-based piracy on WFP supply chains needed to be found.

4. The economics of anti-piracy – lessons of history

In June 2005, hijackers seized the St. Vincent and the Grenadines-registered MV Semlow, 60 kilometers off the coast of Somalia. This is the first time in WFP's history that a ship carrying relief food had been hijacked. The relief effort by the WFP was supplying 3,000 tonnes of food to some 275,000 Somalis each month (Panapress, 2005). As incidents of piracy off the coast of Somalia rose rapidly over the next two years, an international response was eventually implemented. UN Secretary General Ban Ki-moon requested that UN members provide protection for WFP shipments to Somalia, leading to a major international anti-piracy operations being formalized. The European Union (EU) shouldered responsibility for protecting WFP shipments:

> EUNAVFOR Operation Atalanta launched in December 2008. This was the first ever EU naval operation. Launched after only 10 weeks planning it took over protection of WFP shipments, but soon expanded into a more general anti-piracy role. (House of Commons, 2012, p. 28)

Two other separate international anti-piracy naval operations on an ongoing basis followed in short order. In January 2009, a US-led multilateral force, Combined Task Force 151, came into being with a broad-based anti-piracy mandate. This was followed in August 2009 by NATO Operation Ocean Shield, again with a focus on anti-piracy activities, but with added responsibilities to strengthen local anti-piracy capacity (House of Commons, 2012).

The navies involved in these activities all had one major deficiency: they lacked anti-piracy experience. Except for minor local incidents, most navies in developed countries had not engaged in sustained anti-piracy operations in more than a century because piracy had been effectively stamped out globally by the end of the nineteenth century.[1] Over the period from approximately 1500–1900, a great deal of learning by doing had taken place by European and US naval powers, driven in part by the economics of piracy – attempts to reduce the cost of anti-piracy operations. The learning by doing regarding the economics of anti-piracy activities by the navies involved in protecting WFP shipments seems to have been repeated, albeit at a much faster pace than was the case with their predecessors. The parallels are striking, however, and suggest that the lessons of history may have largely been forgotten.

Modern anti-piracy efforts of national navies have their roots in Spanish efforts to protect their shipments of gold bullion and other spoils from their conquests in the Americas from pirates operating in the Caribbean. Prior to this, the major piracy problem for European powers emanated from the Mediterranean, particularly, the Barbary pirates operating out of ports in North Africa. Here, however, instead of engaging in anti-piracy naval activities, the European powers used an alternative – and from their perspective less costly – solution to the piracy problem. They paid bribes to the rulers of the Barbary States to not attack their respective merchant ships (Gewalt, n.d.). This practice continued into the nineteenth century, thus avoiding the need for anti-piracy actions by European navies, and hence, learning strategies to deal with them.[2]

In the wake of their conquests in the Americas, Spain began shipping large quantities of treasure across the Atlantic Ocean. Given the prevailing winds, the route to Spain passed through the Caribbean with its myriad of islands. The Caribbean Sea soon became infested with both freebooting pirates and privateers holding letters of marque from various European governments allowing them to prey on the ships of rivals in times of war. Both were motivated by the incentive of prize money and/or a share in the loot. In response to these threats, Spain quickly resorted to a convoy system. The convoy system was in place from 1566 (less than a 100 years after Christopher Columbus' discoveries) until 1790. There was one return voyage from Spain to the Americas and back per year, determined by the trade winds. Convoys were used in both directions,

---

[1] One exception was anti-piracy patrols maintained by European powers and the United States on Chinese rivers until Communist China's capture of the territory where patrols operated in the 1940s.

[2] It was, in fact, the United States which led to a change in strategy by refusing to pay the bribe once it became independent from the British, who previously paid the bribe which encompassed the ships of its colonies. This led to the US fleet attacking Barbary pirates in Tripoli and elsewhere in North Africa starting in 1801 and eventually ending in 1815 (Kerr, 2013).

although it was the Havana (Cuba) to Seville (Spain) return run treasure convoys where protection was most needed.

The convoys consisted of slow, heavily laden, merchant vessels protected by Spanish naval vessels. These naval ships were purpose designed and built galleons, and represented the capital ships (or ships of the line) of their day – they were primarily designed to do battle against similarly designed galleons of their European rivals. They were heavily armed and more than a match for vessel pirates and most privateers could secure. As long as the weather cooperated and discipline was maintained among the merchantmen, these ships could keep the convoy safe. The system was, in fact, very successful, with the vast majority of convoys safely delivering most of their cargos. If the weather scattered the convoys or a merchant ship could not retain its place in the convoy, then these large lumbering ships were not sufficiently nimble to protect individual merchant ships from quicker pirate ships. Over time, the galleons improved as part of the technological arms race between the European powers. Their improvements kept galleons able to engage in battle with the ships of the line of other navies, but did not make them better escorts for convoys.

This ship of the line phase of anti-piracy operations was, however, extremely resource intensive. It would be the modern-day equivalent of using a guided missile cruiser to defend against a speedboat armed with a machine gun and a few hand-held rockets. While using the guided missile cruiser would be effective, it is not cost-effective. As the nineteenth century progressed, the technological lead of navies over pirates increased, allowing experimentation with less expensive forms of anti-piracy ships (Leiner, 2007). It was easy to see that the dreadnought battleships designed for battle with other naval powers were inappropriate and too expensive for an anti-piracy role.

In essence, the anti-piracy ships of the navy evolved separately from the ships designed to counter the battle fleets of other European powers (and latterly the United States and Japan). The ships were small, able to navigate in confined seas and rivers; technologically superior to whatever the pirates could acquire; and above all inexpensive to build, crew, and run. These were a sub-classification of gunboats whose primary purpose was to suppress piracy (Preston & Major, 2007). These small specialized but eclectic ships were used by all the major naval powers to combat piracy (along with quelling rebellions and protecting lives and property of western nationals on land). They continued to operate in some parts of the world up until after the Second World War. They acted both as escorts for merchant ships and proactive pirate hunters. Their mere presence was often sufficient to deter acts of piracy.

Having merchant vessels able to protect themselves – repel boarders – is an even lower cost method of deterring piracy. This can be accomplished by having military detachments such as marines stationed on merchant ships (Konstam, 2011), hiring private security firms to provide armed guards capable of repelling pirate attacks, or training the ship's crew to use military-grade weapons to stave off pirates. If the area of pirate activity is well defined, the first two options are less costly as personnel can be transferred to new ships once the area of pirate activities is cleared. Thus, both personnel and weapons can be used multiple times whereas a ship's crew and its weapons would be redundant once the ship was no longer in the area where pirates are active. Of course, if merchant vessels transited the area threatened by pirates often, then training and arming their crews could be a lower cost option. The strategy of repelling borders, however, depends on the weapons available to the pirates – if they are superior to those with which merchant ships can be equipped, anti-piracy activities must revert to escorting by technically superior naval vessels.[3]

Convoying imposes additional costs associated with maritime security. There are costs associated with the delays incurred with assembling convoys. The lighter the traffic in the area to be transited, the longer the delays in assembling a sufficient number of ships to justify the naval assets deployed in convoy duty. Furthermore, convoying means that the speed is determined by the speed of the slowest ship; hence, faster ships spend much longer transiting the area at risk from pirates than normal, thus adding to the cost of its voyage. As warships are typically faster than merchant ships, there need not be any time delays in escorting single merchant ships.

Thus, based on the historical experience with anti-piracy activities designed to protect merchant vessels, three approaches have emerged: (1) ships of the line, (2) gunboats, and (3) repel boarders. These are in order of declining cost for providing security for merchant ships. What has been the experience in protecting WFP food shipments? Before this question can be examined, it is necessary to address the important questions of an exit strategy for anti-piracy activities.

5. An exit strategy for anti-piracy activities

Naval activity, on its own, is not a permanent solution to piracy. While anti-piracy naval activities, if at sufficient levels and efficacy, can provide temporary relief from piracy, they cannot provide a permanent solution.

---

[3] Of course, it is also possible for private sector vessels to be used to escort merchant ships. The ships of the British East India Company were historical examples of private sector escorts (Freeman, 2003). With the rise of Somali-based pirate activity, private sector firms have been providing ships for anti-piracy operations, primarily in the Indian Ocean (Pitney & Levin, 2013).

Without an exit strategy, governments are faced with the ongoing expense of naval anti-piracy activities. While naval anti-piracy activities can suppress pirates temporarily, once the naval forces are withdrawn, new pirates will emerge or suppressed pirates will re-emerge. A permanent solution can only be achieved by denying the pirates their land bases. Piracy was largely eradicated in the nineteenth century, not by naval-based efforts, but by denying pirates bases of operation. This was largely accomplished through colonization. As colonial administrations became increasingly effective, they were able to deny pirates their land bases. For example, as various colonial governments in the Caribbean became more effective, they were able to deny pirates their land bases. Piracy in the region disappeared as an important problem and naval forces could be reduced. Along the long route from Europe to India via the Cape of Good Hope, in the wake of the *scramble for Africa* by the European powers, colonial administrations were able to deny land bases all along the route. Similarly in Asia, the increasing effectiveness of the Dutch administration in the sprawling Indonesian archipelago was used to control previously rampant local piracy activities. Spain was less successful in the Philippines, but their administration was eventually replaced by a more effective US one. One of the most difficult areas to suppress local piracy was Malaysia and, in particular, the Strait of Malacca. Incentives for the pirates were high given the heavy traffic through this maritime *choke point*. In addition, local rulers maintained a considerable degree of control over their administrations. Thus, the situation was closer to that of the Barbary pirates. It took considerable effort for the British to eventually suppress piracy. Of course, not all successful efforts to eradicate piracy were colonial. As post-colonial administrations in South and Central America increased in effectiveness, they were able to deny pirates their bases of operation onshore. Once this was accomplished, naval activities could be largely terminated – a successful exit strategy.

It was in areas where control of pirate land bases could not be acquired that anti-piracy naval activity lasted the longest. In China, one found US and European gunboats plying the waters of rivers such as the Yangtze right up until the late 1940s, when the often ineffective Chinese administration was replaced by the more effective, and hostile, communist one (Konstam, 2011).[4] It is clear, however, that the United States, the United Kingdom, and other powers had no exit strategy for anti-piracy activities

---

[4] The sinking of the American gunboat the USS Panay on the Yangtze River by Japanese aircraft in December 1937 was a clear demonstration that, while gunboats were more than able to keep local pirates at bay, they were no match for the modern weapons of the time (Koginos, 1967).

in China – with commensurate ongoing expenditures for naval operations.

6. Protecting WFP shipments from Somali pirates

In the face of a major food security operation by the WFP in Somalia, rapidly increasing acts of seaborne piracy based in the failed state of Somalia and the strategic importance of food as a weapon of reward and control, the international community decided to take action to protect ships chartered by the WFP. Initially, this was done by utilizing whatever ships were available in the area, but formal responsibility was eventually transferred to the European Union under EUNAVFOR Operation Atalanta. In the initial phase, the modern-day equivalents of *ships of the line* were employed to escort WFP ships through areas at risk from pirates, since modern naval powers, such as the United States, the United Kingdom, Russia, France, and more recently China, no longer have an equivalent to gunboats. The ships of these navies are technologically sophisticated and designed to do battle with other modern naval powers – either singly or in cross-supporting groups. They are also designed to counter threats from land-based air and missile attacks and attacks from submarines. Clearly, these types of ships were more than a match for the Somali pirates.

These modern equivalents of ships of the line, however, were an extremely costly option for protecting WFP shipments. Although the exact costs of the early efforts to protect WFP shipments are unavailable, estimates have been made regarding the wider anti-piracy efforts: Operation Atalanta, Operation Ocean Shield, and Combined Task Force (CTF) 151. These estimates (published in 2010) represent the early period of anti-piracy operations:

> Together, the three military efforts make up over 43 vessels operating off the Horn of Africa and the Indian Ocean. We take the estimation given by the 2010 Government Accountability Office (GAO) report on Maritime Security, that one US navy vessel costs around US$82,794 to operate per steaming day. Multiplying this by the total 43 vessels deployed, and 365 days, we approximate the costs of these military vessels to be around US$1.3 billion per year. Adding in the administrative budgets of the three major missions, along with additional independent expenditures from other nations, we come to a rough estimate of US$2 billion being spent on military operations in the region every year. This is also the approximation made by the European Institute in its October 2010 study. (One Earth Future, 2010, p. 16)

Other estimates suggest that deploying a frigate off Somalia costs around US$1.5 million per month (Knott, n.d.). From a budgetary perspective, these are substantial sums.

Because the navies of modern naval powers such as the United States and the United Kingdom are already stretched with their normal responsibilities, they have no spare capacity, and certainly no appropriate capacity, to deal cost effectively with pirates – the opportunity cost of using their ships of the line to escort WPF ships is very high. Given tight budgets and other priorities, these navies are not going to build modern equivalents of nineteenth century gunboats.

Furthermore, in the case of WFP shipments, convoying to more efficiently use the available ships is not an option given the low inventory requirements of the WFP supply chains discussed above. It is probably not surprising then that there has been a major effort to scour the world for spare naval capacity and to harness that capacity in the fight against piracy. This is where EUNAVFOR comes into play in the gunboat era of the Somali anti-piracy campaign. Most of the world's maritime states have some naval capacity. Much of it is underemployed. These navies are often made up of surplus ships of the major naval powers that have been sold to other countries. These ships, often older and/or less technologically sophisticated than those employed by the major naval powers,[5] are easily capable of dealing with pirates. Navies from the smaller maritime powers in Europe have also been drafted into the endeavor. Ships from Belgium, Bulgaria, Demark, Finland, France, Germany, Greece, Italy, the Netherlands, Portugal, Romania, Spain, Sweden, and the United Kingdom have been employed under EUNAVFOR.

It may be a win-win situation for the navies of lesser maritime powers that receive little publicity or even acknowledgment from their countrymen. Having an active role in anti-piracy initiatives can burnish their reputations and possibly ease the acceptance of their budget requests. It may also provide benefits through enhanced training opportunities – the opportunity to gain blue water experience (Kerr, 2013). Still, the cost for individual EU countries was substantial and it appears to have been increasingly difficult for the European Union to convince countries to have their navies participate. For example, to keep the operation going, navies from non-EU countries such as Turkey and Ukraine have also been recruited. The participation of naval vessels in protecting WFP shipments continues, but the costs of this gunboat strategy are substantial. Nevertheless, these naval efforts have produced some results. Compared with 2011, there were about one-third fewer Somalian pirate attacks in 2012 (Rai, 2013).

While the naval vessels from smaller maritime nations may be less expensive to operate and have a lower opportunity cost when deployed in an anti-piracy role than the naval forces of major maritime powers, they still represent an ongoing expense that must be borne by taxpayers. As

---

[5] Of course, the objective of countries that wish to be significant naval powers is to have a technological lead over naval rivals.

one would expect, faced with this ongoing expense, less expensive alternatives are being sought which has led to the third type, and least costly, of the historically observed anti-piracy strategy arising in EUNAVFOR – repel boarders.

In the evolving broader war against piracy in the Indian Ocean, private firms have entered and been increasingly engaged in providing security on a repel boarders basis. These private seaborne security forces largely employ retired military personnel to travel on merchant ships with sufficient weaponry to successfully confront pirates.[6] This is an extremely contentious issue in international maritime law, however, and some countries have refused to allow such mercenaries ashore.[7] Given this controversy, this has not been an option for protecting WFP ships given it is a UN operation. Since 2013, the armed forces of a number of countries have been providing personnel to travel aboard WFP-chartered ships to provide anti-piracy services. Some EU members (Germany, Finland, Estonia, Lithuania, and Croatia) have provided such forces which have proved to be a cost-effective alternative to the use of naval vessels. Whether they will entirely replace naval vessels remains to be seen. Naval vessels also provide considerable positive externalities in being engaged in wider anti-piracy efforts beyond protecting WFP shipments, assisting in local capacity building, and being a reassuring presence in an unstable part of the world.

EUNAVFOR, however, has no exit strategy. Even if it were to move its entire operation to the low-cost repel borders option, there will be considerable ongoing expense to protecting WFP cargos. The pirates still have secure land bases from which to launch anti-piracy operations. In the meantime, Somalia remains a failed state.[8] While the food crisis in Somalia waxes and wanes over the years, the WFP will likely have to continue its programs in Somalia in the foreseeable future. At least, the lessons of history regarding the costs of anti-piracy appear to have been learned again over the period since 2007.

7. Conclusion

According to EUNAVFOR (n.d.), since 2009, 301 WFP ships have been protected, allowing almost one million tonnes of food to be delivered.

---

[6] Although some private firms are investing in ships to be used in the proactive hunting of pirates (Kerr, 2013).
[7] See Kerr (2013) for a discussion of the issues surrounding the use of private sector employees for purposes of repelling boarders.
[8] The nineteenth-century colonization option does not exist in the twenty-first century.

Pirate attacks peaked in 2011 and declined to only two in 2014. There is no doubt the operation has been successful, but at what cost? The early ship of the line phase was very costly, and the gunboat phase is being undertaken at considerable ongoing cost. One can only speculate that if those charged with protecting WFP ships had studied the lessons of history and moved to the repel boarders strategy more quickly, likely a considerable saving of resources could have been achieved while still keeping WFP supply chains functioning securely. Still, one cannot argue with the success of Operation Atalanta supporting WFP efforts to provide food security in Somalia.

References

Bloy, M. (2002). The Irish famine, 1845–1849. *The Victorian Web.* Retrieved from http://www.victorianweb.org/history/famine.html
EUNAVFOR. (n.d.). *Eunavfor.* Retrieved from http://eunavfor.eu/key-facts-and-figures/
Freeman, D. B. (2003). Straits of Malacca: Gateway or gauntlet. Montreal: McGill-Queens University Press.
Gewalt, G. W. (n.d.). *America and the Barbary pirates: An international battle against an unconventional foe* (Jefferson Papers). Washington, DC: Library of Congress. Retrieved from http://memory.loc.gov/ammem/collections/jefferson_papers/mtjprece.html
House of Commons. (2012). *Piracy off the coast of Somalia.* London: Foreign Affairs Committee. Retrieved from https://books.google.ca/books?id=3mDEL2U4cKUC&pg=PA28&lpg=PA28&dq=wfp+shipments+somalia&source=bl&ots=vA4VtK2uz_&sig=ZOc6xvK5XMD2N TOwmX9Xsjx4xN8&hl=en&sa=X&ei=zDndVPDxF4H2oATMkIHIC w&ved=0CDkQ6AEwBjgK#v=onepage&q=wfp%20shipments%20so malia&f=false
Kerr, W. A. (2011). The role of international trade in achieving food security. *Journal of International Law and Trade Policy, 12*(2), 44–53.
Kerr, W. A. (2013). Scourge of the seas – Again!: Anti-piracy services and international trade costs. *Journal of International Law and Trade Policy, 14*(1), 1–17.
Knott, J. (n.d.). *Somalia, the Gulf of Aden, and piracy: An overview of recent developments.* London: Holman, Fenwick, and Willan. Retrieved from http://www.hfw.com/publications/client-briefings/somalia,-the-gulf-of-aden,-and-piracy-an-overview,-and-recent-developments
Koginos, M. T. (1967). *The Panay incident: Prelude to war.* West Lafayette, IN: Purdue University.
Konstam, A. (2011). *Yangtse river gunboats – 1900–49.* Oxon, UK: Osprey Press.

Kraska, J., & Pedrozo, R. (2013). *International maritime security law.* Leiden: Koninklijke Brill.

Leiner, F. C. (2007). *The end of Barbary terror, America's 1815 war against the pirates of North Africa.* Oxon, UK: Oxford University Press.

One Earth Future. (2010). *The economic cost of maritime piracy.* Earth Future Working Paper. Broomfield, Colorado. Retrieved from http://oceansbeyondpiracy.org/sites/default/files/documents_old/The_Economic_Cost_of_Piracy_Full_Report.pdf

Panapress. (2005, July 5). Hijackers oblige WFP to suspend shipment to Somalia. *Panapress.* Retrieved from http://www.panapress.com/Hijackers-oblige-WFP-to-suspend-shipment-to-Somalia–13-568776-18-lang2-index.html

Pitney, J. J., & Levin, J.-C. (2013). Private anti-piracy navies: How warships for hire are changing maritime security. *Google eBook.* Retrieved from https://books.google.ca/books?id=MDFXAgAAQBAJ&dq=anti-piracy+indian+ocean+private+companies&source=gbs_navlinks_s

Preston, A., & Major, J. (2007). *Send a gunboat, The Victorian navy and supremacy at sea, 1854–1904.* London: Conway.

Rai, N. (2013, January 16). Pirates carry out fewer attacks in 2012 – IMB. *gCaptain.* Retrieved from http://gcaptain.com/pirates-carry-attacks-2012/

Sheeran, J. (2008, April 18). *The new face of hunger.* Washington, DC: Center for Strategic and International Studies.

World Food Program. (2012). *Somalia: Trend analysis of food and nutrition insecurity (2007–2012).* Retrieved from http://documents.wfp.org/stellent/groups/public/documents/ena/wfp254879.pdf

World Food Program. (n.d.-a). *Somalia – WFP activities.* Retrieved from https://www.wfp.org/countries/somalia/operations

World Food Program. (n.d.-b). *Logistics.* Retrieved from http://www.wfp.org/logistics/shipping

11

World Population, Food Growth, and Food Security Challenges

William H. Meyers and Nicholas Kalaitzandonakes

University of Missouri, Columbia, 65211-7040, MO, USA
E-mail address: meyersw@missouri.edu and KalaitzandonakesN@missouri.edu

Abstract

Purpose – This paper assesses the projected growth of food supply relative to population growth and estimated food demand growth over the next four decades.

Methodology/approach – World population projections are analyzed for the main developed and developing regions. Implied food demand growth is then compared to grain and oilseed supply projections from a few of the most reliable sources. Three of these are 10-year projections and two extend to 2030 and 2050. To the extent possible, comparisons are made among the alternative projections. Conclusions about food availability and prices are finally drawn.

Findings – Meeting the growth in demand for food, feed, and biofuels to 2050 will not be a steep hill to climb, but there will need to be continued private and public investment in technology to induce increased production growth rates through productivity enhancements and increased purchased inputs.

Practical implications – The main food security challenge of the future, as in the present, is not insufficient production but rather increasing access and reducing vulnerability for food insecure households. The dominance of future population growth in the food insecure regions of Africa makes this challenge even more critical between now and 2050 and even more so in the years beyond 2050 when climate change effects on resource constraints will be more severe.

Keywords: Food supply, population growth, price projection, production growth

JEL classifications: Q18, Q11

Frontiers of Economics and Globalization
Volume 15   ISSN: 1574-8715
DOI: 10.1108/S1574-871520150000015019

1. Introduction

In 2009, FAO issued a report (Bruinsma, 2009) that contained estimates of how much agricultural production needed to increase between 2006 and 2050 to meet the projected growing consumption from increasing population and changing diets. While the most widely used estimate has been that global agricultural production has to double by 2050, the actual estimate in the 2009 FAO report was 70%. More recently, FAO (Alexandratos & Bruinsma, 2012) updated this estimate to 60% increase by 2050. These figures are used later in this paper, but we first examine the broader context for this and other estimates of future needs.

Since the end of World War II, rapid technological change combined with inelastic demand for food has resulted in declining real agricultural prices. Consumers have been the ultimate beneficiaries of agricultural innovation, while farmers have had to expand their operations and become more efficient to offset price declines. Governments in high-income countries have adopted various support and protective trade policies to shelter their farmers from price declines which often contribute to even lower market prices. This long-term decline in real prices has periodically been interrupted by price spikes caused by crop failures or other factors.

From the beginning of 2006 to the end of 2008, the world witnessed the largest surge of commodity and food prices since the early 1970s. After a short and deep price decline, they rose again between 2011 and 2014, and then began another decline in 2015 (Figure 1). The 2007/2008 price surge raised the age-old Malthusian question of whether food

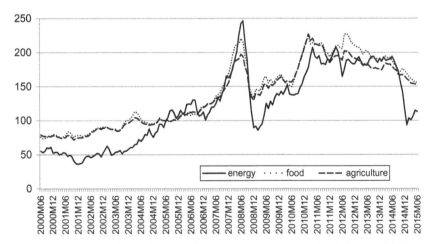

Fig. 1.   World Bank food, agriculture, and energy price indices, 01/00 to 6/15, 2005 = 100. Source: World Bank monthly commodity prices (Pink Sheet), accessed July 11, 2015.

production can keep pace with growing demand. Numerous studies have found complex factors related to this issue. Historically, the main driver of production has been technological progress. Meanwhile, the drivers of consumption have been population growth (which increases the number of mouths to feed) and income growth (which increases the quality and quantity of food consumed per person). Changing diets that accompany both increased incomes and increased urbanization generally lead to more animal-sourced protein consumption per person.

A number of factors have contributed to the rising and more volatile prices since 2007, including declining grain and oilseed stocks, depreciation of the US dollar, poor weather (leading to yield shocks), governmental policy reaction to rising prices, changing diets, and rising demand. It has been in many ways a perfect storm of factors (Abbott, Hurt, & Tyner, 2009; Meyers & Meyer, 2008). In a number of countries, the implementation of policies stimulating biofuel production in pursuit of environmental and farm support objectives has formed a much stronger link between fuel and food markets, a link that can contribute both to the level and the volatility of food prices (FAO, 2008; FAPRI-MU, 2008; Organisation for Economic Co-operation and Development/FAO [OECD/FAO], 2008). These policy changes have increased the profitability of investments in biofuel capacity and the increased use of existing capacity, resulting in more grains and oilseeds being used as feedstock for biofuel production. While the biofuels component of grain and oilseed demand rose strongly from 2005 to 2011, it is not expected to be a major factor in the growth in future food demand (FAPRI-MU, 2015).

Examination of grain and oilseed world markets indicates that the rate of production growth has been decelerating since the 1970s. This has contributed to declining stock positions in global markets (Table 1). While a significant share of the decline in the 1990s was due to the restructuring and reform in the Former Soviet Union (FSU-12), grain production growth would still have been slower than in earlier decades. In comparing growth rates in yield over each decade from 1960 to 2013, there has been a steady deceleration in yield growth rates since the 1970s. Added to this problem is the declaration by the Intergovernmental Panel on Climate Change (IPCC, 2007) that natural disasters may become more frequent and extreme in the future due to climate change, thus contributing to a deceleration in the average growth and yield. Grain area which declined between 1980 and 2000 to less than 1% per annum in production growth has rebounded but not to previous levels.

Consumption growth has been more or less in line with production since the 1960s (Figure 2). This is typical and reveals that production and consumption tend to run parallel over time. Production may temporarily outpace consumption, resulting in the buildup of buffer stocks in years of bumper crops or fast land expansion. Conversely, shrinking land use or adverse weather may lead to lagging production and falling buffer stocks.

Table 1.   Average annual percent change in area, yield, and production, grains and oilseeds

	1960–1970	1970–1980	1980–1990	1990–2000	2000–2010	2010–2013
Grains						
Yield	2.48	1.87	1.82	1.30	1.62	1.11
Area	0.47	0.82	−0.43	−0.43	0.47	0.41
Production	2.98	2.43	1.49	0.62	2.00	1.69
Consumption	3.02	2.31	1.55	0.87	1.67	1.66
FSU-12						
Area	−02.0	0.63	−1.78	−3.03	0.07	0.14
Production	2.82	−0.06	1.15	−3.49	1.80	1.81
Consumption	3.77	2.05	0.68	−5.71	0.84	0.12
World Less FSU-12						
Area	0.62	0.85	−0.18	−0.07	0.52	0.44
Production	3.01	2.79	1.53	1.00	2.01	1.68
Consumption	2.90	2.36	1.68	1.57	1.72	1.75
Grains and oilseeds						
Area	1.44	1.29	−0.15	0.05	0.81	0.71
Production	3.64	2.78	1.63	1.01	2.21	1.88
Consumption	3.71	2.64	1.68	1.20	1.92	1.79

Source: Calculated from PSD database, USDA (2015).

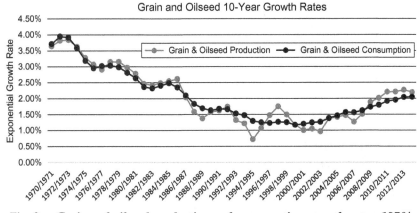

Fig. 2.   Grain and oilseed production and consumption growth rates, 1970/ 1971–2012/2013. Source: Calculated from the PSD database, USDA (2015).

Not surprisingly then, consumption growth rates for total grains and oilseeds have been declining since the 1980s (dropping below the 1% per year level in the 1990s). These, too, have since rebounded, although not to the levels seen in the 1970s and not to the same degree as growth rates in production. This suggests that decelerating population growth rates have not been completely offset by the consumption boosting effects of income growth (Alexandratos, 2008). A major factor in the consumption deceleration of the 1990s was what happened in the FSU-12, when excessive and wasteful feed use was drastically cut by market forces that rationalized grain use. Consumption growth in the rest of the world did not decline substantially in this period.

Sustained reduction in buffer stocks is the hallmark of an imbalance in supply and demand when consumption grows faster than production. Such reductions in grain stocks laid the foundation for the price shocks in the 2006−2008 period. The price surge and the resulting world food crisis captured headlines and stimulated a wide range of analytical activity and policy discourse (Abbott et al., 2009; Meyers & Meyer, 2008). The crisis caused hardship in many developing countries, led to social unrest in many of these countries, and significantly increased global and national efforts for more agricultural investment and food security. With production growth outpacing consumption growth, questions have been raised about the capacity of the global food system to sustain its past success in food and fuel expansion in developing countries.

This paper begins the quest for answers to these food and fuel security questions by analyzing population growth projections and the implications for food demand growth, and then analyzing grain and oilseed supply projections from several sources. Growth in demand and supply for foodstuffs cannot be viewed in isolation from food prices and income growth. Higher incomes stimulate more demand and differing patterns of demand, and prices influence the composition of food consumption. Thus, supply and demand growth are analyzed relative to whether supply−demand pressures will sustain an upward pressure on prices and relative to which supply-side developments may be needed to keep pace with possible demand growth.

2. Population growth dynamics and projections to 2050

The United States Census Bureau (2015) projects that the world population will reach 9.38 billion persons by 2050, an approximate 36.5% increase over the population in 2010. While world population continues to increase, rates of population growth have been decreasing where incomes and education levels increase (Table 2). It is well established that higher income and education levels increase the marriage age of women and reduce the number of children per family. This more than offsets increased life expectancy at birth (which accompanies higher incomes) and reduces population growth rates (Table 2). In the projected aggregate of developed countries, population begins to decline beyond 2040. On the European continent, this decline is projected to commence in 2020 due to low birth rates. In China, with its one-child policy, the population growth

Table 2. Population growth rates, historical and projections in 10-year increments, 1960–2050

Region	1960–1970	1970–1980	1980–1990	1990–2000	2000–2010	2010–2020	2020–2030	2030–2040	2040–2050
World	1.82	1.66	1.58	1.29	1.10	0.96	0.78	0.62	0.48
Developing	2.20	2.00	1.90	1.53	1.28	1.11	0.91	0.72	0.56
Developed	0.89	0.68	0.51	0.39	0.32	0.25	0.14	0.04	-0.04
Africa	2.27	2.47	2.53	2.23	2.23	2.09	1.89	1.70	1.50
North America	1.48	1.28	1.12	1.21	0.93	0.80	0.67	0.50	0.38
South America	2.48	2.13	1.89	1.48	1.13	0.90	0.68	0.43	0.20
Europe	0.76	0.50	0.35	0.10	0.11	0.09	-0.06	-0.16	-0.26
Oceania	1.91	1.45	1.45	1.29	1.27	1.07	0.85	0.62	0.46
Asia	2.09	1.86	1.72	1.34	1.04	0.85	0.61	0.39	0.22
China	2.13	1.67	1.41	0.87	0.47	0.37	0.05	-0.22	-0.37
India	2.00	1.95	1.85	1.68	1.40	1.12	0.88	0.67	0.48

Source: International database, US Census Bureau (2015).

rate is projected to go negative in 2033 and be below the developed country level by 2050.

Another important aspect of global population growth is regional distribution. From 1970 to 2010, 63% of the world population growth was in Asia and 21% in Africa (Figure 3). These numbers change dramatically between 2010 and 2050, when total share of population growth will be about 42% in Asia and 48.5% in Africa. More than 1.2 billion people are projected to be added in Africa, which well exceeds the 1.0 billion projected for Asia. This dramatic shift in shares of population in Asia and Africa may have a significant impact on global food consumption patterns and food security because the most food insecure regions are growing the fastest. Meanwhile, Europe's population which has been at essentially zero growth since 1990 is expected to decrease from 11% of the world population in 2010 to 7.5% in 2050. The shares of total population in North America and South America are projected to be around 7% each in 2050. With the expected 2.67 billion additional people between 2010 and 2050 and nearly half of these in Africa, there will be future food security challenges.

3. Potential income and demand growth

As an approximation of the growth in demand for food, if there were no change in per capita consumption in each country, food demand would grow at a slower rate than population simply because the populations with lower per capita consumption levels also tend to have higher population growth rates (Alexandratos, 1999). In addition, per capita

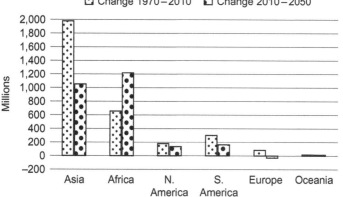

Fig. 3. *Regional population changes over 40 year periods past and future.*
Source: *International database. US Census Bureau (2015).*

consumption tends to grow with income in low-income populations, where the diet is often inadequate. At higher income levels, where there is an adequate diet, the income effect is insignificant. The percent growth in demand for food for 1% growth in income is called income elasticity of demand. We can illustrate this by comparing the calculated growth in demand for food with no change in per capita consumption (or no income effect) compared to scenarios where the income elasticity of demand for food is 0.2 or 0.4, meaning that food consumption would grow by 2% or 4% for every 10% growth in income, assuming that nothing else changes (i.e., there is no change in prices or other factors that may influence food demand).

Food demand growth = population growth + (income elasticity * per capita income growth). This calculation requires a projection of the growth in per capita income for which we use the projected growth in real gross domestic product (GDP) per capita. These GDP figures reflect an average growth rate of 2% or slightly higher on a per capita basis and between 3% and 3.5% per annum, including population growth. Applying the different income elasticities and using the world population growth rates from the previous section, we obtain food demand growth rates that range from about 2% per annum for the higher-income elasticity to about 1% per annum when there is no income effect or no change in per capita consumption (Figure 4). To check which of these may be closest to a recent long-term projection of food demand growth, we use the FAO (Alexandratos & Bruinsma, 2012) projection for growth rate of demand for all commodities and all uses. For the period of 2000–2030, the estimated average growth rate is 1.4% per annum which is virtually identical to the middle calculation from 2015 onward (Figure 4). Since

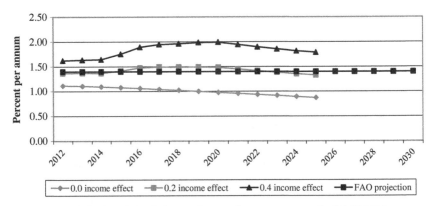

Fig. 4. Calculated food demand growth rate compared with FAO long-term projections. **Source: *GDP growth rates are IHS Global Insight projections used in the FAPRI January 2015 baseline.***

population growth rates are declining, it is likely that future food demand growth will be lower.[1]

We do not want to dwell too much on food demand growth without speaking of supply and price conditions, but it is useful to have a reference point when speaking of potential growth in supply. When looking at supply growth, we focus on grains and oilseeds since they are the basic commodities from which most foods are derived. When incomes grow, people tend to shift from direct consumption of grains to indirect consumption of grain through meat (animals eat grain as a feedstuff). This is reflected in the income effect represented by the income elasticity; that is, more grain per capita is used when meat constitutes an increasing percentage of the national diet.

4. Supply projections for cereals from different sources

As discussed earlier, several factors have contributed to the slow production growth in cereals. A key market factor was the extended period of declining real prices that reduced market incentives to invest and produce. The result was a decline in grain area (Table 1) at the same time that yield growth rates were decelerating.

Another important factor in slowing yield growth rates (Figure 5) was the diminishing national and international public investment in agricultural research and development (R&D) that began in the 1990s. The international research investments of the 1960s were deliberate policies to enhance agricultural productivity in developing countries which resulted in the high yielding Green Revolution wheat and rice varieties that spurred yield growth and enhanced multiple cropping opportunities with shorter growing seasons. Along with continuing public and private agricultural R&D in industrial countries, improved technologies supported grain yield growth of nearly 2.5% and production growth of 3% annually from 1960 to 1970. While yield growth remained relatively high in the 1970s and 1980s, grain area declined and finally plateaued in the 1990s.

Numerous World Bank, FAO, and International Food Policy Research Institute (IFPRI) documents have established that investment in agricultural development has been lagging, especially in developing countries. Developing countries have underinvested in agriculture since the 1990s (World Bank, 2007a). Only 4% of total public R&D goes to agriculture in developing countries where 75% of the world's poor live in

---

[1] This global illustration greatly oversimplifies the process used in conducting such projections. Generally, projections of demand growth must be conducted in more disaggregated ways and preferably country by country (Alexandratos, 1997).

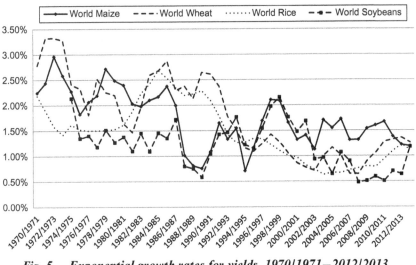

Fig. 5.   Exponential growth rates for yields, 1970/1971–2012/2013.
Source: *Calculated from the PSD database, USDA (2015).*

rural areas. Pardey, Beintema, Dehmer, and Wood (2006) find that growth in public agricultural R&D spending (which was critical to the Green Revolution) declined by more than 50% in most developing countries from 1980 onward and turned negative in high-income countries from 1991 onward. While there have been important exceptions in China and India (World Bank, 2007b), national governments and international organizations have mainly neglected these investments despite the high rates of return demonstrated in past R&D projects.

It is noteworthy that crop yield growth rates since 2000 have been significantly higher for corn than for soybeans, wheat, and rice (Figure 5). This reflects the role of private investments in the biotechnology development and commercialization of corn germplasms.

Grain and oilseed area and production have been increasing in response to a commodity price surge and increasing biofuels feedstock demand since 2006 (Figure 2). Another contributing factor has been the steady recovery and growth of the crop sectors in the FSU-12 since 2000. It is in this context that the most recent 10-year projections of future supply have been conducted. These projections are also conducted in the context of public R&D deficiency because, even if urgent action were taken to reverse the investment path for agriculture, such action would constitute the beginning of a long-term endeavor.

A comparison of grain and oilseed production projections is made from three well-known annual global market assessments. The first is by FAPRI-MU with assistance from the University of Arkansas on global rice market analysis (FAPRI-MU, 2015). The second is by the United

States Department of Agriculture (USDA, 2015). The third is conducted jointly by the OECD and FAO (OECD/FAO, 2014). The implications of all three projections are quite similar.

Grains (except for rice) and oilseeds have had significant growth in production, primarily in response to rapidly rising prices and agricultural recovery in the FSU-12 since 2000 (Table 3). Projected production growth rates for 2014–2023 are lower, with only wheat production growth rates remaining higher than in the 1990s. Wheat is a special case in the United States because the decoupling of payments from base acres in the mid-1990s led to a large shift of land from wheat to soybeans in the 1990–2000 period. The comparison of FAPRI with USDA and OECD/FAO projections serves to show a considerable agreement on production growth rates.

Finally, we compare these 10-year projections to long-term projections conducted by FAO (Alexandratos & Bruinsma, 2012) and by IFPRI (Rosegrant, Simla Tokgoz, & Bhandary, 2013). The long-term projections use different kinds of modeling systems than the 10-year projections. FAO essentially assumes constant real prices and projects that the use of grains and oilseeds for biofuels feedstock will not grow beyond 2020. IFPRI's projections also estimate prices and incorporate models of bio-fuel feedstock demands. The long-term estimates also take account of water and land resource constraints in the analysis. We use the FAPRI results for comparison and find a rather consistent outlook (Table 4).

Comparing FAO and IFPRI analyses, they are very similar in terms of total cereals. Their figures suggest that there will be about a 50% increase in cereal production over the next 30 years, compared to a 22% increase over the last 10 years.

Regional patterns of production are also important because production growth in areas closer to faster growing populations and

Table 3. Comparison of growth rates for grains and oilseeds production, % per annum

Crop	1990–2000	2000–2014	FAPRI 2014–2023	USDA 2014–2023	OECD/FAO[a] 2014–2023
Rice	1.48	1.28	1.03	0.89	1.06
Wheat	0.38	1.38	0.90	0.63	0.91
Corn/coarse grains[a]	1.98	3.57	1.40	1.31	1.08
Total grains above	1.24	2.25	1.14	1.00	1.03
Soybeans/ oilseeds[a]	5.25	3.98	2.24	2.38	1.57

Sources: FAPRI-MU (2015), OECD (2014), and USDA (2015). Historical figures use three-year average of production.
[a]OECD does aggregate coarse grains and oilseeds.

**Table 4.   Comparison of growth rates for grains and oilseeds production,
% per annum**

Crop	FAPRI 2014–2023	FAO[a] 2006–2030	FAO[a] 2006–2050	IFPRI 2010–2050
Rice	1.03	–	–	–
Wheat	0.90	–	–	–
Corn	1.40	–	–	–
Total above/ cereals[a]	1.14	1.20	0.90	0.84
Soybeans	2.24	1.0	1.3	N/A
Population	1.00	1.04	0.87	0.87

Sources: Alexandratos and Bruinsma (2012), FAPRI-MU (2015), Rosegrant et al. (2013).
[a]FAO data are for all cereals.

**Table 5.   Regional pattern of agricultural production growth rates,
historical and FAO projection, % per annum**

	1961–2007	1987–2007	1997–2007	2005/ 2007–2030	2030–2050
World	2.2	2.2	2.2	1.3	0.8
Developing countries	3.3	3.5	3.1	1.6	0.9
Excluding China and India	2.9	3.0	3.3	1.8	1.2
South Asia	2.9	2.7	2.4	1.9	1.3
East Asia	4.0	4.2	3.3	1.3	0.5
Sub-Saharan Africa	2.6	3.2	3.1	2.5	2.1
Latin America and the Caribbean	2.9	3.3	3.8	1.7	0.8
Near East/North Africa	3.0	2.7	2.6	1.6	1.2
Developed countries	0.9	0.2	0.5	0.7	0.3
44 countries with over 2,700 kcal/person/day in 2005/2007[a]	2.6	2.9	2.0	1.1	0.5

Source: Alexandratos and Bruinsma (2012, p. 95).
[a]Accounting for 57 percent of the world population in 2005–2007.

consumption reduces transport costs and reduces losses in quality and quantity associated with transporting commodities from production to consumption centers. Between 1997 and 2007, the rate of total agricultural production growth increased in Latin America and decreased or remained nearly the same in most other regions. Future cereal production growth rates are projected to be higher in developing countries than in industrial or transitional countries (Table 5). In the 2006–2050 projection period, the agricultural production growth rate is projected to be highest in Sub-Saharan Africa. Although all rates are projected to decrease between 2030 and 2050, production growth rates in developing countries

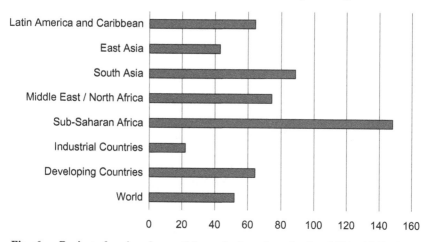

Fig. 6.   Projected regional growth in agricultural production 2010–2050 (%).
Source: *Alexandratos and Bruinsma (2012).*

are expected to be higher than in industrial countries, with the highest projected growth rate being in Sub-Saharan Africa. Growth rates in agricultural production imply that production will more than double in Sub-Saharan Africa, will increase by 90% in South Asia, and will increase more than 50% for the world as a whole (Figure 6).

5. Commodity and food price projections

Projections of commodity and food prices are also important. The FAPRI, OECD/FAO, and USDA projection models include a wide range of production, consumption, trade, and price information for crops and livestock/dairy products. From these projections, we cannot view the production and consumption outlook without referencing prices. Price spikes in 2007/2008 and shortly thereafter have opened a dialog on whether the downward path of real commodity prices has come to an end. The FAPRI price projections that accompany the most recent outlook do not answer this question. It is a price path that is neither increasing nor returning to the lowest levels seen at the beginning of the twenty-first century (Figure 7). Price projections of FAPRI include a stochastic price band that makes it clear that prices will continue to be volatile whether the long-term path is increasing or decreasing. The demand for grains and oilseeds as feedstock for biofuels adds to the traditional demands for food grains and animal feeds. The demand for biofuels will depend on future petroleum prices and continued recovery from the recent economic crisis. Declining petroleum prices have lessened price pressures in the near future.

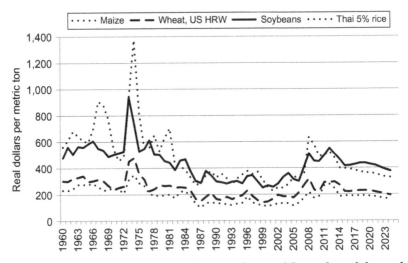

***Fig. 7. World grain price projections consistent with supply and demand projections.* Source:** *History from World Bank Pink Sheet, projections calculated from FAPRI 2015 baseline.*

The IFPRI projection clearly signals that it would take increased real prices to achieve the rates of production growth they estimate would be needed to meet rising demand by 2050 (Rosegrant et al., 2013). This is in opposition of the FAPRI projection of constant or slightly declining real prices. IFPRI also evaluated how much productivity growth would be required to maintain the real prices experienced in 2010. They estimated that productivity growth rates would have to increase by 32% for rice, 65% for wheat, and 100% for maize. This indicates a rather large difference with the FAO analysis which has approximately the same growth rates in cereal production to 2050 but implicitly assumes constant real prices. We cannot resolve these differences here, but rather present the alternative futures as a further indication of the uncertainty facing food security analysis for the future.

A study by Wise (2013) of alternative analyses and modeling approaches to projecting future food needs highlights the post-2050 timeframe as being more challenging because climate change impacts will be more pronounced, especially in Africa (Figure 8). The projections cited in this paper do not attempt to estimate the possible impacts of reducing food loss and waste which in some locations could be a substitute for increasing production at the farm level (Segrè, Falasconi, Politano, & Vittuari, 2014). Questions on the cost effectiveness of policies and how such actions could improve food security need more careful assessment (Koester, 2014).

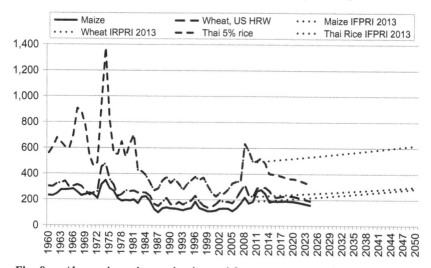

Fig. 8.   Alternative price projections with status quo and high yield growth.
Source: 2050 projection from Rosegrant et al. (2013) added to World Bank
Pink Sheet and FAPRI projections.

6. Conclusions and implications

Since 2000, declining stocks and a series of market shocks have led to markedly higher prices that have induced increased land use and a more rapid growth of yields and production. Limits on future agricultural land-use expansion and water sources are constraints on both production and consumption growth. Prices are likely to be volatile for some time. It does appear that meeting the growth in demand for food, feed, and biofuels to 2050 will not be difficult to achieve, but there will need to be continued private and public investment in technology to induce increased production growth rates through productivity enhancements and increased purchased inputs. There will be greater pressure on land and water use and on food import costs, to meet food demand and provide greater food security among low-income households, especially in developing food-importing countries.

Most of these baseline projections assume a continuation of technology growth patterns of the recent past, which has seen a deceleration of yield growth rates. An alternative future would see an increased rate of technological advancement through higher private and public R&D investment which would generate a higher yield growth path, permit substitution of technology for cropland, and benefit farmers through higher productivity and consumers through lower food prices. Such an alternative higher technological future would improve the well-being of consumers, especially in developing countries, and contribute to long-term sustainability of agricultural resources by substituting technology for land, thereby reducing pressure on cropland.

The main food security challenge of the future, as in the present, is not insufficient production but rather increasing access and reducing vulnerability for food insecure households. The dominance of future population growth in the food insecure regions of Africa makes this a significant challenge between now and 2050 and even more so in the years beyond 2050 when climate change effects on resource constraints will be more severe. These are also the regions where waste reduction could be a cost-effective alternative to increased production, but ideally both of these means to increase availability should be pursued simultaneously.

References

Abbott, P. C., Hurt, C., & Tyner, W. E. (2009, March). *What's driving food prices?* Oakbrook, IL: Farm Foundation. Retrieved from http://purl.umn.edu/48495

Alexandratos, N. (1997). The world food outlook: A review essay. *Population and Development Review, 23*(4), 877–888.

Alexandratos, N. (1999). World food and agriculture: Outlook for the medium and longer term. *Proceedings of the US National Academy of Sciences, 96*, 5908–5914.

Alexandratos, N. (2008). Food price surges: Possible causes, past experiences, relevance for exploring long-term prospects. *Population and Development Review, 34*(4), 663–697.

Alexandratos, N., & Bruinsma, J. (2012). *World agriculture towards 2030/ 2050: The 2012 revision* (ESA 12-03). Rome: Food and Agriculture Organization of the United Nations.

Bruinsma, J. (2009, June). *The resource outlook to 2050: By how much do land, water and crop yields need to increase by 2050?* Rome: Food and Agriculture Organization of the United Nations. Retrieved from http://ftp.fao.org/agl/aglw/docs/ResourceOutlookto2050.pdf

Food and Agricultural Policy Research Institute at University of Missouri [FAPRI-MU]. (2008, July). *Model of the US ethanol market.* FAPRI-MU Report #07-08. Columbia, MO: University of Missouri.

Food and Agricultural Policy Research Institute at University of Missouri [FAPRI-MU]. (2015, March). *2015 US baseline briefing book.* FAPRI-MU Report #01-15. Columbia, MO: University of Missouri.

Food and Agriculture Organization of the United Nations [FAO]. (2008). Biofuels: Prospects, risks and opportunities. In *State of food and agriculture 2008*. Rome: FAO.

Intergovernmental Panel on Climate Change [IPCC]. (2007). *Climate change 2007: Impacts, adaptation and vulnerability. Contribution of working group II to the fourth assessment report of the intergovernmental panel on climate change*. Cambridge, UK: Cambridge University Press.

Koester, U. (2014). Food loss and waste as an economic and policy problem. *Intereconomics, 49*(6), 348–354.

Meyers, W. H., & Meyer, S. (2008, December). *Causes and implications of the food price surge.* FAPRI-MU Report #12-08. Columbia, MO: University of Missouri. Retrieved from http://www.fapri.missouri.edu/wp-content/uploads/2015/02/FAPRI-MU-Report-12-08.pdf

OECD. (2014, July). *OECD-FAO agricultural outlook 2014–2023.* Paris: OECD.

Organisation for Economic Co-operation and Development [OECD]. (2008, July). *Biofuel support policies: An economic assessment.* Paris: OECD.

Pardey, P. G., Beintema, N., Dehmer, S., & Wood, S. (2006, August). *Agricultural research: A growing global divide?* Washington, DC: International Food Policy Research Institute.

Rosegrant, M. W., Simla Tokgoz, S., & Bhandary, P. (2013). The new normal? A tighter global agricultural supply and demand relation and its implications for food security. *American Journal of Agricultural Economics, 95*(2), 303–309.

Segrè, A., Falasconi, L., Politano, A., & Vittuari, M. (2014). *SAVE FOOD: Global initiative on food loss and waste reduction.* Background paper on the economics of food loss and waste (Working paper). Rome: FAO.

United Stated Department of Agriculture [USDA]. (2015, February). *International long-term projections to 2022.* Washington, DC: USDA.

United States Census Bureau. (2015). *International database* [Online database]. Washington, DC: US Census Bureau. Retrieved from http://www.census.gov/population/international/data/idb/informationGateway.php

Wise, T. A. (2013, September). *Can we feed the world in 2050?* A scoping paper to assess the evidence (Working Paper No. 13-04). Somerville, MA: Tufts University, Global Development and Environment Institute.

World Bank. (2007a). *World Bank development report 2008: Agriculture for development.* Washington, DC: World Bank.

World Bank. (2007b, October 17). *Press release 2008/080/DEC.* Washington, DC: World Bank.

12

Genetic Engineering and Food Security: A Welfare Economics Perspective

Prithviraj Lakkakula[a], Dwayne J. Haynes[b] and Troy G. Schmitz[c]

[a]*Department of Agribusiness and Applied Economics, North Dakota State University, Fargo, ND, USA 58102*
E-mail address: prithviraj.lakkakula@ndsu.edu
[b]*Food and Resource Economics Department, University of Florida, Gainesville, FL, USA 32611*
E-mail address: nygator3@ufl.edu
[c]*Morrison School of Agribusiness, Arizona State University, Tempe, AZ, USA 85287*
E-mail address: Troy.Schmitz@asu.edu

Abstract

Purpose — This chapter analyzes the economic implications of genetic engineering for food security. We discuss the asynchronous nature of genetically modified (GM) crop regulation and labeling requirements among countries, associated politics, and consumer perceptions of GM crops.

Methodology/approach — We perform an *ex-ante* analysis of the introduction of a GM rice variety in major rice exporting and importing countries (including potential producer and consumer impacts) within the framework of a partial equilibrium trade model.

Findings — Although the introduction of a GM rice variety that increases global yield by 5% could result in a consumer gain of US$23.4 billion to US$74.8 billion, it could also result in a producer loss of US$9.7 billion to US$63.7 billion. The estimated net gain to society could be US$11.1 billion to US$13.7 billion. Overall, we find a positive economic surplus for major exporters and importers of rice based on a 5% supply increase with a GM rice variety.

Practical implications — The adoption of transgenic (GM) rice varieties would have a far greater impact on rice prices for poorer counties than for richer countries. Therefore, GM rice may help ensure that more people throughout the world would have food security.

Keywords: GMOs, genetically modified crops, transgenic rice, welfare economics

Frontiers of Economics and Globalization
Volume 15   ISSN: 1574-8715
DOI: 10.1108/S1574-871520150000015020

JEL classification: D6, F61, Q1

1. Introduction

The Food and Agricultural Organization of the United Nations (FAO, 2015) estimates that the global population will reach 9.5 billion by 2050. The World Health Organization (WHO) defines food security as the condition when everyone has continuous access to safe, nutritious food to maintain a healthy life (WHO, 2015). An increasing global population presents a challenge in fulfilling the standards set by this definition. To meet this challenge, agricultural scientists must find ways to increase food production in progressively unfavorable environmental conditions and climate change.

Genetic Engineering (GE)[1] is one way to address global food security. Many advancement in agriculture have been made since the advent of GE in the early 1980s, particularly in gene markers/mapping technology. These advancements have led to the creation of various transgenic and bioengineered organisms called genetically modified organisms, or GMOs. The United States Department of Agriculture defines GMOs as the "manipulation of an organism's genes by introducing, eliminating, or rearranging specific genes using the methods of modern molecular biology, particularly those techniques referred to as recombinant DNA (rDNA) techniques" (United States Department of Agriculture, n.d.).

Genetically modified (GM) crops were first commercially released for cultivation in 1996 (Qaim, 2009). By 2013, GM crops were being cultivated in 27 countries, covering 175.2 million hectares, or approximately 25% of global arable land (International Service for the Acquisition of Agri-Biotech Applications (ISAAA), 2013). The planted areas of GM crops in developing countries exceeded than in developed countries after 2011 (Figure 1).

Scientists place GMOs into three categories: first, second, and third generation. First-generation GMOs involve splicing plant genes to increase crop resistance to pests or herbicides. These high-yielding GM crops (e.g., corn, soybeans, and canola) are for human and animal consumption (Moss, Schmitz, & Schmitz, 2006). Figure 2 presents a timeline of the percentage of acres planted with GM crops in the United States from 1996 to 2014.

Second-generation GMOs involve mixing the DNA of one species with the DNA of an unrelated species to produce a transgenic, value-enhanced food. For example, beta-carotene is biosynthesized with rice to create a product called golden rice. These GM foods are for human and animal consumption.

---

[1] In this chapter, we use the terms: genetic engineering (GE), genetically modified (GM) and transgenic crops interchangeably.

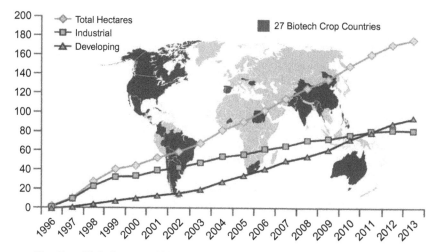

Fig. 1. **Global area of biotech crops, million hectares (1996–2013).**
Sources: *James (2013).* **Note:** *A record 18 million farmers, in 27 countries, planted 175.2 million hectares (433 million acres) in 2013, a sustained increase of 3% or 5 million hectares (12 million acres) over 2012.*

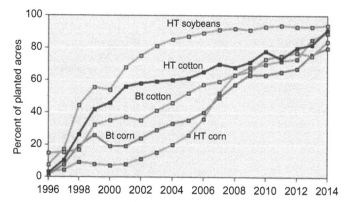

Fig. 2. **Adoption of genetically engineered crops in the United States, 1996–2014.** Sources: **USDA, Economic Research Service using data from Fernandez-Cornejo and McBride (2002) for the years 1996–1999 and USDA, National Agricultural Statistics Service, June Agricultural Survey for the years 2000–2014.** Note: *Data for each crop category include varieties with both HT and Bt (stacked) traits.*

Third-generation GMOs are plants that are used in factories to produce substances such as antibodies, enzymes, vaccines, therapeutic drugs for humans and livestock, and materials for research and industry. Unlike first-generation or second-generation GMOs, third-generation GMOs are not intended for human or animal consumption. The final product is extracted from plants that are then discarded. These GMOs are referred to as plant-made pharmaceuticals (PMPs). Either food plants (e.g., corn or rice) or non-food plants (e.g., tobacco or algae) can be used to produce PMP products. The United States Food and Drug Administration (FDA) has approved numerous third-generation GMO, protein-based drugs (Williams, 2006, 2007).

This chapter focuses on first-generation GMOs with brief examples of how second-generation and third-generation GMOs can impact food security. A discussion on GM crop regulation, associated politics, and consumer perceptions of GM crops is followed by an *ex-ante* analysis of a transgenic rice variety in major rice exporting and importing countries (including potential producer and consumer impacts), within the framework of a

Table 1. Major publicly funded GM crop research

S. No	Organization	Project	Trait improvement in the crop
	First-generation GMOs		
1.	University of Hawaii/Cornell	Rainbow Papaya	Highly resistant to ringspot virus
2.	Texas A&M, Florida, UC-Davis	Oranges	Resistant to citrus greening with a spinach gene
3.	SUNY-ESF	American Chestnut Tree	Resistant to blight with a wheat gene
4.	USDA-ARS	Honeysweet plum	Highly resistant to plum pox potvirus (PPV)
5.	INRA	Grape rootstock	Resistant to grapevine fanleaf virus
6.	Rothamsted	Wheat	Produces aphid repelling odor
7.	Bangladeshi	Bt eggplant	Pest-resistant Bt eggplant
	Second-generation GMOs		
8.	CSIRO	Wheat	Alter wheat carbohydrate content to reduce glycemic response and improve metabolic health
9.	Bill & Melinda Gates Foundation; National Root Crop Research Institute of Nigeria; Donald Danforth Plant Science Center	Biocassava	Cassava with increased nutrient (i.e., zinc, iron, protein, and vitamin A) levels, increased shelf life, reductions in toxic cyanogenic glycosides, and resistance to viral disease for Africa
10.	USAID; Syngenta Foundation; HarvestPlus; Bill & Melinda Gates Foundation	Golden Rice	Rice enriched with beta-carotene

Source: Van Eenennaam (2014).

partial equilibrium trade model. Table 1 lists some of the major publicly funded GM crop research projects (seven first-generation GM crops and three second-generation GM crops) in the United States.

2. GM crop regulation, politics, and consumer perception

The level of regulation of GM crops varies greatly across countries. For example, regulations are stricter in the European Union than in the United States (Moss et al., 2006). Unlike in the United States, legislation in the European Union makes a clear distinction between traditional and GM crops (Europa, 2014; Schmitz, Moss, Schmitz, Furtan, & Schmitz, 2010). Also, labeling of GM foods is mandatory in the European Union, whereas it is voluntary in the United States (Moss et al., 2006). Globally, approximately 64 countries have labeling laws on products containing GMOs (Millstein, 2015). Hence, a significant problem with alleviating global food insecurity via GM crops lies in the asynchronous nature of GM crop regulation among different countries.

Politics play a role in dealing with food security issues. In the United States, President Eisenhower signed the Food for Peace Program (Public Law 480) into law in 1954 as a means of distributing food to developing countries and increasing global food security. The creation and use of such global food aid programs is important because there is a significant portion of the world population that is food insecure (food insecurity can be chronic or acute). As some of this food aid comes in the form of GM crops, resistance to GM food consumption may cause political issues that can be detrimental to the overall goals of food aid programs. Notable cases have occurred in Africa where, despite widespread starvation, certain countries have refused to accept US food aid because of the possibility of consuming GMO food products (Lewin, 2007; Zerbe, 2004). These countries were also concerned about the potential for GM seed contamination of traditional crops which would limit their food exports to Europe.

Within the United States, there is an ongoing discussion regarding GMO labeling laws. The regulation of GM crops in the United States is coordinated through three government agencies: the Department of Agriculture, the Environmental Protection Agency, and the Food and Drug Administration (Pollack, 2015). The FDA, which is responsible for food labeling laws in the United States, does not require mandatory GMO labeling because it does not consider GMOs as potentially harmful.

In a world of decreasing natural resources, increasing agricultural productivity is important for ensuring food security (von Braun, 2007). The use of GMOs can accomplish this. First-generation GMOs help alleviate poverty through higher yielding crops (Fan, Chan-Kang, Qian, and Krishnaiah, 2005; Qaim, 2009). Second-generation GMOs help alleviate malnutrition through value-enhanced crops (Bouis, 2007; Unnevehr, Pray, & Paarlberg, 2007).

Despite the researched benefits of GM crops, concerns over their production, distribution, and safety persist in society. In developing countries, there are concerns about the potential monopolization of GE seed markets due to intellectual property rights (IPRs) (Sharma, 2004), and the loss of export market shares due to GMO regulations in countries such as Japan and the European Union. Below, we highlight five of the major misconceptions surrounding GM crops.

2.1. Misconception 1: GM foods are unsafe

There have been concerns about the safety of consuming GM foods. A 12-year research study by Nicolia, Manzo, Veronesi, and Rosellini (2013) finds no significant hazards directly connected with GM crops. This is an important finding considering that GE technology has been used for approximately 30 years. The WHO (2015) supports this finding since it also has not discovered any negative effects on human health so far.

2.2. Misconception 2: GM animal feed alters the DNA of livestock

There have been safety concerns about GM animal feed genetically altering livestock animals so that food products (meat, dairy, and eggs) from these animals become dangerous for human consumption. Research suggests that GM crops are safe for both human and animal consumption and should not require special labeling (Van Eenennaam, 2014).

2.3. Misconception 3: Mandatory GMO labeling will not impact food prices

GMO labeling will create separate supply chains for GM and non-GM food manufacturing processes, whereby additional production costs will be passed on to the end consumer in the form of higher prices. Lesser (2014) estimates that mandatory GMO labeling would increase food costs for a family of four by $500 per year.

2.4. Misconception 4: GM crops harm the environment

Concerns regarding the impact of GM crops on the environment include the potential consequences of increased use of pesticides and the development of resistance in both insects and weeds. There are a number of studies that highlight the advantages (economic and environmental) of GM crop adoption. Carpenter (2013) states that GMOs improve crop yield, particularly in developing countries. A meta-analysis by Klümper and Qaim (2014) on the impact of GM crops finds that GMO adoption reduces chemical pesticide use by 37%, increases crop yield by 22%, and increases farmer profit by 68%. GM crops with pest-resistant traits have reduced the use of pesticides in many cases (Fernandez-Cornejo & Caswell, 2006).

2.5. Misconception 5: GMOs are not a good solution for food security

There are concerns about using GMOs to solve global food insecurity. Research has shown that GM crops can be a viable component in the overall strategy for food security through better nutrition for everyone and higher incomes for farmers, particularly in developing countries (Bethell, 2006; Zavaleta et al., 2007). Qaim and Kouser (2013) show how the adoption of GM cotton improves crop yields and increases farm household income while reducing food insecurity by almost 20%. Ventria Bioscience (2007) highlights the potential of third-generation GMOs (PMPs) as nutritional supplements in foods.

3. Producer and consumer impacts of GM rice: An ex-ante analysis

Rice is one of the most important staple food crops in the world (especially in Asian countries), accounting for approximately 20% of global food calorie consumption (Wailes, 2005). The world's major rice exporters are Thailand (30%), Vietnam (20%), India (11%), and the United States (10%) (Trading Economics, 2014). Figure 3 shows the 1965–2014 global rice supply, demand, and stocks, with both global supply and global demand showing an increasing trend. Given that severe weather conditions (capable of reducing crop yields, or even eliminating crops completely) frequently exist in areas where rice production is significant, the development of transgenic (GM) rice varieties (especially those that are resistant to either drought or flood conditions) could help meet future global food requirements.

A partial equilibrium trade model is employed to analyze the effect of transgenic rice varieties in an international rice market. Consider Figure 4, where a two-country, one-good (rice) model is depicted. S and D are the supply and demand schedules in the net exporting country, S' and D' are the supply and demand schedules in the net importing country, and the world price of rice is p_f. In the exporting country, Q_1 is production, Q_3 is domestic demand, $(Q_1 - Q_3)$ are exports, and consumer and producer surpluses are (gbp_f) and (adp_f), respectively. In the importing country, Q_4 is production, Q_6 is domestic demand, $(Q_6 - Q_4)$ are imports, and consumer and producer surpluses are $(hp_f q)$ and $(p_f km)$, respectively.

In the event of transgenic rice adoption that results in a global outward shift in supply, there are several impacts on both the net exporting and net importing countries. In the exporting country, a shift in supply from S

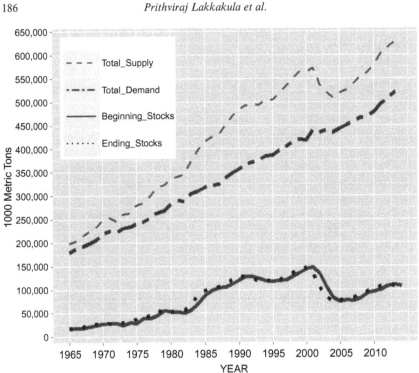

Fig. 3. *Global rice supply and demand, 1965–2014.* Source: *USDA PS&D (2015).*

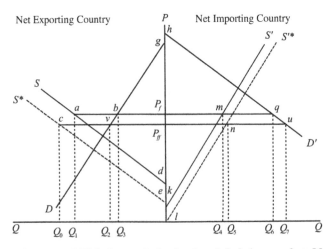

Fig. 4. *Impact of GM rice varieties in the global rice market.* **Note:** *As discussed in the theory, when determining the producer surplus impact, a cutoff price may be used (not depicted here).*

to S* occurs, causing a price decrease from p_f to p_{ff}. Now, Q_0 is production, Q_2 is domestic demand, $(Q_0 - Q_2)$ are exports, and consumer and producer surpluses are (gvp_{ff}) and (cep_{ff}), respectively. In the importing country, after a shift in supply from S' to S'^*, the new output is Q_5, domestic demand has increased to Q_7, $(Q_7 - Q_5)$ are imports, and the new consumer and producer surpluses are $(hp_{ff}u)$ and $(p_{ff}ln)$, respectively.

The resulting gains in consumer surplus for the net exporting and net importing countries are $(bvp_{ff}p_f)$ and $(p_fp_{ff}uq)$, respectively. While the consumer surplus gains are certain (i.e., given the increase in production and the decrease in prices *Ceteris paribus*), positive producer gains are not. For example, the producer surplus gains to the net exporting and net importing countries are $[(cep_{ff}) - (adp_f)]$ and $[(p_{ff}ln) - (p_fkm)]$, respectively; however, the outcome depends heavily on the price elasticities of supply and demand.[2] It is possible that under highly inelastic conditions, the adoption of transgenic rice could result in negative producer gains. In addition, the magnitude of the consumer gains are dependent on the supply and demand elasticities. The more price inelastic the supply and demand schedules are, the greater is the consumer gain from an outward shift in supply. This model can be utilized to assess the potential global impact of transgenic rice adoption.

To analyze the economic viability of adopting GM technology in rice production, we examine the producer and consumer surplus in major rice exporters and importers and provide an extension to the global market for rice. For purposes of illustration, we assume that (1) there is a 5% increase in domestic rice supply in each country with the introduction of a transgenic rice variety, (2) all rice will be transgenic, and (3) consumers

Table 2. Rice elasticities for selected countries

Country	Supply	Demand (own-price elasticities)
Thailand	0.193	−0.100
Vietnam	0.232	−0.190
India	0.108	−0.150
Indonesia	0.103	−0.139
Philippines	0.152	−0.148
Nigeria	0.400[a]	−0.300

Source: Mohanty, Wailes, and Chavez (2010).
[a]Assumed for this study.

[2] Within an empirical context, the calculation of the producer surplus could be altered given the inclusion of a cutoff price. For example, in the case where the price elasticity of supply is highly inelastic, a portion of the producer surplus would extend into negative prices, rendering the interpretation of the change in producer gain impractical.

fully adopt the new rice variety. We also assume the following in our analysis. First, we do not consider the differentiated rice types. Second, we
assume linear supply and demand curves and a parallel shift in the supply
curve for domestic rice given the introduction of the transgenic variety.
Third, we use supply and demand elasticities found in the literature
(Table 2). Figure 4 represents the case of a net rice exporter, and net rice
importer market and associated consumer and producer impacts with the
potential introduction of transgenic rice variety that causes a 5% increase
in production/supply.

The empirical analysis uses 1985–2014 international rice price (Thai
5% broken rice) data (World Bank, 2014). The summary statistics used in
the above model are presented in Table 3 (United States Department of
Agriculture, Production, Supply and Distribution, USDA PS&D, 2015).
We consider three rice exporters (Thailand, Vietnam, and India) and three
rice importers (Indonesia, the Philippines, and Nigeria). In the case of
exporters, effective supply is total supply minus ending stocks. In the case
of importers, effective supply is production. Effective supply, domestic

Table 3. Mean statistics of selected global rice exporters and importers

Country	Effective supply (1,000 MT)	Domestic demand (1,000 MT)	Total exports (1,000 MT)	Total imports (1,000 MT)	Yield (MT/HA)
Exporters					
Thailand	17,675	9,642	8,033	–	1.63
Vietnam	23,188	18,233	4,955	–	2.74
India	91,114	86,211	4,903	–	1.97
Importers					
Indonesia	32,886	34,216	–	1,330	2.88
Philippines	8,248	9,295	–	1,047	2.05
Nigeria	6,548	7,229	–	681	1.71

Source: USDA PS&D (2015).

**Table 4. Global producer and consumer surplus estimates given a 5%
increase in rice supply**

Component	US Billion Dollars
	Supply/demand elasticities, 0.07 and −0.12, respectively
Producer surplus impact	−63.6
Consumer surplus impact	74.6
	Supply/demand elasticities, 0.53 and −0.40, respectively
Producer surplus impact	−9.7
Consumer surplus impact	23.4

Source: Authors' computations.

demand, total exports, and yield statistics are averages for the 1985–2014 period.

Table 4 includes consumer and producer surplus estimates associated with a 5% shift in supply in the global market for rice. A US$100/ metric ton cutoff price was factored into the producer surplus estimates. In addition, results are presented under two sets of supply and demand elasticities, respectively: (1) 0.07 and −0.12 and (2) 0.40 and −0.53. Under the first set of elasticities, producer and consumer surplus changes are − US$63.7 billion and US$74.8 billion, respectively. The second set of more elastic elasticities yielded more modest results of − US$9.7 billion and US$23.4 billion in surplus changes for producers and consumers, respectively. These results indicate that price elasticities have a substantial role in determining surplus changes from an increase in supply. Taken the analysis a step further, if we relate elasticities to country wealth (i.e., assuming that richer countries possess more elastic supply and demand curves than do poorer countries), the adoption of transgenic rice varieties in poorer countries would have a far greater impact on rice prices than would be the case in richer countries.

We now consider the differing impacts of transgenic rice adoption on net exporting countries and net importing countries. Table 5 presents the consumer and producer surplus changes in select countries (net exporters − Thailand, Vietnam, and India) as a result of a 5% increase in supply due to the adoption of transgenic rice varieties. In column A, we assume that 50% of the increased supply is exported, and in column B, 85% of the increased supply is exported. The producer surplus calculations include a US$100/metric ton cutoff price (as discussed in an earlier section). Specifically regarding net exporters, the consumer gains and

Table 5.   Economic surplus change given a 5% increase in rice supply (US million dollars)[a]

Surplus change in net exporting countries	A	B
Thailand		
ΔCS	1,455	430
ΔPS	−1,666	−410
Vietnam		
ΔCS	998	296
ΔPS	−691	−89
India		
ΔCS	4,954	1,473
ΔPS	−2,893	−404

Source: Authors' computations.
[a]Where ΔCS (area $bvP_{ff}P_f$) and ΔPS (area $[(P_{ff}ce) - (P_f ad)]$) are changes in consumer surplus and producer surplus for the selected countries, respectively. Results are based on supply and demand elasticities from Table 2. A and B refer to estimates where (1) we assume 50% of the increased supply is exported, and (2) 85% of the increased supply is exported.

Table 6.   Economic surplus change given a 5% increase in rice supply (US million dollars)[a]

Surplus change in net importing countries	C
Indonesia	
ΔCS	3,901
ΔPS	−2,280
Philippines	
ΔCS	917
ΔPS	−488
Nigeria	
ΔCS	359
ΔPS	−171

Source: Authors' computations.
[a]Where ΔCS (area $P_f P_{ff} uq$) and ΔPS (area $(P_{ff} nl - P_f mk)$) are changes in consumer surplus and producer surplus for the selected countries, respectively. Results are based on supply and demand elasticities from Table 2. C refers to estimates where we assume that all the 5% increase in supply is absorbed domestically.

producer losses were US$1.455 billion and US$1.666 billion, respectively for Thailand; correspondingly, they were US$4.954 billion and US$2.893 billion for India.

Regarding net importers, the consumer gains and producer losses were US$3.901 billion and US$2.280 billion, respectively, for Indonesia; correspondingly, they were US$359 million and US$171 million, respectively, for Nigeria (Table 6).

Our analysis indicates that transgenic rice adoption would yield considerable benefits to global rice consumers via a significant decrease in price. However, if transgenic rice production was adopted, producers would likely face surplus losses in the process. Therefore, partly depending on elasticities, even if transgenic rice varieties were commercially available, they might not be adopted.

4. Conclusions

Food security contains many facets. Research indicates that GM crops can increase both crop yield and farm incomes worldwide (Barclay & Clayton, 2013). With GMO labeling regulations varying from country to country and surplus losses at stake, producers worry about the costs associated with identity preservation of non-GM foods. Thus, export markets have been hesitant to take on the risks associated with introducing GM foods. With the asynchronous global regulatory environment, key players in the global market have a plethora of considerations to make before adopting GM crops.

The issue is not so much the science behind GM crops as it is the perception of GM crops. Indeed, our analysis illustrates that there exist potential gains to both producers and consumers worldwide (especially those in poorer countries) from the adoption of GM crops, such as transgenic rice varieties. Increased production caused by the adoption of high-yielding genetically engineered crop varieties may positively impact the availability of food. Also, as this chapter suggests, an increase in consumer surplus brought about by the potential adoption of GM crops may lead to an increase in the entitlement component of food security through both a price and an income effect. Looking into the future, GM crops may help ensure that people are more food secure.

References

Barclay, A., & Clayton, S. (2013). The state of play: Genetically modified rice. *Rice Today*. Retrieved from http://irri.org/rice-today/the-state-of-play-genetically-modified-rice/

Bethell, D. (2006). *Lactiva and lysomin: Helping to save lives by improving oral rehydration solution.* Sacremento, CA: Ventria Bioscience. Retrieved from http://www.ventria.com/news/ORS%20Article%202005-06.asp

Bouis, H. (2007). The potential of genetically modified food crops to improve human nutrition in developing countries. *Journal of Development Studies, 43*, 79−96.

Carpenter, J. E. (2013). The socio-economic impacts of currently commercialized genetically engineered crops. *International Journal of Biotechnology, 12*(4), 249−268.

Europa. (2014). *Commission publishes compendium of results of EU-funded research on genetically modified crops.* Retrieved from http://europa.eu/rapid/press-release_IP-10-1688_en.htm?locale=en

Fan, S., Chan-Kang, C., Qian, C.-K., & Krishnaiah, K. (2005). National and international agricultural research and rural poverty: The case of rice research in India and China. *Agricultural Economics, 33*, 369−379.

Fernandez-Cornejo, J., & Caswell, M. F. (2006). *The first decade of genetically engineered crops in the United States.* EI Bulletin 11. Washington, DC: USDA/ERS.

Fernandez-Cornejo, J., & McBride, W. D. (2002). *Adoption of bioengineered crops.* Agricultural Economic Report (AER) No. 810, ERS/USDA. Retrieved from http://www.ers.usda.gov/media/259028/aer810_1_.pdf

Food and Agricultural Organization of the United Nations. (2015). *FAOSTAT.* Rome: FAO.

James, C. (2013). *Global status of commercialized biotech/GM crops: 2013.* International Service for the Acquisition of Agri-Biotech Applications (ISAAA) Brief No. 46. ISAAA: Ithaca, NY.

Klümper, W., & Qaim, M. (2014). *A meta-analysis of the impacts of genetically modified crops.* Retrieved from http://journals.plos.org/plosone/article?id=10.1371/journal.pone.0111629

Lesser, W. (2014). *Costs of labeling genetically modified food products in New York.* Retrieved from http://consumersunion.org/wp-content/uploads/2014/05/NY_GE_lbl_costs_5_14.pdf

Lewin, A. (2007). Case study #4-4, Zambia and genetically modified food aid. In P. Pinstrup-Andersen & F. Cheng (Eds.), *Food policy for developing countries: Case studies.* Ithaca, NY: Cornell University. Retrieved from http://cip.cornell.edu/dns.gfs/1200428165

Millstein, R. L. (2015). *GMOs? Not so fast.* Retrieved from http://commonreader.wustl.edu/c/gmos-not-so-fast/

Mohanty, S., Wailes, E. J., & Chavez, E. C. (2010). The global rice supply and demand outlook: The need for greater productivity growth to keep rice affordable. In S. Pandey, D. Byerless, D. Dawe, A. Dobermann, S. Mohanty, & B. Hardy (Eds.), *Rice in the global economy: Strategic research and policy issues for food security* (pp. 175–187). Los Baños: International Rice Institute.

Moss, C. B., Schmitz, A., & Schmitz, T. G. (2006). First-generation genetically modified organisms in agriculture. *Journal of Public Affairs, 6*(1), 46–57.

Nicolia, A., Manzo, A., Veronesi, F., & Rosellini, D. (2013). An overview of the last 10 years of genetically engineered crop safety research. *Critical Reviews in Biotechnology, 34*(1), 77–88.

Pollack, A. (2015). *White house review of rules for genetically modified crops.* Retrieved from http://www.nytimes.com/2015/07/03/business/white-house-orders-review-of-biotechnology-regulations.html?_r=0

Qaim, M. (2009). The economics of genetically modified crops. *Annual Review of Resource Economics, 1,* 665–693.

Qaim, M., & Kouser, S. (2013). Genetically modified crops and food security. *PLOS One, 8*(6), e64879.

Schmitz, A., Moss, C. B., Schmitz, T. G., Furtan, H. W., & Schmitz, H. C. (2010). *Agricultural policy, agribusiness, and rent-seeking behavior.* Toronto: University of Toronto Press.

Sharma, D. (2004). *GM food hunger: A view from the south.* New Delhi: FBFS.

Trading Economics. (2014). *Rice: 1981–2015.* Retrieved from http://www.tradingeconomics.com/commodity/rice

United States Department of Agriculture. (n.d.). *Glossary of agricultural biotechnology terms.* Retrieved from http://www.usda.gov/wps/portal/usda/usdahome?contentid=biotech_glossary.html

United States Department of Agriculture, Production, Supply and Distribution. (2015). *PS&D online.* Retrieved from http://apps.fas.usda.gov/psdonline/psdquery.aspx

Unnevehr, L., Pray, C., & Paarlberg, R. (2007). Addressing micronutrient deficiencies: Alternative interventions and technologies. *AgBioForum*, *10*, 124–134.

Van Eenennaam, A. (2014). *GMO technology: What do the facts say?* Retrieved from http://mediasite.video.ufl.edu/Mediasite/Play/6b427993a 59d45fb9d207dffa4255ed41d

Ventria Bioscience. (2007, July 27). *Ventria product benefits and economic analysis.* Sacramento, CA: Ventria Bioscience.

von Braun, J. (2007). *The world food situation: New driving forces and required actions.* Food Policy Report 18. Washington, DC: IFPRI.

Wailes, E. J. (2005). *Rice: Global trade, protectionist policies, and the impact of trade liberalization.* Retrieved from http://siteresources. worldbank.org/INTPROSPECTS/Resources/GATChapter10.pdf

Williams, C. (2006). *Finding the fit between molecular farming and organic farming opportunities in North Carolina: Report on a roundtable discussion.* Durham, NC: Duke University.

Williams, C. (2007). The fit between organic and pharma crops in North Carolina. *Nature Biotechnology*, *25*(2), 166–167.

World Bank. (2014). *Overview of commodity markets.* Retrieved from http://econ.worldbank.org/WBSITE/EXTERNAL/EXTDEC/EXTDE CPROSPECTS/0,,contentMDK:21574907~menuPK:7859231~pagePK: 64165401~piPK:64165026~theSitePK:476883,00.html

World Health Organization. (2015). *Food security.* Retrieved from http:// www.who.int/trade/glossary/story028/en/

Zavaleta, N., Figueroa, D., Rivera, J., Sanchez, J., Alfaro, S., & Lonnerdal, B. (2007). Efficacy of rice-based oral rehydration solution containing recombinant human lactoferrin and lysozyme in Peruvian children with acute diarrhea. *Journal of Pediatric Gastroenterology and Nutrition*, *44*(2), 258–264.

Zerbe, N. (2004). Feeding the famine? American food aid and the GMO debate in Southern Africa. *Food Policy*, *29*(6), 593–608.

13

Who Will Feed the Growing Population in the Developing Nations? Implications of Bioenergy Production

Won W. Koo and Richard Taylor

Agribusiness and Applied Economics, North Dakota State University, Fargo, ND 58106, USA
E-mail address: Won.koo@ndsu.edu, Richard.taylor@ndsu.edu

Abstract

Purpose – This chapter examines whether the supply of food is large enough to feed an increasing world population for the 2012–2050 period. Special attention is given to the implications of bioenergy production on global and regional food security.

Methodology/approach – For this analysis, a global food security simulation model was developed to determine if the global and regional supply of food, in terms of calories, is large enough to meet the demand and also to estimate the impact on food prices.

Findings – This chapter found that the global supply of food in terms of calories is insufficient to satisfy food demand in 2050, with food shortages especially significant in Africa.

Practical implications – The estimated shortage of food may result in significant food-price inflation by 2050.

Keywords: Calorie, per capita GDP, equilibrium, simulation, bioenergy

1. Introduction

Thomas Malthus, in *Essay on the Principle of Population* (1798), predicted that food production would not grow fast enough to feed the growing world population, thus causing a major food shortage in the future. More recently, Lester Brown, in *Who Will Feed China?: Wake-up Call for a*

Frontiers of Economics and Globalization
Volume 15   ISSN: 1574-8715
DOI: 10.1108/S1574-871520150000015021

Small Planet (1995), claimed that food production was not growing fast enough to feed the increasing population in China which could result in higher food prices in China and the world, under globalization. So far, his claim has only been realized on a regional basis rather than on a global basis. The main reason food production has kept up with food demand is because of significant increases in world crop yields since 1980: a 57.4% increase in corn yield, a 52.1% increase in soybean yield, a 61.6% increase in rice yield, and a 65.2% increase in wheat yield for the 1980–2011 period (Food and Agriculture Organization of the United Nations, FAO, 2013b).

However, other questions arise. How about the next 50 years? Can we produce enough food to feed everyone in the world so all the population can maintain an active and healthy lifestyle? The world population is expected to grow about 30% from 7.2 billion in 2011 to 9.3 billion in 2050 (United States Census Bureau, 2013). The populations of developing countries are growing much faster than those of developed countries. According to the United States Census Bureau (2013), the population in Sub-Saharan Africa is expected to grow by about 54% during the 2012–2050 period, whereas East Asia is expected to grow only 0.7% for the same period, followed by the Former Soviet Union (5.7%) and Europe (10.6%). However, agricultural productivity in developing nations is generally less than that in developed countries. As a result, food shortage has already been severe in some developing nations although, globally, the food supply is large enough to meet the demand (International Food Policy Research Institute [IFPRI], 2012). These trends tend to exacerbate the problem. In addition, the average consumption of calories per person has increased and is expected to increase with future income growth (FAO, 2006).

A significant amount of agricultural commodities has been used to produce bioenergy in the United States, the European Union (EU), and Brazil. For example, in 2015, the United States is expected to use about 81 million tons of corn equivalent to produce approximately 15 billion gallons of corn-based ethanol under the Energy Security and Independence Act (ESIA) of 2007. That amount of corn would provide enough calories for 412 million persons per year (Resourcemedia.org, 2012). In addition, the total agricultural commodities used for bio energy production in other nations, such as the European Union and Brazil, are approximately 3.6 billion bushels to produce 13.3 billion gallons of bioenergy annually (Worldwatch Institute, 2013). It has been estimated that the total amount of the agricultural commodities used for global bioenergy production may be able to feed over 700 million persons for one year. Many studies argue that bioenergy production was one of several causes of price increases for food in 2007, 2008, and 2011 (Baek & Koo, 2010; Congressional Research Service, 2008; The World Bank, 2012).

This chapter presents the results of an analysis to determine whether the supply of food is large enough to feed the world population for the 2012–2050 period. Special attention is given to the implications of bioenergy production on global and regional food security. Food security can be measured globally and regionally. If regional supply is smaller than regional demand, then regional food security depends not only on the regional supply and demand for food but also on the capability to import excess demand from surplus regions. Global food security depends on the aggregate supply and demand for food on a global scale. Food security can be expressed in terms of food price; a food-shortage region experiences higher food prices while a surplus region experiences lower food prices. Thus, food flows from surplus regions to deficit regions through commercial trade and/or food aid. If the supply of food, including imports, in a country/region is still not large enough to satisfy the demand for food in the country/region, the area will experience a food shortage and higher food prices. The food price increases, even in surplus regions, if the global demand for food is larger than the global supply of food in a globalized trade environment.

Global food security can also be observed from both a short-run and long-run perspective. On the one hand, short-run food security depends on volatility in the food supply, mainly stemming from severe weather conditions (e.g., drought or flood) or climate changes (severe hot or cold temperatures) during the growing season (Jiang & Koo, 2011). On the other hand, long-run food security depends on a general demand trend caused by population growth and changes in diet, as well as the supply of food affected by factors such as arable land, farming technology, and alternative uses for agricultural commodities, including bioenergy production in the United States (under the Energy Independent and Security Act of 2007) and other agricultural-exporting countries/regions such as Brazil and the European Union.

Many studies have focused on analyzing regional and/or global food security issues using different approaches. Baek and Koo (2010) use a time-series econometric approach to find factors affecting food-price inflation for the 2007/2008 period in the United States. They conclude that bioenergy production was one of the main causes for rising food prices during that period. Cordell, Drangert, and White (2009) examine the demand for phosphorus to increase agricultural productivity in the developing and developed world. Anderson and Strutt (2012) analyze the food supply for Asia in 2030. They project the agricultural productivity in 2030 under several assumptions related to the trade policies adopted by nations in the region. The International Food Policy Research Institute (IFPRI, 2010) has completed a comprehensive study for global food security that focuses on factors affecting the supply and demand for food, including climate change, biofuel production, land degradation, population, and the food-delivery system. In addition, Paarlberg (2010),

Pinstrup-Andersen (2010), and Pinstrup-Andersen, Pandya-Lorch, and Rosegrant (2001) discuss policy alternatives to reduce global and regional food insecurity. Shapouri et al. (2011) focus on food security in terms of the number of food-insecure people in each of 77 countries for 2011−2021, projecting that the number of food-insecure people will decline during this period. Subramanian and Deaton (1996) use food calories to represent various food items and estimate the demand for calories for rural Maharashtra, India. Roberts and Schlenker (2010) convert major food commodities (wheat, corn, soybeans, and rice) into calories and estimate the demand and supply of calories to evaluate the causes of food-price inflation in 2007 and 2008. They conclude that, under the Energy Act of 2005, ethanol production caused an increased corn price in 2007 and, consequently, food-price inflation in 2007 and 2008. Meade and Rosen (2013) focusing on 76 low- and middle-income countries, as classified by the World Bank, conclude that the food security situation is expected to deteriorate for the 2013−2023 period based on the number of food-insecure people. According to their study, the number of food-insecure people will increase from 707 million in 2013 to 868 million in 2023.

Unlike previous studies, our study used a system approach by developing a global food security simulation model to analyze the balance between the global and regional demand for and supply of food, as well as the impact on the food price. To simplify the modeling procedure, we used the calorie to represent all food items produced and consumed in the world, following the lead of Subramanian and Deaton (1996) and Roberts and Schlenker (2010). To capture the regional economic and noneconomic characteristics, the world was divided into 12 regions for this study. Calorie intake differed from one region to another; with the highest intake in North America, and the lowest take in Africa (The World Bank, 2013). According to the World Health Organization (WHO, 2013) and FAO estimates (2013a), there were 870 million undernourished people worldwide, with 98% of the undernourished people living in the developing world, and 62% of those living in South Asia and Sub-Saharan Africa. This was because population growth outdistanced agricultural productivity in the developing world.

The next section discusses the development of a global food security econometric simulation model based on the demand for and supply of calories by region. This section includes specifying and estimating the supply and demand models for calories in each region used in the simulation model. The results include the predicted demand and supply of calories as well as the impacts on food prices under different levels of bioenergy production. The last section discusses the implications and policy alternatives to resolve the food-shortage problems during the next 40-year period.

2. Development of a Global Food Security Simulation Model

A global partial equilibrium econometric simulation model was developed for this study. To capture the regional economic and noneconomic characteristics for food supply and demand, the world was divided into 12 regions: China, East Asia, Other Asia, India/South Asia, North Africa, South Africa, Sub-Saharan Africa, Europe, the Former Soviet Union (FSU), North America, South America, and Oceania.

As shown in Table 1, the world population is predicted to increase 11.3% during 2012–2025 and 32.6% during 2012–2050. However, there are major differences in population growth among the regions. Each region is different in population growth for the 2010–2050 period; the fastest growth is in Africa (88%), followed by North Africa (55.4%). The population is predicted to increase by 10% in Europe and only 0.7% in East Asia (United States Census Bureau, 2013).

Each region also has unique economic and noneconomic characteristics. The per capita consumption of calories is low in India/South Asia (2,300 calories/day) and Sub-Saharan Africa (2,400 calories/day) while it is high in North America (3,452 calories/day). Per capita gross domestic product (GDP) is low in Sub-Saharan Africa (US$640) and high in North America (US$39,808). In contrast, arable land per capita (per person) is low in Sub-Saharan Africa (0.17 ha/person) and high in Oceania (14.9 ha/person).

Following Subramanian and Deaton (1996) and Roberts and Schlenker (2010), we use calories to represent all food items produced and consumed in each region. The demand for and supply of calories are estimated for each region and are incorporated into the simulation model.

Table 1. World population growth by region

Country/region	2012	2025	Change	2050	Change
	Million		%	Million	%
China	1388.0	1450.0	4.5	1600.0	15.3
India/South Asia	1617.6	1888.5	16.7	2452.9	51.6
East Asia	206.6	207.2	0.3	208.0	0.7
Other Asia	1120.0	1221.0	9.0	1300.0	16.1
North Africa	171.3	200.9	17.3	262.8	53.4
South Africa	58.5	65.3	11.5	79.3	35.4
Sub-Saharan Africa	868.0	1094.1	26.0	1565.2	80.3
Europe	514.8	533.4	3.6	569.3	10.6
Former Soviet Union	281.9	287.3	1.9	297.9	5.7
North America	368.8	398.9	8.2	453.9	23.1
South America	623.8	684.7	9.8	783.4	25.6
Oceania	33.7	38.8	15.0	46.7	38.6
Total	7253.0	8070.1	11.3	9319.3	32.6

Source: United States Census Bureau (2013).

The simulation model is solved for the price of calories by equating the aggregate demand for calories with the aggregate supply of calories.

This study is based on several assumptions in examining global food security for the 2014–2050 period. The first assumption is that agricultural production resulting from farming technology increases at a decreasing rate (log linear). This nonlinear trend for productivity is similar to that of the previous three decades. Figure 1 shows the US and world productivity indices for 1948 through 2011. Three major technical innovations have occurred since 1900. Hybrid corn was developed in 1908, and was adopted in over 90% of the United States by 1940. In 1910, the process of extracting nitrogen fertilizer from the air was perfected; it became available for US agriculture during the 1950s and was widespread by the 1970s. Genetically modified (GM) crop technology became available in 1996, predominately in corn and soybean crops. From Figure 1, there appears to be no apparent shocks in agricultural production due to these major changes. The growth in United States and world agricultural production began decelerating in 2000 and 2008, respectively. The assumption that farming technology follows a log-linear trend is based on the idea that all biological entities have a productivity limit at some level.

The second assumption is that there will be no significant changes in agricultural productivity as a result of changes in weather due to greenhouse gas emissions. Because there is no substantiated evidence to support the negative effects of climate change on agricultural productivity, the effect of climate change is not included in the study. Any changes in climate that may occur will be slow and have minor impacts on agricultural production.

The third assumption is that there is no shortage of water to produce agricultural commodities in each of the 12 regions. Water may become a major issue in the future; however, the severity and the location of the crises will be unknown (Falkenmark, 2008).

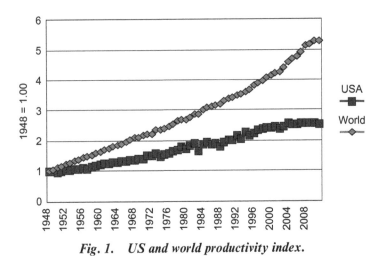

Fig. 1.   US and world productivity index.

The fourth assumption is that there are no significant changes in arable land. Since 1950, world agricultural land area has increased about 10%, so it can be assumed that the land base will remain stable until 2050 (FAO, 2013a).

The fifth assumption is that there will not be any significant changes in farming conditions and structure that could affect agricultural productivity.

3. Mathematical presentation of the model

The model is based on demand and supply of calories in each of the 12 regions. The demand for and supply of calories are specified as follows and are estimated with time-series data using an econometric technique.

3.1. Specification of the demand for calories

The individual consumer's demand for good j, which maximizes consumer utility subject to its budget constraint, can be specified as

$$D_j^i = f(P_1, P_2...P_n, Y) \quad \text{for } i = 1, 2, ... n \tag{1}$$

where D_j^i is individual i's demand for good j, P_j represents the price of good j, and y represents individual i's disposable income.

Because calories are used to represent all food items, Equation (1) is rewritten as

$$D_c^i = f_c(P_c, Y) \tag{2}$$

where D_c^i is individual i's consumption of food in terms of calories per year, P_c is the price of calories, and Y is individual i's disposable income. Because it is difficult to calculate the average price of calories representing all food items for a given time, the consumer price index for food is used as a proxy for the average price of calories in each region.

Based on Equation (2), an empirical demand model for an individual's calories, in a linear functional form with time-series data, is specified as

$$D_{ct}^i = a_0 + a_1 P_{ct} + a_2 Y_t + a_3 \text{TR} + e_t \tag{3}$$

where TR denotes a general trend in calorie consumption representing the consumer's preference for diet in each region. It is expected that $\alpha_1 < 0$ and $\alpha_2 > 0$ based on demand theory. The sign of α_3 is unknown.

Aggregate demand for calories in a region is the product of the individual demand for calories and the population in the region:

$$D_c^r = D_c^i \times \text{POP}^r \tag{4}$$

where D_c^r is the aggregate demand for calories in region r and POP^r denotes the region's population.

3.2. Specification for the calorie supply

The total supply of calories in a region is determined by the price of calories, production technology, and other factors affecting food production:

$$S_c^r = f(P_c, T, G) \tag{5}$$

where S_c^r is the aggregate supply of calories in region r; T represents production technology; and G represents other factors affecting food production, including changes in available land and climate change. As mentioned previously, it is assumed that production technology increases agricultural productivity at a decreasing rate for the 2012−2050 period. An econometric supply model of calories with time-series data is specified as follows:

$$S_{tc}^r = \beta_0 + \beta_1 P_{ct} + \beta_2 \ln TR + V_{ct} \tag{6}$$

where S_{tc}^r represents the aggregate supply of calories in time t, P_{ct} is price of calories in time t, and TR represents a trend that captures the improvement for farming technology and changes in arable land. Since agricultural productivity is assumed to increase at a decreasing rate, we used a logarithmic trend rather than a linear trend in Equation (6). According to historical data for crop yields in major agricultural producing regions, crop yields have increased at a decreasing rate since 1950. It is expected that $\beta_1 > 0$ and $\beta_2 > 0$ under an assumption that positive effects of farming technology are greater than the negative effects for the expected decrease in arable land.

4. Econometric estimation of the demand for and supply of calories

The data used to estimate the demand for and supply of calories are annual data from 1989 to 2011. The data for caloric consumption prior to 1989 are unavailable. The annual caloric consumption for each region comes from FAOSTAT (FAO, 2013b). Consumer price indices for food and per capita GDP for each region come from International Monetary Fund (IMF, 2013).

An ordinary least squares estimator is used with a correction of the first-order autocorrelation to estimate the per capita consumption of calories in each region. The estimated coefficients for the price variable are statistically significant and have a negative sign, as expected, based on demand theory. The per capita income variables are all positive, indicating that consumers increase their caloric consumption as their incomes increase, but the variables are marginally significant. The trend variables are positive and statistically significant, indicating that most consumers in each region increase their caloric consumption through improved diets.

In the supply equation (Equation 6), we use a log trend instead of a linear trend under the assumption that agricultural technology increases agricultural productivity at a decreasing rate. The price variables are statistically significant at the 5% critical level and have a positive sign, indicating that caloric supply increases with increases in caloric price. The log trend variable is statistically significant at the 5% critical level in all supply equations except that of North America. In North America, agricultural productivity depends not only on agricultural technology but also on exogenous factors stemming from the structural changes in the agricultural sector since 1950.

Table 2 shows price elasticities for caloric demand and supply. The estimated price elasticities of the demand for calories are very inelastic, ranging from −0.01 in Africa to −0.10 in North America. This is mainly due to the aggregated data used for demand estimation. Also, the demand data represent consumption of calories which is necessary for daily activities with reasonable health. However, price elasticities for caloric supply are much more elastic than are the demand elasticities. The estimated elasticities range between 0.12 in Europe and 0.54 in North America. The extremely inelastic demand elasticities relative to the supply elasticities are similar to those in Roberts and Schlenker (2010). The numbers in parentheses represent the *t*-values of the estimated elasticities. Demand elasticities are significant at the 10% level for North Africa, China, South America, and Oceania; they are insignificant in the other regions. In

Table 2.   Estimated price elasticities for the demand and supply in each region

Region	Demand	Supply
North Africa	−0.02 (1.87)	0.11 (3.71)
South Africa	−0.01 (0.34)	0.30 (1.93)
Sub-Saharan Africa	−0.04 (1.00)	0.27 (9.35)
China	−0.02 (1.81)	0.10 (4.20)
India/South Asia	−0.02 (0.28)	0.10 (4.20)
East Asia	−0.04 (0.70)	0.14 (0.60)
Other Asia	−0.02 (0.94)	0.15 (6.50)
Former Soviet Union	−0/12 (0.86)	0.16 (6.94)
Europe	−0.03 (0.94)	0.12 (6.48)
North America	−0.01 (1.49)	0.54 (38.14)
South America	−0.01 (4.65)	0.14 (9.01)
Oceania	−0.06 (7.58)	0.20 (21.31)

contrast, supply elasticities are significant at the 5% level in all regions, except that of East Asia.

5. Simulation model

We developed a global econometric simulation model for calories which includes the 12 previously identified regions. Each region has its own caloric demand and supply equations. The simulation is based on a partial equilibrium approach where the aggregate demand for calories is equal to the aggregate supply of calories:

$$\sum_{r=1}^{12} D_{ct}^r(P_{ct}, Y_t, \text{TR}) = \sum_{r=1}^{12} S_{ct}^r(P_{ct}, \ln\text{TR}) \tag{7}$$

Because the price of calories is endogenous and other variables, such as population and income, are assumed to be exogenous, the equation is solved for price of calories. The equilibrium price obtained from Equation (7) is converted to the regional price of calories. Then, the demand for and supply of calories in each region are calculated under the regional price at time t. These processes are simulated for 2012 through 2050.

Two different simulations, based on the estimated demand for and supply of calories, are conducted. The first simulation is to project the demand for and supply of calories using the estimated demand and supply equations. In the demand and supply equations, the price of calories in each region is endogenous while other variables are exogenous. In this first simulation, it is assumed that the real price of calories is constant at the 2012 level. The projected value of other variables is obtained from different sources; the population is from the United States Census Bureau (2013), and per capita income is from United States Department of Agriculture, Economic Research Service, USDA/ERS (2012).

6. The base and alternative models

Because a large amount of agricultural commodities, 222 million tons, is used to produce bioenergy in the United States, the European Union, and Brazil, it is hypothesized that bioenergy production increases the demand for agricultural commodities (corn, oilseeds, and sugar) and affects food security negatively. Two base models and two alternative models are developed to test this hypothesis. Base model 1 assumes that the food price in real terms remains at the 2012 level for the simulation period while base model 2 uses a partial equilibrium approach to obtain the equilibrium price of calories. Both base models assume that the current level of bioenergy production will remain constant until 2050. Alternative model 1 is based on a 25% increase in bioenergy production for the 2012−2050 period under a partial equilibrium approach (base model 2) while alternative model 2 assumes a 50% increase in bioenergy production.

The total amount of agricultural commodities used for bioenergy production is converted to calories and added to the caloric demand for each region as an additional demand for industrial use. Thus, the initial effect of bioenergy production is to increase the price of calories, so the increased price will stimulate the supply of calories and the reduced demand for calories in the model to establish equilibrium in the global food industry.

7. Simulation results

We estimate the total supply and demand for calories in each region under the assumption that the real price remains constant for the 2012−2050 period (base model 1). The aggregate demand for calories in a region can be calculated by multiplying the population in a region by the region's per capita consumption of calories. Because per capita GDP is an exogenous variable, we use the per capita income projected by USDA/ERS (2012) to estimate the demand for calories during the 2012−2050 period. Tables 3 and 4 present the actual supply and demand for calories in 2012 and projected supply and demand for calories in 2025 and 2050.

For the 2012−2025 period, the global demand for calories is expected to grow by 15.5% (Table 3) while the global supply of calories is predicted to grow by 13% (Table 4), indicating a shortage of food, in terms

Table 3.   Projected demand for calories in each region under base model 1

Demand	2012	2025	Change	2050	Change
	Million		%	Million	%
China	4,317,357	4,615,860	6.9	5,294,602	22.6
India/South Asia	3,747,715	4,607,137	22.9	6,277,907	67.5
East Asia	610,553	615,686	0.8	634,281	3.9
Other Asia	2,739,550	3,189,969	16.4	3,740,640	36.5
North Africa	531,840	649,220	22.1	895,525	68.4
South Africa	165,365	203,313	22.9	272,887	65.0
Sub-Saharan Africa	2,084,338	2,961,608	42.1	5,093,234	144.4
Europe	1,749,290	1,821,665	4.1	1,965,686	12.4
Former Soviet Union	901,024	924,928	2.7	976,300	8.4
North America	1,274,393	1,383,881	8.6	1,585,742	24.4
South America	1,845,441	2,092,908	13.4	2,453,415	32.9
Oceania	112,037	130,372	16.4	160,556	43.3
Total	20,078,904	23,196,546	15.5	29,350,775	46.2

Table 4. Projected supply of calories in each region under base model 1

Supply	2012	2025	Change	2050	Change
	Million		%	Million	%
China	4,317,357	4,748,977	8.6	5,180,463	18.5
India/South Asia	3,746,850	4,759,296	27.0	5,917,437	57.9
East Asia	607,689	612,263	0.8	617,496	1.6
Other Asia	2,716,180	3,077,558	13.3	3,490,941	28.5
North Africa	530,292	589,857	11.2	657,993	24.1
South Africa	166,243	170,762	2.7	175,932	5.8
Sub-Saharan Africa	2,040,336	2,281,802	11.8	2,558,016	25.4
Europe	1,781,189	1,951,675	9.6	2,146,695	20.5
Former Soviet Union	985,195	1,032,955	7.8	11,189,473	16.7
North America	1,260,337	1,390,433	10.3	1,539,251	22.1
South America	1,827,921	2,072,159	13.4	2,345,071	28.3
Oceania	108,845	118,610	9.0	129,607	19.1
Total	20,115,850	22,806,348	13.4	25,877,375	28.6

of calories by 2025. The total supply of calories is capable of meeting 95.4% of the total caloric demand in the same year. However, the supply and demand for calories differ across the regions. The total supply of calories is larger than the demand in China, India/South Asia, Europe, North America, and South America, while Africa and Oceania is expected to have food shortage. Food shortage is especially severe in Sub-Saharan Africa; the caloric supply is predicted to grow by 12% while the demand is expected to grow by 42% for the 2012−2025 period. The demand for calories is mainly caused by fast population growth and an expected increase in per capita calorie consumption as a result of higher per capita income. In East Asia and South America, supply of calories is approximately equal to demand for calories.

In 2050, the aggregate supply of calories is projected to meet 88% of the aggregate demand. The demand for calories is predicted to grow by 46% while the supply is only expected to grow by 27% for the 2012−2050 period. Europe and the Former Soviet Union are expected to have an adequate supply of calories in 2050. Europe is expected to have a surplus of food because the calorie supply is projected to grow by 17% while demand only increases by 8%. Supply of calories in the Former Soviet Union is expected to grow faster than demand of calories. North America is expected to have a shortage of food, but not at significant levels; the supply of calories is expected to grow by 22.1% for the period, while demand for calories is expected to grow by 24.4%. All other regions will experience food shortages by 2050. Food shortages are anticipated to be extremely severe in Sub-Saharan Africa, where demand is predicted to grow by 144% for the 2012−2050 period and the supply is only expected to grow by 25%.

The shortage of calories in 2025 and 2050 can be explained in terms of increased food prices. The food price is predicted to increase by 9% in 2025 and by 73% in 2050 to accommodate a balance between the global demand for and the supply of calories under base model 2 (Table 5). The increased price will reduce the consumption of calories and raise caloric supply, resulting in equilibrium in the global food industry. However, food shortages may exist regionally with the increased prices; Asia, Europe, North America, and South America will have sufficient calories, but other regions will experience a shortage of calories in 2025 and 2050. At those prices, the food in-security problem can be solved if the food-shortage regions can afford to import calories from the surplus regions. If these regions cannot afford imports, food insecurity will exist in the region even though global food supply is equal to global food demand.

Bioenergy production contributes to the demand for agricultural commodities and further increases the food price. If bioenergy production were to increase by 25% (alternative model 1), food price would increase by 13% in 2025 and by 85% in 2050, compared to 9% and 73% increases, respectively, under base model 2. With a 50% increase in bioenergy production (alternative model 2), the food price would increase by 18% in 2025 and by 95% in 2050.

It is important to note that the global food price is projected to increase at an increasing rate for the 2012–2050 period. This implies that a shortage of food will increase exponentially on the basis of the projected demand and supply of calories. For example, the price of corn increased from a long-run average of $2.27/bushel in the late 1990s to $6.07/bushel in 2012 due, in part, to corn-based ethanol production, causing food-price inflation (Taylor & Koo, 2011).

8. Conclusions and policy implications

Given agricultural production conditions and technology, it is projected that the estimated total calorie production (25.8 trillion calories) will not be large enough to satisfy the required consumption of calories for an active and healthy lifestyle (29.3 trillion calories) in 2050; the total supply of calories will be 12% smaller than total caloric consumption. The resulting food shortage will be especially severe in Africa, where the caloric

Table 5.　Food prices under base and alternative models

Model	2012	2025	2050
Base model 2	100	109.2	173.2
Alternative model 1	100	113.0	185.4
Alternative model 2	100	118.1	195.5

supply is expected to increase by 25% while demand for calories is expected to grow by 144% during the 2012–2050 period. A sharp increase in caloric consumption in Africa is mainly due to a rapidly increasing population.

A global food shortage will result in increased food prices. Under base model 2, where bioenergy production remains at its current level, the world's average food price is expected to increase 9% by 2025 and 73% by 2050. Bioenergy production from corn, sugar, and other agricultural commodities will significantly increase the demand for calories, resulting in a further increase in food prices. This study reveals that, by 2025, the food price will increase by 13% with a 25% increase in bioenergy production, an additional increase of 4% from the base model 2; a corresponding increase of 85% will occur by 2050, an additional increase of 12% from the base. The increase in food price from base model 2 associated with a 50% increase in bioenergy production would be 9% and 22% in 2025 and 2050, respectively. The high price of food will reduce social welfare in low-income, developing countries, including many nations in central Africa and Asia. It also increases the number of undernourished people in the developing world to beyond 870 million in 2013 (FAO, 2006).

International organizations, such as FAO and WHO, must remain cognizant of the potential for food shortages and the resulting food-price inflation. Policy alternatives must be developed to ease the projected shortages of food. A global effort should be devoted to increase agricultural productivity by improving farming technology at a global scale and making appropriate technologies available in food-deficit developing nations. To accomplish this, all the nations should invest more resources to improve agricultural technologies and disseminate the technologies among developing nations. Furthermore, international organizations should assist developing nations in enhancing their agricultural infrastructure, such as the development of irrigation systems to supply water to arable land to increase agricultural productivity. To ease expected shortages of food, in the short-run, it may be wise to establish a moratorium on further agricultural commodity-based increases in bioenergy production.

References

Anderson, K., & Strutt, A. (2012). Agriculture and food security in Asia by 2053. *Farm Policy Journal, 19*(4), 21–33.

Baek, J., & Koo, W. (2010). Analyzing factors affecting U.S. food price inflation. *Canadian Journal of Agricultural Economics, 58*, 303–320.

Brown, L. L. (1995). *Who will feed China? Wake-up call for a small planet.* The Worldwatch Environmental Alert Series. New York, NY: Norton.

Congressional Research Service. (2008). *Food price inflation: Causes and impacts* (CRS Report to Congress, Order code RS22858). Washington, DC: Library of Congress.

Cordell, D., Drangert, J., & White, S. (2009). The story of phosphorus: Global food security and food for thought. *Global Environmental Change, 19*(2), 292–305.

Falkenmark, M. (2008). Water and sustainability: A reappraisal. *Environment, 50*(2), 4–16.

Food and Agriculture Organization. (2006). *Food security*. Rome: FAO. Retrieved from http://www.fao.org/forestry/13128-0e6f36f27e0091055-bec28ebe830f46b3.pdf

Food and Agricultural Organization. (2013a). *FAOSTAT food supply*. Rome: FAO. Retrieved from http://www.fao.org/corp/statistics/en/

Food and Agriculture Organization. (2013b). *FAOSTAT statistical yearbook*. Rome: FAO. Retrieved from http://www.faostat3.fao.org/faostat-ateway/go/to/download/Q/*/e

International Food Policy Research Institute. (2010). *Food security, farming and climate changes to 2050: Scenarios, results, policy options*. Washington, DC: IFPRI. Retrieved from http://www.ifpri.org/publication/food-security-farming-and-climate-change-2050

International Food Policy Research Institute. (2012). *Global food policy reports*. Washington, DC: IFPRI.

International Monetary Fund. (2013). *International financial statistics*. Washington, DC: IMF.

Jiang, Y., & Koo, W. W. (2011). *The role of weather in local crop production* (Policy Brief No 19). Fargo, ND: North Dakota State University.

Malthus, T. R. (1798). *An Essay on the Principle of Population*. London: Joseph Johnson.

Meade, B., & Rosen, S. (2013). *International food security assessment, 2013-2023* (GFA-24). Washington, DC: USDA/ERS. Retrieved from http://www.ers.usda.gov/media/1138077/gfa-24a.pdf

Paarlberg, R. (2010). *Food politics: What anyone needs to know*. Oxford, UK: Oxford University Press.

Pinstrup-Andersen., P. (2010). *The African food system and its interaction on human health and nutrition*. Ithaca, NY: Cornell University Press.

Pinstrup-Andersen, P., Pandya-Lorch, R., & Rosegrant, M. (2001). Global food security: A review of the challenges. In P. Pinstrip-Andersen & R. Pandya-Lorch (Eds.), *The unfinished agenda* (pp. 7–17). Washington, DC: IFPRI.

Resourcemedia.org. (2012). *Food not fuel*. Retrieved from http://www.resource-media.org/food-not-fuel/

Roberts, M., & Schlenker, W. (2010). *Identifying supply and demand elasticities of agricultural commodities: Implications for the U.S. ethanol mandates*. NBER 15921. Cambridge, MA: NBER. Retrieved from http://www.ewi-ssl.pitt.edu/econ/files/seminars/101118_sem757_Wolfram %20Schlenker.pdf

Shapouri, S., Rusen, S., Tandom, S., Gale, F., Mancino, L., & Bai, J. (2011). *International food security assessment, 2011–2021.* GFA-22 Report. Washington, DC: USDA/ERS. Retrieved from http://www. ers.usda.gov/media/123436/gfa22.pdf

Subramanian, S., & Deaton, A. (1996). The demand for food and calories. *Journal of Political Economy, 104*, 133–162.

Taylor, R., & Koo, W. W. (2011). *The role of ethanol on the U.S. and world corn and soybean industries* (Policy brief No. 18). Fargo, ND: North Dakota State University.

The World Bank. (2012, July 30). *Food price volatility, a growing concern, World Bank stands ready to respond* (press release). Washington, DC: World Bank.

The World Bank. (2013). *The World Bank website.* Washington, DC: World Bank. Retrieved from http://www.data.world.org/topic

United States Census Bureau. (2013). *Total population of the world by decade, 2010–2050 (historical and projected), international database.* Washington, DC: US Census.

United States Department of Agriculture, Economic Research Service. (2012). *International macroeconomic dataset.* Washington, DC: USDA/ ERS.

World Health Organization. (2013). *World health statistics, Part III. Global Health Indicators.* Luxembourg: WHO.

Worldwatch Institute. (2013). *Biofuels make a comeback despite tough economy.* Washington, DC: Worldwatch Institute. Retrieved from http://www.worldwatch.org/biofuels-make-comeback-despite-tough-economy

14

Food Security and Conflict

Donna Mitchell[a], Darren Hudson[a], Riley Post[b], Patrick Bell[c] and Ryan B. Williams[a]

[a]Texas Tech University, Lubbock, TX, USA
E-mail address: donna.m.mitchell@ttu.edu, darren.hudson@ttu.edu, ryan.b.williams@ttu.edu
[b]US Special Operations Command Central (USSOCCENT), MacDill AFB, Florida, USA
E-mail address: ryan.b.williams@ttu.edu
[c]United States Military Academy, West Point, NY, USA
E-mail address: patrick.bell@usma.edu

Abstract

Purpose — The objective of this chapter is to discuss the pathways between climate, water, food, and conflict. Areas that are exhibiting food insecurity or have the potential to be food insecure are typically located in areas that experience poverty and government corruption. Higher rates of conflict occur in areas with lower caloric intake and poor nutrition.

Methodology/approach — We identify key pathways between these variables and discuss intervening factors and compound effects.

Findings — The pathways between water, food security, and conflict are complicated and are influenced by many intervening factors. A critical examination of the literature and an in-depth analysis of the reasons for conflict suggest that food insecurity is a multiplier, or facilitator, of the opportunities for and benefits from conflict.

Practical implications — To most effectively reduce the risks of conflict, policies must adequately and simultaneously address each of the four dimensions of food security — availability, stability, utilization, and access. Careful attention to alleviating food insecurity will help alleviate some of the underlying rationale for conflict.

Keywords: Food security, conflict, water scarcity

Frontiers of Economics and Globalization
Volume 15   ISSN: 1574-8715
DOI: 10.1108/S1574-871520150000015022

1. Introduction

According to the Food and Agricultural Organization of the United Nations (FAO, 1996), food security exists when everyone has continuous access to safe, nutritious food for a healthy lifestyle. That is not the case for over 800 million people in 76 countries who are currently food insecure (FAO, 2014; Meade & Rosen, 2013). One in nine of that number suffers from extreme starvation (FAO, 2014). The number of globally food insecure will increase by 23% by 2023 as population increases. World population is expected to rise to 9.6 billion by 2050 (Meade & Rosen, 2013), with developing countries contributing 98% of that population growth. Sub-Saharan Africa, Latin America, and Asia are at risk for becoming the most food insecure (Global Assessment Report, 2013) due to a variety of factors.

As defined by FAO (2009), food security is based on four dimensions: availability, access, stability, and utilization. The impacts of climate change, water availability, population growth, and migration all potentially impact food security, and the lack of food security may be a source of local and regional conflict. Water scarcity by either natural or manmade causes will have the most impact on food availability, with 40% of the world's population living in water scarce regions and 60% of global crop production being rain-fed (Arnell, 1999).

Before proceeding, it is useful to delineate three related, but different sources of water scarcity. Most broadly is climate change. Over longer periods, shifts in climate may alter weather patterns and permanently (or at least over long-time scales) alter rainfall, snowfall, and other sources of fresh water. Other weather phenomena such as droughts or floods which may or may not be tied to climate change contribute to water scarcity.[1] Finally, there are manmade causes of water scarcity such as damming stream flows or over-use. Any of these may affect water availability and food production, and each cause may have a different impact due to how they interact with other variables.

The potential impacts of water scarcity, regardless of source, are important for many reasons. First, the impacts on food security, migration, and potential conflict are vital for military and humanitarian planners to prepare for potential food shortages, large-scale migration, political and civil instability, and outright war. Second, identifying and delineating causal pathways can help development professionals and organizations focus attention on those issues that are likely to bring greater overall stability through food security and conflict mitigation. The objective of this chapter is to discuss the relationships between climate,

---

[1] For example, the weather effects of *El Niño* can lead to temporary (2–4 year) cyclical weather patterns that are not directly tied to increasing temperatures or other climate change impacts.

water, food, and conflict. We identify key pathways between these variables and discuss intervening factors and compound effects.

2. Pathways to and from food security to conflict

A key to understanding the relationship between food security and conflict is to sketch the potential pathways by which the disparate variables that ultimately impact the potential for social and military conflict can be examined. Figure 1 provides a simplified view of these pathways with an emphasis on the factors that affect food security. The complexity of these pathways is complicated by the significant feedback loops which makes identifying directions of causality difficult at best.

Climate/weather has important impacts on macro variables such as population migration and water availability. Major weather factors such as long-term drought and flooding (be they related to long-term climate change or not) can directly lead to both acute and long-term population migration. Acute migration is an immediate stressor on food supplies/security which can directly challenge government legitimacy and resiliency, lead to famine, and increase the probability of intra-state or inter-state conflict (Barnett & Adger, 2007; Findley, 1994; McLeman & Smit, 2006; Nordas & Gleditsch, 2007; Raleigh, Jordan, & Salehyan, 2008; Raleigh & Urdal, 2007). At the same time, long-term migration which is most closely related to climate change can place stress on food production and distribution systems, thus stressing government legitimacy and/or directly leading to conflict. Even more indirectly, migration can stress water availability which affects food production systems and government legitimacy.

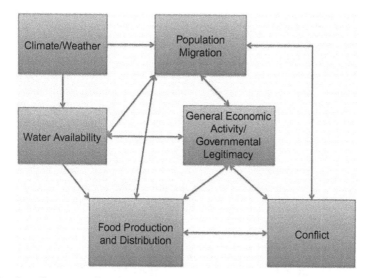

Fig. 1.   Conceptualization of the pathways from food security to conflict.

Households in developing countries adapt to climate change and acute weather events by migration. The pathways between natural resource degradation and migration have become increasingly relevant as the number of people affected by climate change has increased. Water scarcity in Africa and Asia is expected to cause an estimated 250 million environmental refugees by 2020 (Piguet, 2011). In 2011, 2.3 million Somalian refugees were forcibly displaced in the Horn of Africa due to the worst drought in 60 years. Almost one million refugees fled to Kenya, Ethiopia, and Djibouti (UNHCR, 2014). While Somalia ranked first in the Failed State Index for 2011, neighboring states were not far behind and the influx of migrants only exacerbated resource scarcity issues in those nations (Fund for Peace, 2011).

Both climate/weather and man-made factors directly affect water availability which directly affects agricultural production. Some areas are naturally more suited to agricultural production, and there exist other mitigating factors that affect the relationship between food production, food security, and conflict. However, in countries that are economically challenged, or where food security is already an issue, food production is a key pathway to government legitimacy, population growth and migration, economic growth, and conflict.

Climate forecasts suggest that nations located in arid to semi-arid areas, such as the Middle East and North Africa (MENA), are expected to experience more severe weather events such as drought and increased rainfall variability that will place stressors on water availability (IPCC, 2007). Because they lack water to produce agricultural products, nations in arid and semi-arid regions must rely on food imports to establish food security. Rural populations (subsistence farmers who depend on agriculture for survival) would be left extremely vulnerable if the forecasts are correct. Unfortunately, nations with large subsistence farmer populations often have regimes that lack stability and legitimacy where political insecurity and corruption occur. Unstable and illegitimate regime types encourage unsustainable agricultural production practices, leading to environmental degradation and production on marginal land. In Central Asia, for example, the former Soviet Union mismanaged their water resources to encourage intensive, continuous cotton monoculture. This practice eventually led to the desiccation of the Aral Sea and left a legacy of policies that still discourage productivity.

Water scarcity has not been proven to cause war, but it can be a destabilizing factor. Most disputes over trans-boundary water resources lead to treaties and cooperation; but in Ethiopia/Egypt[2] and Uzbekistan/Tajikistan, water scarcity potentially increases the probability of conflict. Furthermore, places like the Great Plains in the United States have

---

[2] As of this writing, Egypt and Ethiopia (and others) have reached a tentative agreement to share the waters of the Blue Nile.

suffered significant periods of severe drought over the last 100 years with little social or civil conflict, although early in the 1900s, droughts were accompanied by migration. Figure 1 is a simplification of the causal factors affecting conflict. Obviously, there are many factors affecting government legitimacy and other factors that directly influence conflict. Much of the available literature suggests that food security is not a direct causal factor, but a stressor that enhances the chances of conflict where other instability is already in place. Food insecurity, *per se*, may not cause conflict, but the feedback mechanisms between food, population, economic growth, and government legitimacy suggest that food security can be a key driver for conflict in some situations. Next, we discuss some of the mitigating factors that may help alleviate food insecurity and its role in conflict.

3. Intervening factors in the pathways

Food production is not necessarily the same as food security. While food production/availability is a necessary condition for food security, it is insufficient. Both the ability to acquire food for the household and the ability of food to be moved effectively from production sources to demand points are part of the food security equation as well.

The distinction between demand and effective demand, or the ability to purchase, is critical in food security. Total potential food demand is obtained by multiplying daily caloric requirements by the population. But, household income in most at-risk areas limits what can be purchased, suggesting large gaps between potential demand and effective demand. Effective demand is significantly related to general economic growth, but even in countries with robust economic growth, skewed income distribution can leave large swaths of the population with insufficient income to purchase sufficient food supplies to be food secure. Both economic growth and income distribution are directly related to government policy and, as such, are related to the structure of the government and government legitimacy. For example, countries that support private property rights generally incentivize landowners to invest in agricultural production (Norton, Alwang, & Masters, 2010). Countries with significant private property rights also generally enjoy greater economic growth and more equal income distribution, thus promoting effective food demand (O'Driscoll Jr. & Hoskins, 2003; Powell, 2003).

In addition to food production and effective demand, food distribution is also a key element in food security. Food distribution is related to overall economic growth as well as government policy and legitimacy. Infrastructure investments; provision of a business environment favorable to investments in processing and transportation; and policies fostering food safety, production, and processing all assist with the translation of food availability into overall food security. For countries that are currently in conflict, the government's ability to provide security for food production and processing contribute to food security as well.

Another key intervening factor is the presence of natural resources or other sources of income that can be used to import food. For example, oil-rich Middle Eastern countries are often water scarce and face significant constraints on food production. However, with ample exportable oil, they can easily import sufficient food to meet needs under normal conditions (when they are not already in conflict or the subject of sanctions). This concept of virtual water allows at least some water scarce countries to import necessary water *via* food imports to circumvent the water scarcity issue (Allan, 1997; Wichelns, 2001). Whether these countries utilize the alternative natural resources in this way to enhance food security is not guaranteed, however, and, if not, could contribute to social instability.

4. Policy and food production

Areas that are food insecure or have the potential to be food insecure are located in countries with weak institutions and fragile economies. Land tenure laws and labor-displacing technologies can negatively affect overall economic growth.

Without established property rights, there are no incentives for farmers to adopt new technologies, manage natural resources, and make land-based investments. These inefficiencies lead to environmental degradation and unsustainable agricultural practices, creating more poverty and famine. Property rights that are structured properly will benefit food security because they provide access to international markets and technologies. However, some countries are still constrained by dependency on labor which inhibits the adoption of labor-displacing technologies.

In labor abundant countries such as Uzbekistan, agriculture may be the only means of achieving food security and meeting the demand for calories. The Uzbekistani government has used policies such as minimum production quotas and input subsidies to artificially increase cotton production due to its revenue-making abilities, resulting in forced child labor laws. Producers lack the ability to make farm management decisions from an inability to own land coupled with state-mandated fixed acreage assignments which have prevented producers from capturing economies of scale or maximizing profit. The potential for conflict in this region is increasing with the failure of water allocation policies established during the Soviet Union era and an inability to sustain deteriorating irrigation systems.

5. Pathways to conflict

In the winter of 2010/11, food insecurity, as measured by FAO, reached a historic peak (FAO, 2011). At the same time, the MENA region experienced a wave of violent, history altering revolts. This confluence of events inspired a number of pithy news articles identifying the seeds of conflict, or human insecurity, as having been sown in the soil of food insecurity. This section examines such claims, weighing the evidence for food insecurity causing conflict. Along the way, we articulate the most commonly understood pathways from food to human insecurity. This section ends by tackling the challenges of creating stability for food security in the midst of conflict and by considering for future risk mitigation.

While water rights and land disputes both contribute to food insecurity and may precipitate inter-state wars, for the purposes of this chapter, we concern ourselves primarily with intra-state conflict. Importantly, the term "conflict" is broader than "war." Food insecurity is related to armed conflict as well as civil disobedience, riots, and other forms of political and social violence (Salehyan et al., 2011).[3] As defined, the correlation between food insecurity and internal conflict is clear. The majority of the world's food insecure population lives in India, China, the Democratic Republic of Congo, Bangladesh, Indonesia, Pakistan, and Ethiopia (FAO, 2011). Of these, all but China have seen civil conflict in the past decade. More specifically, several researchers have found higher rates of conflict in areas with lower caloric intake and poor nutrition (Pinstrup-Andersen & Shimokawa, 2008; Sobek & Boehmer, 2009). The connection between food security and violence also appears to be sensitive to income. Joachim von Braun, for example, found that the ratio of violent to non-violent food price related protests was consistently higher in low-income countries (von Braun, 2008). Taken together, this body of research reveals a significant correlation between food insecurity and conflict at the societal level.

At the micro or individual level, theories linking hunger and conflict are plentiful. These theories are generally built on two related foundations: grievance (relative deprivation) and opportunity cost. In these narratives, individuals and collectives are pushed toward conflict as their food-related suffering increases and the opportunity cost of rebellion decreases. Food insecurity impacts these calculations by eroding economic well-being, reducing government capacity, and necessitating the migration to urban areas.

---

[3] Salehyan et al. (2011) note that while Kenya never experienced an intra-state or inter-state war between 1990 and 2009, over 4,000 Kenyans died in food-related riots and communal conflict during that time.

5.1. Grievance

On its face, internal conflict stems from irreconcilable grievances. Political scientist Ted Gurr articulated this as an issue of relative deprivation, where the likelihood of rebellion is driven by a discrepancy between what an individual believes ought to be and what is (Gurr, 1970). The intensity and scope of this relative deprivation, then, sets the conditions for future conflict. Generally, microeconomic and macroeconomic research is increasingly linking increased poverty to increased violence (Miguel, 2007). One of the primary links in this relationship is related to food security. Threats to food security are particularly likely to create massive grievance in a short period of time due to food's highly inelastic demand. Small fluctuations in supply can produce sharp increases in price which can quickly escalate into a life-threatening issue for individuals living in poverty. Indeed, increases in the price of staple foods increase the poverty gap in low-income countries, having a greater impact in urban areas than rural (Ivanic & Martin, 2008). Similarly, fluctuations in world food prices and inadequate government food security programs can also lead to food insecurity grievances (Walton & Seldon, 1994). This trend was particularly evident in 2007—2008 as record-high food prices triggered protests in 48 countries (Brinkman & Hendrix, 2011).

The initial grievance created by food insecurity is often compounded by secondary effects on government capacity and migration to urban areas. These two secondary effects feedback on each other and cannot be discussed in isolation. For example, in a widespread drought, the government of an agrarian society receives significantly less tax revenue at the same time that its citizens require more government assistance. This increases citizens' grievances with their local and national government. In fact, several researchers have linked decreased agricultural production during turbulent climatic events to reduced government capability and have linked it to increased violence as well (Chassang & Padro-i-Miquel, 2009; Dube & Vargas, 2013). As drought worsens, many farmers, desperate for any form of employment and income, will migrate to urban areas, causing some researchers to identify this large-scale population migration as a contributor to increasing urban violence (Barrios, Bertinelli, & Strobl, 2006).

The civil war in Syria and the rise of the Islamic State is a recent and stark example of this compounding effect and its connection to conflict (Kelley, Mohtadi, Cane, Seager, & Kushnir, 2015). As severe drought set in across Syria in 2006/07, the country's agricultural system disintegrated. Most farmers and herders faced zero or negative production rates in 2008. With the Assad government unable or unwilling to provide a safety net for these farmers, migration to urban areas became the only recourse for most. An estimated 1.5 million Syrians joined the swelling Iraqi refugee population in Syria's largest cities, including Damascus, Aleppo,

Homs, and Latakia (Ali, 2010; Kelley et al., 2015). Comprising as much as 20% of these urban areas, the refugee community lived in sub-standard housing, faced rampant unemployment, and received little, if any, support from the government. These communities, not surprisingly, became the fountainhead of the Syrian revolution.

5.2. Opportunity costs

As important as grievance is, it is an insufficient condition for conflict, even in the most extreme cases. For example, communities can rally around one another, and international aid agencies can temporarily alleviate some sources of grievances. Rather, grievance is important primarily as a component of the opportunity cost individuals face as they decide if rebellion is a viable course of action. To engage in rebellion, a potential rebel must have an alternative opportunity that is likely to produce a better outcome than the *status quo*. Fearon and Laitin (2003) and others have argued for such an opportunity cost model of insurgency where both grievance with the current system and viability of the next-best alternative are considered. In these models, conflict increases when either the potential benefits of fighting increase or the cost of fighting decreases. The opportunity cost of violent action, then, is affected heavily by local factors such as food security and the capability of government security forces. If individuals like those in the slums of Aleppo are unemployed, poor, sick, uneducated, and hungry, they are not losing much by joining the resistance. Similarly, as food insecurity strains a government's coffers by robbing the government of tax revenue and necessitating additional requests for social provision, properly funding police and military forces becomes exceedingly more difficult. Regardless of their source, shocks to agricultural production appear to induce this simultaneous increase of grievance and decrease in the cost of rebellion. Where they exist, the incentive to resort to violence appears to increase (Miguel, Satyanath, & Sergenti, 2004). However, even the most hungry, desperate peasant may not rise up because the same regime that is exacerbating the widespread famine may also be willing to massacre protesters (Goodwin, 2001). Because context matters, a discussion of opportunity costs in rebellion indirectly brings us back to the broader question of the causal link between hunger and conflict.

The narrative of food insecurity causing conflict is appealing and, in some cases, appears to carry weight. However, this is not the whole story. If it were, the high plains of America would be embroiled in a bloody civil war following what has now been years of record drought. The fact that similar meteorological circumstances in Aleppo, Syria and Lubbock, Texas bring about such varied outcomes requires us to dig a bit deeper into issues that may cause *both* food insecurity and conflict.

Hunger and conflict do not happen on the moon; they are societal outcomes that must be understood in their broader political, economic, and
social contexts (Tilly, 1978). For the past twenty plus years, the majority
of the conflict around the world has taken place in poor countries; countries that are also chronically food insecure. Hunger and conflict, then,
appear to be symptoms of a deeper problem; one of broken institutions
(Blattman & Miguel, 2010; Collier, Lani, Anke, Mara, & Nicholas, 2003).
Furthermore, we might view the relationship between food and human
insecurity as one of amplifying existing failure. For example, the drought
in the Tuareg region of Mali created significant hardship, but it was the
government's theft of donated food aid that drove many to take up arms
(Benjaminsen, 2008). The more fragile the society, the more likely food
insecurity is to lead to violence (Bora, Ceccacci, Delgado, & Townsend,
2010). Such was the situation across much of the MENA region in the
spring of 2011. In states with broken institutions and populations already
living on the edge, food insecurity provided the catalyst for rebellions
that had been years in the making. Strong grievances and few alternatives
drove hundreds of thousands of people to the streets and eventually to
take up arms against their governments.

5.3. Risk mitigation

If food insecurity contributes to and amplifies conflict, actors in this space
must create policies that mitigate risk by attacking the pathways that lead
from food to fighting. More broadly, they need policies that minimize
grievances and increase the opportunity costs of conflict, particularly in
our three primary pathways: economic well-being, migration, and government capacity. In each of these areas, food security is the starting point.
An effective food security policy acts to control measures that influence
long-term food security and also works to reduce the short-term destabilizing effects of market shocks that can have long-term effects. In this
way, effective policies are forward-looking and can absorb market shocks
by building in excess government capacity. In the process, the policies
increase economic well-being, improve governmental capacity, and reduce
the likelihood for migration.

It is important to recognize that even the best governmental policies
have limitations. Natural disasters, for example, are impossible to prevent, but a sound government policy takes proactive measures to reduce
the effects of disasters when they hit and prepares emergency response
plans that can be quickly implemented to minimize suffering. Similarly,
food security policies should not be limited to a sound long-term plan
focused on the four dimensions of food security, but also must be able to
respond to emergencies to minimize the risks associated with short-term
food insecurity. To most effectively reduce the risks of conflict, policies

must adequately and simultaneously address each of the four dimensions of food security: availability, stability, utilization, and access (FAO, 2009). Ultimately, food availability is the dimension of chief long-run importance since proper food utilization, access, and stability would be fruitless without the sufficient availability of food. Immediate improvements to food security can be achieved by combating underutilization and increasing the nutritional value of citizens' diets which has been shown to improve public health and reduce poverty (Pena & Bacallao, 2002). For the short run, however, a policy that ensures the stability of food supplies when unpredictable forces (such as droughts and natural disasters) disrupt the normal supply, and helps hold prices to an acceptable range of price fluctuations, can greatly ease the burdens on society and on government capacity. Likewise, ensuring universal access to food is a key contributor to reducing the migration from rural to urban areas that can similarly strain government capacity. Planning for and monitoring these four dimensions of food security provides an early warning and enables a government time to react before the situation becomes untenable.

Recognizing that no policy can create 100% food security, governments should allocate their resources where they can have the greatest impact. That is most often in the area of food stability and is accomplished through reduced volatility of both food supply and food prices (FAO, 2013). Shocks to food supply and prices can wreak havoc on consumers in low-income countries, such as Egypt, where it is not uncommon for a household to spend over 40% of income on food (WFP, 2013). Price controls have proven effective at improving food price stability (Poulton, Kydd, Wigins, & Dorward, 2006). Along these lines, governments often implement price ceilings, regulating the maximum price at which products can be sold. While these price ceilings reduced some food price volatility in Egypt, Tunisia, and Yemen (World Bank, 2011), it was not without a cost. Government subsidies to support price ceilings can heavily strain the already stressed government coffers. Consequently, to be sustained for a prolonged period of time, price controls require a significant amount of excess capacity within the government's budget.

An optimal strategy combines market-based risk management instruments, such as weather derivatives and improving access to credit markets, with countercyclical safety nets, such as food-for-work programs, that ease the burden on the poorest citizens (Byerlee, Myers, & Jayne, 2005). Along the lines of the market-based instruments, having ample foreign exchange reserves can spur imports and reduce the vulnerability in the food supply (FAO, 2013). This can be extremely important for safety net food importing countries, including the vast majority of MENA and Sub-Saharan African countries (Valdes & Foster, 2012). Although these policies do not eliminate all volatility in food supply and prices, they can reduce their inherent uncertainties and consequently reduce many of the sources of grievance felt by their citizens.

To reduce the opportunity costs associated with rebellion, it is critical to either make rebellion less desirable or make a different course of action more desirable. States can make rebellion less desirable by increasing their police presence and/or toughening punishments for criminal offenders. Doing either of these increases the potential cost of fighting, and thus increases the likelihood of stasis. On the other hand, states can also increase the attractiveness of alternatives beyond revolution and stasis, so that a solution other than conflict becomes the highest valued alternative. By targeting those suffering the most, social safety nets can be particularly effective at reducing the contributors to conflict. Food insecurity and lack of viable farming options has been linked to massive migration from rural to urban areas and increasing the strain on the government's ability to provide for its citizens, Ensuring safety nets that make food available, accessible, and affordable for rural citizens should significantly decrease the likelihood of a mass migration and preserve government legitimacy and capacity.

Taken as a whole, these measures for risk mitigation do not eliminate the possibility of future conflict. However, understanding the pathways from food insecurity to conflict will help the international community reduce both the risk of food insecurity and its probability of producing violence, while informing policymakers how to better focus government resources. Better food policy increases the well-being of the population, minimizes forced migration, and allows the government to better provide for its citizens in both the present and the future. As a result, the grievance that often sparks armed conflict is minimized and rebellion is largely unattractive to the average citizen.

6. Conclusions

The pathway between water, food security, and conflict is complicated and is influenced by many intervening factors. A critical examination of the literature and an in-depth analysis of the reasons for conflict suggest that food insecurity is a multiplier, or facilitator, of the opportunities for and benefits from conflict. Promoting food security is, therefore, a necessary but insufficient condition for conflict mitigation.

References

Ali, M. (2010). *Years of drought: A report on the effects of drought on the Syrian Peninsula*. Heinrich Böll-Stiftung. Retrieved from http://lb. boell.org/sites/default/files/uploads/2010/12/drought_in_syria_en.pdf

Allan, J. A. (1997). *Virtual water: A long-term solution for water short Middle Eastern economies*. London: University of Leeds.

Arnell, N. W. (1999). Climate change and global water resources. *Global Environmental Change*, *9*, 31–49.

Barnett, J., & Adger, W. N. (2007). Climate change, human security, and violent conflict. *Political Geography*, *26*, 639–655.

Barrios, S., Bertinelli, L., & Strobl, E. (2006). Climatic change and rural-urban migration: The case of Sub-Saharan Africa. *Journal of Urban Economics*, *60*, 357–371.

Benjaminsen, T. A. (2008). Does supply-induced scarcity drive violent conflicts in the African Sahel? The case of the Tuareg rebellion in Northern Mali. *Journal of Peace Research*, *45*(6), 819–836.

Blattman, C., & Miguel, E. (2010). Civil War. *Journal of Economic Literature*, *48*(1), 3–57.

Bora, S., Ceccacci, I., Delgado, C., & Townsend, R. (2010). *Food security and conflict*. Washington, DC: World Bank.

Brinkman, H., & Hendrix, C. S. (2011). Food insecurity and violent conflict: Causes, consequences, and addressing the challenges. *Occasional Paper*, *24*, 513–520.

Byerlee, D., Myers, B., & Jayne, T. (2005). *Managing food price risks and instability in an environment of market liberalization* (Report 32727). Washington, DC: World Bank.

Chassang, S., & Padro-i-Miquel, G. (2009). Economic shocks and civil war. *Quarterly Journal of Political Science*, *4*(3), 211–228.

Collier, P., Lani, E., Anke, H., Marta, R., & Nicholas, S. (2003). *Breaking the conflict trap*. Washington, DC: World Bank.

Dube, O., & Vargas, J. (2013). Commodity price shocks and civil conflict: Evidence from Colombia. *The Review of Economic Studies*, *80*(4), 1384–1421. doi:10.1093/restud/rdt009

Fearon, J. D., & Laitin, D. D. (2003). Ethnicity, insurgency, and civil war. *American Political Science Review*, *97*(1), 75–90.

Findley, S. (1994). Does drought increase migration? A study of migration from rural Mali during the 1983–1985 drought. *International Migration Review*, *28*(3), 539–553.

Food and Agricultural Organization of the United Nations. (1996). *Rome declaration on world food security*. Rome: FAO.

Food and Agricultural Organization of the United Nations. (2009). *Declaration of the world summit on food security*. Rome: FAO.

Food and Agricultural Organization of the United Nations. (2011). *Food prices reach new historic peak*. Retrieved from http://www.fao.org/news/story/en/item/50519/icode/

Food and Agricultural Organization of the United Nations. (2013). *The state of food insecurity in the world*. Retrieved from http://www.fao.org/docrep/018/i3434e/i3434e00.htm

Food and Agricultural Organization of the United Nations. (2014). *The state of food insecurity in the world, 2014*. Retrieved from http://www.fao.org/publications/sofi/2014/en/

Fund for Peace. (2011). *Failed states index.* Retrieved from http://ffp.sta-tesindex.org/rankings-2011-sortable

Global Assessment Report. (2013). *Global assessment report on disaster risk reduction, 2013.* Retrieved from http://www.unisdr.org/we/inform/gar

Goodwin, J. (2001). No other way out: States and revolutionary movements, 1945–1991. Cambridge: Cambridge University Press.

Gurr, T. R. (1970). *Why men rebel.* Princeton, NJ: Princeton University Press.

Intergovernmental Panel on Climate Change (IPCC). (2007). *Climate change 2007: Synthesis report.* Retrieved from http://www.ipcc.ch/publications_and_data/ar4/syr/en/spms3.html

Ivanic, M., & Martin, W. (2008). Implications of higher global food prices for poverty in low-income countries. *Agricultural Economics, 39*(1), 405–416.

Kelley, C. P., Mohtadi, S., Cane, M. A., Seager, R., & Kushnir, Y. (2015). *Climate change in the fertile crescent and implications of the recent Syrian drought.* PNAS, *112*(11), 3241–3246.

McLeman, R., & Smit, B. (2006). Migration as an adaptation to climate change. *Climatic Change, 76,* 31–53.

Meade, B., & Rosen, S. (2013). *International food security assessment, 2013–2023.* Washington, DC: USDA/ERS.

Miguel, E. (2007). Poverty and violence: An overview of recent research and implications for foreign aid. In L. Brainard & D. Chollet (Eds.), Too poor for peace? Global poverty, conflict and security in the 21st century (pp. 50–59). Washington, DC: Brookings Institution Press.

Miguel, E., Satyanath, S., & Sergenti, E. (2004). Economic shocks and civil conflict: An instrumental variables approach. *Journal of Political Economy, 112*(4), 725–753.

Nordas, R., & Gleditsch, N. P. (2007). Climate change and conflict. *Political Geography, 26,* 627–638.

Norton, G., Alwang, J., & Masters, W. (2010). *Economics of agricultural development: World food systems and resource use* (2nd ed.). New York, NY: Routledge.

O'Driscoll, G. P., Jr., & Hoskins, L. (2003). *Property rights: The key to economic development* (Cato Policy Analysis No. 482). Retrieved from http://www.cato.org/publications/policy-analysis/property-rights-key-economic-development

Pena, M., & Bacallao, J. (2002). Malnutrition and poverty. *Annual Review of Nutrition, 22*(1), 241.

Piguet, E. (2011). *The migration/climate change nexus: An assessment.* Retrieved from http://www.network-migration.org/rethinking-migration-2011/2/papers/Piguet.pdf

Pinstrup-Andersen, P., & Shimokawa, S. (2008). Do poverty and poor health and nutrition increase the risk of armed conflict onset? *Food Policy, 33*, 513−520.

Poulton, C., Kydd, J., Wiggins, S., & Dorward, A. (2006). State intervention for food price stabilisation in Africa: Can it work? *Food Policy, 31*(4), 342−356.

Powell, B. (2003). *Private property rights, economic freedom, and well-being* (Working Paper 19). Fairfax, VA: George Mason University.

Raleigh, C., Jordan, L., & Salehyan, I. (2008). *Assessing the impact of climate change on migration and conflict.* Washington, DC: World Bank.

Raleigh, C., & Urdal, H. (2007). Climate change, environmental degradation, and armed conflict. *Political Geography, 26*, 674−694.

Salehyan, I., Hendrix, C. S., Case, C., Linbarger, C., Stull, E., & Williams, J. (2011). *The social conflict in Africa database: New data and applications.* Working Paper. Denton, TX: University of North Texas.

Sobek, D., & Boehmer, C. (2009). *If they only had cake: The effect of food supply on civil war onset, 1960−1999.* Retrieved from http://works. bepress.com/charles_boehmer/4

Tilly, C. (1978). *From mobilization to revolution.* New York, NY: McGraw-Hill.

United Nations High Commissioner for Refugees (UNHCR). (2014). *Crisis in the Horn of Africa.* Retrieved from http://www.unhcr.org/ pages/4e1ff4b06.html

Valdes, A., & Foster, W. (2012). *Net food-importing developing countries: Who they are, and policy options for global price volatility.* Retrieved from http://www.ictsd.org/downloads/2012/08/net-food-importing-developing-countries-who-they-are-and-policy-options-for-global-price-volatility.pdf

von Braun, J. (2008). *Food and financial crises: Implications for agriculture and the poor.* Free downloads from IFPRI.

Walton, J., & Seldon, D. (1994). *Free markets and food riots.* Oxford: Blackwell.

Wichelns, D. (2001). The role of 'virtual water' in efforts to achieve food security and other national goals, with an example from Egypt. *Agricultural Water Management, 49*(2), 131−151.

World Bank. (2011). *Middle East and North, Africa: Facing challenges and opportunities.* Washington, DC: World Bank.

World Food Program (WFP). (2013). *The status of poverty and food security in Egypt: Analysis and policy recommendations.* Retrieved from https://www.wfp.org/content/egypt-status-poverty-food-security-analysis-policy-recommendations-may-2013

15

Major Trends in Diets and Nutrition: A Global Perspective to 2050

Siwa Msangi and Miroslav Batka

Environment and Production Technology Division, International Food Policy Research Institute (IFPRI), Washington, 20006, DC, USA
E-mail address: s.msangi@cgiar.org and m.batka@cgiar.org

Abstract

Purpose – In this chapter, we explore the future global supply and demand trends for key agricultural products under baseline assumptions of socioeconomic changes in population and income. We examine nutritional trends under this baseline to highlight countries that lag behind in attaining key dietary sufficiency targets.

Methodology/approach – Using a global multimarket agricultural model, we disaggregate the key macronutrients within food commodities to understand how progress toward target dietary intake levels of nutrients compares across various regions. We look particularly at those regions whose populations fall into the bottom sixth of nutritional attainment (the Bottom Billion) and note their slow projected progress toward achieving dietary sufficiency in key macronutrients.

Findings – Many countries falling into the Bottom Billion category of nutritional attainment are in Africa and Asia. Colombia is the only Latin American country that fell into this category. Most populations in the Bottom Billion are deficient in carbohydrate, protein, and fiber intake.

Practical implications – Policies aimed at eliminating hunger and improving the nutritional status of populations must be aligned with evolving socioeconomic patterns and changes that shape food consumption and dietary patterns. This analysis evaluates regions of the world in greatest need of attaining sufficient dietary intake of important nutrients, and sets the stage for a deeper discussion of policy options for improving these regions' food security.

Keywords: Agriculture, food, nutrition, socioeconomic growth

Frontiers of Economics and Globalization
Volume 15   ISSN: 1574-8715
DOI: 10.1108/S1574-871520150000015023

1. Introduction

Sharp increases in food prices in global and national markets over the 2006–2008 period made policy makers and agricultural economic analysts aware of the stresses facing global food systems and ecosystems. The rapid increase in prices of key food grain commodities such as maize, wheat, and rice tended to mirror the increase in prices of bioenergy, thus strengthening the perception that bioenergy and agricultural markets are becoming more closely linked (Schmidhuber, 2006). Some are concerned about the effect of high food prices and increased volatility in food markets on the welfare of vulnerable populations in developing countries that are net consumers of these products (Evans, 2008; Food and Agriculture Organization of the United Nations [FAO], 2008).

The underlying factors of the rapid increase in food prices vary both in nature and in their relative strength in driving market dynamics across food commodities (Oxfam International, 2008; Runge & Senauer, 2008). Comprehensive discussions have assessed these factors based on macroeconomics and the decline of the dollar relative to other currencies (Abbot, Hurt, & Tyner, 2008). A result of the privatization of agriculture operations and the adoption of just-in-time management (Trostle, 2008), the steady decline in cereal stocks worldwide is cited as a factor in reducing the ability of national governments to stabilize consumer and producer prices (Organisation for Economic Co-operation and Development [OECD], 2008). Overall, most researchers cite a complex interaction between coincidental factors rather than any one specific cause for the current world food situation.

Policy debate centered on the underlying causes of the food price spike of 2006–2008 continues (Headey & Fan, 2010). While not a sufficient explanatory factor for the short-term dynamics of agricultural markets, demand growth is a factor in the long-term evolution of market conditions. Growth in food and feed consumption largely determines the pace at which food supply must evolve to keep up with domestic and export demand for agricultural goods. Little research exists to demonstrate how changes in consumption would affect nutrition and food security. Looking beyond China and India, other evolving regions exist in which increases in urbanization and income will have a profound effect on global food security.

In this chapter, we explore some major trends of diet and nutrition projected to the year 2050 based on model-generated, baseline projections of global food market dynamics. We examine the demand side of agricultural markets and consumption trends to help meeting the goals for the recommended daily intake (RDI) as defined by international health organizations. We also highlight the Bottom Billion consumers who have made the least progress toward meeting nutritional food intake goals, and discuss where these consumers are located along with the policies and drivers of socioeconomic change that best support them.

2. Drivers of change in food systems

A number of underlying factors drive the long-term trends in food supply and demand that have contributed to the tightening of global food markets. These trends are driven by environmental and socioeconomic changes and by agricultural and energy policies. Figure 1 illustrates the interactions between various key drivers of change in global food systems and their links to nutrition and health. While it does not examine all the significant factors, this schematic incorporates the main elements of global environmental and economic change in food production and consumption systems.

Socioeconomic change (in the form of increasing growth in population numbers and total income) and urbanization are among the major factors driving consumer demand for food, fiber, and energy products. Changes in consumption and consumption preferences increase the pressure on food and energy systems to meet demand. In turn, producers who supply the products may be constrained by resource scarcity or degraded land

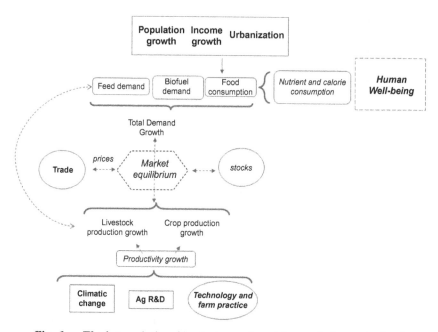

Fig. 1. *The interrelationships between key drivers of change in food systems and their connection to human nutrition and well-being.*

and water quality. Over time, constraints can reduce investments in crop and energy technology, creating upward pressure on prices as consumer demand outpaces supply growth.

A thorough overview of policy drivers by Headey and Fan (2010) illustrates the importance of country-level policy decisions (e.g., grain reserves and trade) regarding supply and demand. The role of improving crop yield growth and productivity to meet future demand, as well as to conserve resources, becomes increasingly critical.

Figure 1 shows a variety of entry points for policy or technological intervention. These entry points offer options for policy makers for coping with stresses on food and energy systems and for mitigating the severity of future stresses. We discuss these issues in the context of food and energy supply and demand systems.

3. Socioeconomic factors

The main socioeconomic factors driving food demand are increases in population, income, and urbanization. As measured by per capita gross domestic product (GDP), incomes are expected to grow significantly in recently industrialized nations such as East Asia (United Nations Environment Program [UNEP], 2007; World Bank, 2007). Using the rates in the International Model for Policy Analysis of Agricultural Commodities and Trade developed by the International Food Policy Research Institute (IFPRI IMPACT) (von Braun, 2008), our research suggest the per capita GDP in China and India are expected to increase by 5.2% and 4.5%, respectively. Figure 2 shows the growth of total population to 2050 in various regions of the world based on the medium variant population projections of the United Nations [UN] (2008).

Most future population growth will come from developing countries, with the most sizable shares occurring in Sub-Saharan Africa and South Asia (Figure 2). This has important consequences for the future demand for food and feed. Urbanization also has implications for changes in future consumer preferences in terms of increased demand for higher-value animal-sourced protein food products rather than plant-sourced food products. Figure 3 shows expected changes by 2050 in the share of population living in urban areas.

We obtain a more complete picture of the key drivers of change if we add a projection of per capita income growth up to 2050 (Figure 4). Note the substantial increase in the incomes of the highest income countries in both 2030 and 2050, with the emerging countries of Asia and Latin America experiencing more substantial growth relative to previous decades.

The combination of rising income and urbanization is changing diets worldwide. Rapidly rising incomes in the developing world has led to

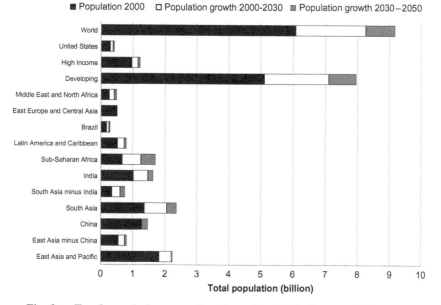

Fig. 2. Total population growth projected to 2050. Source: Calculated from UN medium variant population projections.

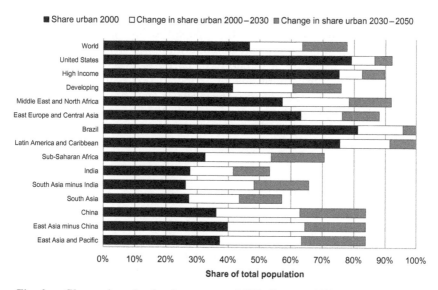

Fig. 3. Change in urbanization rates to 2050. Source: UN medium variant population projections.

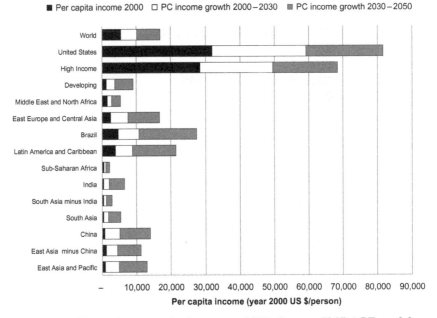

Fig. 4. Change in per capita income to 2050. Source: IMPACT model baseline assumptions.

increased demand for animal-sourced protein foods and for processed foods (Rosegrant, Paisner, Meijer, & Witcover, 2001). Animal-sourced proteins place additional pressure on land resources for pasture as well as coarse grain markets for livestock feed. By 2020, over 60% of animal-sourced protein consumption are projected to occur in the developing world and the production of these products at least doubling from their 1993 levels (Delgado, Rosegrant, Steinfeld, Ehui, & Courbois, 1999). Figure 5 shows the close correlation between income and animal-sourced protein consumption (Delgado et al., 1999).

4. Policy factors in shaping food futures

We consider several policy intervention factors to address the current global food situation. As shown in Figure 1, a number of policies can be considered from both the demand side and the supply side (Sarris, 2009). For example, demand-side policies that govern the use of food-based feedstock crops for biofuel production could be altered so that nonfood feedstock or feedstock conversion technologies are used instead of grain-based food and feed sources. Supply-side policies that accelerate the improvement of crop technologies can be accomplished through improved seed technologies or the expansion of irrigated production.

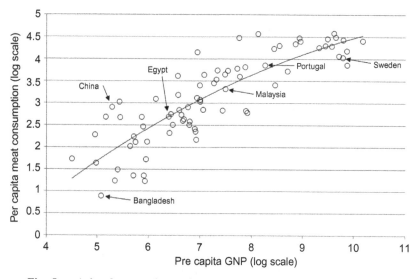

Fig. 5. Animal-sourced protein consumption and per capita income.
Source: *Authors' calculations with World Development Indicators*
(WDI) data.

5. How diets shape food futures

The IFPRI IMPACT model is a partial equilibrium agricultural model for crop and livestock commodities that is used to project future global food supply and demand, and food security (Rosegrant et al., 2001). This model links international trade between countries and regions using a series of linear and nonlinear equations to approximate underlying production and demand functions. The model contains four categories of commodity demand: food, feed, biofuels feedstock, and other uses. Demand is a function of prices, income, and population growth. World agricultural commodity prices are determined annually. Growth in crop production in each country is determined by crop and input prices, the rate of productivity growth, investment in irrigation, and water availability. The baseline results of the IFPRI IMPACT model (Rosegrant, Cai, & Cline, 2002; Rosegrant et al., 2001) illustrate how socioeconomic and demographic changes factor into the long-term evolution of food consumption for key commodity groups.

6. Baseline results from the IMPACT model

The exogenous trajectories of socioeconomic changes lead to changes in food consumption patterns based on the relationship between income growth and per capita food consumption. For most regions, the per capita levels of animal-sourced protein consumption tend to increase with additional per capita income, while those based on plant-sourced (cereals, especially coarse grains) protein consumption tend to decrease. Figure 6 shows how per capita plant-sourced protein consumption is expected to change as a result of socioeconomic drivers.

On average, there is a worldwide decline in the level of per capita plant-based (cereal) protein consumption, with the strongest decreases coming from the developing world. The developing world starts with a higher initial level of per capita plant-based protein consumption in 2000 compared to high-income countries. A wide range of regional variation exists in this pattern, with the Middle East and North Africa experiencing increases in per capita plant-based protein consumption levels, whereas areas of East Asia experience decreases in per capita plant-based protein consumption levels.

An even more dynamic picture emerges of behavioral change over the long term in relation to animal-sourced protein consumption. Figure 7 shows higher annual growth in per capita animal-sourced protein consumption in high-income countries as compared to low-income countries.

As regards other food categories, growth in per capita fruit and vegetable consumption shows a dynamic trajectory in the Middle East, North Africa, and East Asia, with China's level of fruit and vegetable consumption exceeding that of the United States by 2030. On average,

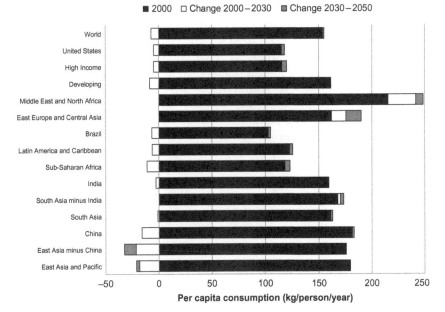

Fig. 6.   Growth in per capita plant-sourced (cereal) protein consumption to 2050. Source: IMPACT model projections.

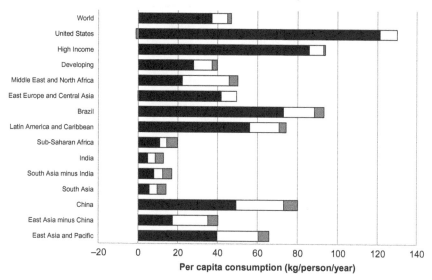

Fig. 7. Growth in per capita animal-sourced protein consumption to 2050. Source: IMPACT model projections.

the level of growth in per capita fruit and vegetable consumption in high-income countries is less than that seen in developing countries up to 2030, but accelerates thereafter. In terms of per capita root and tuber consumption, nearly all regions show very modest increases in the levels of per capita consumption to 2030.

7. Global nutrition trends and the Bottom Billion

Nutrition is important for food security. To describe the nutritional content of food, we define macronutrients and micronutrients as the basic elements needed for health and well-being. Loosely speaking, the body requires a larger amount of macronutrients than micronutrients to maintain good health. Table 1 provides a description of the kinds of macronutrients and micronutrients that are commonly considered when discussing the nutritive value of foods.

Macronutrients describe the bulk properties of foods often associated with a healthy diet. They are easier to measure and quantify in terms of daily intake than micronutrients (Bouis, 2007), and provide most of the caloric value of food. Therefore, we discuss macronutrients because it is easier to quantify their bioavailability in foods within the framework of our model.

Table 1. Description of macronutrients and micronutrients

Macronutrients	Micronutrients	
	Vitamins	Minerals and trace elements
Energy	Vitamin A	Calcium
Protein	Thiamin	Chromium
Fat	Riboflavin	Copper
Carbohydrate	Niacin	Fluoride
Dietary fiber	Vitamin B6	Iodine
Water	Vitamin B12	Iron
	Folate	Magnesium
	Pantothenic acid	Manganese
	Biotin	Molybdenum
	Choline	Phosphorus
	Vitamin C	Potassium
	Vitamin D	Selenium
	Vitamin E	Sodium
	Vitamin K	Zinc

Source: Government of Australia, Ministry of Health (2005).

8. Defining the Bottom Billion for nutrition

Focusing on nutritional deficiencies, we use the observed levels of average, national intakes of key macronutrients to identify those regions with the lowest levels macro-nutritional intake. We use data from the World Health Organization (WHO) and the FAO to define the parameters of a healthy diet. The WHO Technical Report (2003) provides a rough outline of the intake requirements of key macronutrients necessary for maintaining human health. Table 2 lists some of the recommended intake quantities of macronutrients.

A more detailed outline of requirements would include demographics (e.g., age and sex) associated with the physical needs of the body at various stages of development. The RDI requirements provided by the US Food and Nutrition Board of the Institute of Medicine (National Academy of Sciences, 2004) are based on demographics. Therefore, we use the RDI in the IMPACT model (UN, 2008). We distinguish the nutrient intakes simulated at the national level for each country and then rank them by how closely they match the healthy diet guidelines in Table 3.

We focus on the three key macronutrients (carbohydrates, proteins, and fiber) that offer the most straightforward means of quantifying caloric intakes in all the target countries. Most dietary energy intake comes from proteins and carbohydrates. Fiber helps the body absorb and use macronutrients and micronutrients. Water quality has a similar function as fiber in that it helps the body retain or absorb nutrients. In the IMPACT model, access to clean water is an important determinant of

Table 2.   General description of healthy diet macronutrient requirements

Dietary factor	Goal (% of total energy, unless otherwise stated)
Total fat	15%−30%
Total carbohydrate	55%−75%
Protein	10%−15%
Cholesterol	<300 mg per day
Sodium chloride (sodium)	<5 g per day (<2 g per day)
Fruits and vegetables	5,400 g per day
Total dietary fiber	From foods

Source: WHO (2003, Table 6).

child malnutrition (Smith & Haddad, 2000), underscoring the importance of utilizing nutrients from food.

In *The Bottom Billion*, Collier (2007) describes the political, socioeconomic, and historical factors that lead to the persistence of malnutrition and poverty in developing regions of the world. We identify regions that are consistently insufficient in delivering adequate levels of the three target macronutrients (protein, carbohydrates, and fiber). The countries in Table 3 fall roughly into the bottom 20% of the global ranking of sufficient intake, and fall below the 40% ranking of RDI intake. In relation to recommended intakes, rankings for fiber and protein were below 20% and 25%, respectively. While we recognize that these aggregated indicators can potentially mask the heterogeneity in per capita intake, our results provide important implications for some of the world's most food insecure populations. In the projection horizon, a number of regions are at or near 60% of the RDI level for carbohydrates. Latin America leads aggregate regions, followed by South Asia, Europe and Central Asia, the Middle East and North Africa, and Southeast Asia. These countries provide a stark contrast to Sub-Saharan Africa, which is heavily represented among the Bottom Billion for nutritional outcomes.

9. Baseline trends for macronutrients

We present some projections for macronutrient intakes that characterize future trends for key regions of the world. In particular, our analysis shows how macronutrient availability compares to RDIs weighted by demographics for each region. Table 4 shows projected improvements in the achievement of RDI levels of carbohydrates for key global sub-regions.

Table 4 also shows the projected improvements in the protein RDI achievements for the target key sub-regions. Many regions are already at or approaching the 10%−15% range of protein RDI achievement described in Table 3. In this profile, the Middle East and North Africa

**Table 3.   Description of the Bottom Billion countries falling below
20%—40% of target intake for key macronutrients**

	Africa	Asia	Latin America
All three macronutrients	Benin Burundi Chad Congo Democratic Republic of the Congo Côte d'Ivoire Kenya Madagascar Malawi Mozambique Rwanda Tanzania Togo	Bangladesh Cambodia Laos Myanmar Nepal North Korea Sri Lanka	
Fiber and protein	Cameroon Central America and Caribbean South Africa Uganda Zimbabwe		Colombia
Fiber and carbohydrates	Central African Republic Mauritania	Mongolia Vietnam	
Protein and carbohydrates	Burkina Faso Ethiopia Mali Niger		

Source: Authors' calculations.
Notes: Indicates countries that fall below the threshold daily intake for key macronutrient categories, which is 20% of recommended daily intake (RDI) for fiber, 25-30% of RDI for protein, and 40% of RDI for carbohydrates

almost reach the level of high-income countries by 2050. The developing region average is well below the level of protein RDI achievement observed for the high-income countries. Once more, the population in the Bottom Billion lies below the developing country average.

Dietary fiber RDI achievements are much lower (Table 4). Only the regions of Europe and Central Asia, and the Middle East and North Africa finish above the 40% level. Latin America ranks only slightly above the Bottom Billion.

We do not construct an aggregate index to describe how the RDIs of these three particular macronutrients (carbohydrates, protein, and dietary fiber) translate into an overall measure of nutritional performance. To do so would be beyond the scope of our analytical framework. It is striking how much the Bottom Billion ranks below the rest of the sub-regions. With these nutritional gaps, global food insecurity will continue to exist.

Table 4.   Baseline projections of achievement of recommended intakes of carbohydrates, protein, and fiber for global sub-regions (as percentage of RDI met)

	Carbohydrates		Protein		Fiber	
	2006	Change 2006–2050	2006	Change 2006–2050	2006	Change 2006–2050
World	56%	12%	27%	5%	23%	6%
High income	49%	7%	40%	6%	28%	8%
Developing	57%	12%	24%	6%	22%	6%
Middle East and North Africa	58%	22%	32%	10%	31%	11%
Europe and Central Asia	59%	25%	29%	8%	31%	9%
Latin America	99%	18%	30%	4%	18%	3%
Sub-Saharan Africa	38%	2%	23%	5%	23%	6%
South Asia	66%	17%	19%	4%	20%	6%
East Asia	43%	9%	25%	8%	22%	4%
Southeast Asia	57%	9%	27%	8%	23%	10%
Bottom Billion	42%	1%	17%	1%	15%	2%

Source: IMPACT model projections.

10. Conclusions

In this chapter, we focused on baseline projections of agricultural markets and food demand in various regions of the world. We focused particularly on the Bottom Billion, where the least progress has occurred. We noted that the populations in the Bottom Billion made the least progress toward reaching target RDI levels for key macronutrients. Although we do not designate certain macronutrients as especially important, energy from carbohydrates and protein is among the most consequential for human health and well-being.

Policies aimed at eliminating hunger and improving countries' nutritional status need to align with the socioeconomic patterns of evolution as well as the changes that shape consumption and dietary patterns. Solving nutrition-based problems requires a long-term effort to alter food consumption patterns and nutrient intake. Such interventions often provide benefits far beyond the short-term horizon of politically minded policy makers, and must be maintained through consistent and optimal policies that sustain progress over the long term.

References

Abbot, P. C., Hurt, C., & Tyner, W. E. (2008). *What's driving food prices?* Oak Brook, IL: Farm Foundation.

Bouis, H. E. (2007). The potential of genetically modified food crops to improve human nutrition in developing countries. *Journal of Development Studies, 43*(1), 79—96.

Collier, P. (2007). *The bottom billion: Why the poorest countries are failing and what can be done about it.* Oxford: Oxford University Press.

Delgado, C. L., Rosegrant, M. W., Steinfeld, H., Ehui, S., & Courbois, C. (1999). *Livestock to 2020. The next food revolution* (2020 Vision for Food, Agriculture, and the Environment. Discussion Paper No. 28). Washington, DC: IFPRI.

Evans, A. (2008). *Rising food prices: Drivers and implications for development* (Briefing Paper 08/02). London: Chatham House.

Food and Agriculture Organization of the United Nations. (2008). *Soaring food prices: Facts, perspectives, impacts, and actions required.* Rome: FAO.

Government of Australia, Ministry of Health. (2005). *Nutrient reference values for Australia and New Zealand.* Retrieved from https://www. nhmrc.gov.au/_files_nhmrc/publications/attachments/n35.pdf

Headey, D. C., & Fan, S. (2010). *Reflections on the global food crisis: How did it happen? How did it hurt? And how can we prevent the next one?* (IFPRI Research Monograph 165). Washington, DC: IFPRI.

National Academy of Sciences. (2004). *Dietary reference intakes.* Washington, DC: Food and Nutrition Board, Institute of Medicine, National Academies.

Organisation for Economic Co-operation and Development. (2008). *Rising food prices: Causes and consequences.* Paris: OECD.

Oxfam International. (2008). *Another inconvenient truth: How biofuels policies are deepening poverty and accelerating climate change* (Briefing Paper 114). Oxford: Oxfam.

Rosegrant, M. W., Cai, X., & Cline, S. (2002). *World water and food to 2025: Dealing with scarcity.* Washington, DC: IFPRI.

Rosegrant, M. W., Paisner, M. S., Meijer, S., & Witcover, J. (2001). *Global food projections to 2020: Emerging trends and alternative futures.* Washington, DC: IFPRI.

Runge, C. F., & Senauer, B. (2008). *How ethanol fuels the food crisis.* Retrieved from http://www.foreignaffairs.org/20080528faupdate87376/ c-ford-runge-benjamin%20senauer/how-ethanol-fuels-the-food-crisis. html

Sarris, A. (2009). *Evolving structure of world agricultural trade and requirements for new world trade rules.* Rome: FAO. Retrieved from ftp://ftp. fao.org/docrep/fao/012/ak979e/ak979e00.pdf

Schmidhuber, J. (2006). *Impact of an increased biomass use on agricultural markets, prices and food security: A longer-term perspective.* Retrieved from http://www.fao.org/fileadmin/templates/esa/Global_persepctives/ Presentations/BiomassNotreEurope.pdf

Smith, L., & Haddad, L. (2000). *Explaining child malnutrition in developing countries: A cross-country analysis* (IFPRI Research Report 111). Washington, DC: IFPRI.

Trostle, R. (2008). *Global agricultural supply and demand: Factors contributing to the recent increase in food commodity prices (WRS-0801).* Washington, DC: USDA/ERS.

United Nations Environment Program. (2007). *Global environmental outlook* (GEO4): Environment for Development. Nairobi: United Nations Environment Program.

United Nations. (2008). *World population prospects: 2008 revisions.* New York, NY: UN.

von Braun, J. (2008). *The world food situation: New driving forces and required actions.* Washington, DC: IFPRI.

World Bank (2007). *Global economic prospects: Managing the next wave of globalization.* Washington, DC: The World Bank.

World Health Organization [WHO]. (2003). *Diet, nutrition and the prevention of chronic diseases* (WHO Technical Report Series 916). Geneva: WHO.

16

Dietary Change and Global Drivers of Change: How Can We Improve the Nutritional Status of the Bottom Billion?

Siwa Msangi and Miroslav Batka

Environment and Production Technology Division, International Food Policy Research Institute (IFPRI), Washington, 20006, DC, USA
E-mail address: s.msangi@cgiar.org and m.batka@cgiar.org

Abstract

Purpose – This chapter explores policy implications of deliberately targeted interventions aimed at closing the gap between nutrition baseline trends and desirable levels of nutrition intake according to World Health Organization/Food and Agriculture Organization of the United Nations guidelines. Special attention is paid to the implications for those at the bottom of the nutrition achievement range (Bottom Billion).

Methodology/approach – We conduct a forward looking evaluation with a global multimarket model for agriculture within the context of key drivers of change. We observe the effect of interventions on nutrition intake for the most food-insecure regions as transmitted through food prices, changes in country-level food trade, and other market-driven outcomes. We demonstrate the nutrition-enhancing effects that occur when animal-sourced protein consumption, livestock production, and livestock feed demand decrease in developed countries. We also show the effect of a significant growth in agricultural productivity and household incomes.

Findings – Our analysis shows that the most effective intervention boosts household income to facilitate adequate intake of food and key nutrients. Diet changes have notable effects but are harder to implement on a practical level. Enhancing agricultural productivity (especially in regions with historically low yields) is also effective in improving nutrition outcomes.

Practical implications – Short of social protection and direct assistance programs, the ability of policy to effect short-term changes in nutritional status is limited. We highlight the effectiveness of pathways that promote

Frontiers of Economics and Globalization
Volume 15   ISSN: 1574-8715
DOI: 10.1108/S1574-871520150000015024

longer-term socioeconomic growth and productivity gains as ways of improving the nutrition and health status of consumers.

Keywords: Diet change, nutrition, poverty, agriculture, economic policy

1. Introduction

The growing demand for food, feed, and fiber − and its implications for the global agricultural system − has raised issues concerning future food security (Food and Agriculture Organization of the United Nations [FAO], 2010). Based on increasing future demand, projections point to increasingly tighter markets for food and feed (Rosegrant, Tokgoz, & Bhandary, 2013). In addition, intensive production of animal-sourced protein may have a negative environmental impact (FAO, 2006; World Bank, 2013).

The evolution of diets from a concentration in plant-sourced to animal-sourced protein has raised concerns about the health implications of high-fat, caloric-intensive foods (Nellemann et al., 2009; Popkin, 2006, 2009). International health organizations have become involved in campaigning for more plant-sourced protein for healthier diets (WHO, 2003). The policy of steering consumers toward healthier diets is not always easy to implement (Stehfest, van den Berg, Woltjer, Msangi, & Westhoek, 2013; Westhoek et al., 2011). For example, emerging middle-income countries such as Brazil, Russian Federation, India, and China (BRIC) are increasing per capita meat and dairy consumption as their populations become wealthier (Delgado, Rosegrant, Steinfeld, Ehui, & Courbois, 1999). This diet change has increased obesity and health-related diseases in these countries (Msangi & Rosegrant, 2012; Ross, 2013).

This chapter explores the policy implications of deliberately targeted interventions aimed at closing the gap between nutrition baseline trends and the desirable levels of nutrition intake according to WHO/FAO guidelines. Special attention is paid to the implications for those at the bottom of the nutrition achievement range (the Bottom Billion) (Collier, 2007).

We conduct an evaluation using a global multimarket model for agriculture within the context of key drivers of change to observe the effect of interventions on nutrition intake for the most food-insecure regions. We also demonstrate the nutrition-enhancing effects that occur when animal-sourced protein is replaced with plant-source protein in the diet.

2. Modeling diet change

Consumer preferences provide a powerful force for change in food systems. We use the global, agricultural multimarket model of the International

Food Policy Research Institute (IFPRI IMPACT model) (Rosegrant, Cai, & Cline, 2002; Rosegrant, Paisner, Meijer, & Witcover, 2001) to carry out simulations of supply and demand dynamics to 2050. We also incorporate plant-sourced protein diet changes into the IMPACT model to reflect the effects of healthier diets over time. To model this case, we forced a solution for targeted regions toward consumption patterns that conform to a healthy diet as defined by the World Health Organization (WHO, 2003). Table 1 summarizes the diet changes in higher-income countries.

The numbers in Table 1 represent the average proportional change of per capita consumption in higher-income countries relative to the 1999−2001 average per capita consumption figures. On average, per capita cereal consumption increases by 45%, whereas per capita meat consumption decreases by more than 50%. In solving the IMPACT model, the per capita consumption path of each country within the target is fixed by reducing the baseline path of consumption $pcQD_{c,t}^{EU}$ (for the prescribed commodities) by a prescribed proportion ($redc_{c,t}$) over time (t) such that the per capita consumption amount in the target region becomes $pcQD_{c,t}^{EU} = pcQD_{c,t}^{baseline} \times redc_{c,t}$. At the same time, food consumption in all the other regions of the IMPACT model evolves according to the normal price-based interaction and response to changing levels of income over time ($pcQD_{c,t} = f(P_c, P_{-c}, pcInc | \Theta s)$). In the IMPACT model, the prices of other commodities are P_{-c}, per capita income is $pcInc$, and the behavioral response parameters are summarized in a vector Θ. The adjustment factor ($redc_{c,t}$) is applied uniformly to all countries within the targeted regions,[1] and the time period for adjustment is implemented such that changes begin in 2008 and are complete by 2015.

Table 1. *Proportional changes in per capita consumption implemented in alternative diet scenarios for high-income countries*

Product	High-Income Countries
Cereals	1.45
Beef	0.45
Pork	0.45
Poultry	1.30
Other meats	0.40
Milk products	0.80
Eggs	1.00

[1] For the purposes of defining these scenarios, high-income countries are identified as those in North America, the OECD region (including the original EU-15 members), Australia, New Zealand, Japan, South Korea, Israel, and the wealthy Gulf states.

Table 2. *Per capita cereal consumption under baseline and alternative*
(HIC) diet scenarios (kg per capita/year)

Location	2000	2030 baseline	2030 HIC diet change
United States	115.3	111.0	161.0
China	181.3	167.6	162.3
India	158.6	160.0	156.3
Brazil	102.9	98.9	97.1
East Europe/Central Asia	161.9	177.3	193.8
HICs	115.6	111.8	161.3
Sub-Saharan Africa	118.3	109.5	107.2
Developing countries	161.0	155.6	153.2
World	153.8	149.5	154.4

Source: IMPACT model projections.
Note: HIC, high-income country.

Table 3. *World prices of key commodities under baseline and alternative*
(HIC) diet scenarios ($/ton)

Product	2000	2030 baseline	2030 HIC diet change
Beef	1,970	2,081	1,677
Pork	899	875	665
Lamb/Goat	2,831	2,926	2,553
Poultry	1,244	1,223	1,368
Eggs	764	737	744
Milk	308	346	340
Rice	207	291	306
Wheat	114	164	182
Maize	88	149	157
Other coarse grains	67	127	138
Soybeans	203	352	356
Potatoes	211	307	312
Sweet potatoes/Yams	472	524	532
Cassava	63	89	91
Meal	189	370	364

Source: IMPACT model projections.
Note: HIC, high-income country.

3. Impacts of alternative diet changes on consumption

Using the results on food consumption generated by the model under
these diet change scenarios, the effect on per capita cereal consumption in
2030 (Table 2) is significant and positive for the United States, East
Europe, and Central Asia for the first variant (high-income countries only).

Under this variant, in which high-income countries adopt a healthy diet,
the emerging transitional BRIC countries experience a decrease in per capita
cereal consumption due to the increase in world cereal prices (Table 3).

Table 4.   Per capita meat consumption under baseline and alternative (HIC) diet scenarios (kg per capita/year)

Location	2000	2030 baseline	2030 HIC diet change
United States	121.4	129.4	103.5
China	49.4	72.5	76.5
India	4.8	8.5	9.4
Brazil	73.0	87.5	94.1
Eastern Europe/Central Asia	41.9	49.4	43.4
HICs	85.8	92.3	69.8
Sub-Saharan Africa	10.9	14.3	15.8
Developing countries	27.9	36.9	38.5
World	37.1	44.6	42.9

Source: IMPACT model projections.
Note: HIC, high-income country.

Table 5.   Per capita eggs and milk consumption under baseline and alternative (HIC) diet scenarios (kg per capita/year)

Location	2000	2030 Baseline	2030 HIC diet change
United States	133.3	131.0	107.6
China	24.2	33.4	33.5
India	45.5	50.5	50.9
Brazil	111.4	109.9	110.5
East Europe/Central Asia	124.1	133.5	127.9
HICs	91.8	91.5	75.8
Sub-Saharan Africa	23.7	21.6	21.9
Developing countries	45.4	48.0	47.9
World	52.8	54.0	51.8

Source: IMPACT model projections.
Note: HIC, high-income country.

In the case of per capita meat consumption (Table 4), the consumption in the United States and the overall grouping of high-income countries decreases. The consumption in the transitional and developing regions increases due to lower meat prices.

Under diet change in the high-income countries, per capita egg and milk consumption (Table 5) decreases in the United States. The consumption in China and India increases.

The price effects underlying these changes in food demand are also tied to changes in animal feed demand, mainly from coarse grains. Table 6 shows the effect of diet change on animal feed demand – there is a notable drop in tonnage for most of the regions. An increase in cereal consumption offsets a lower meat demand's effect on the release of grain for food use.

**Table 6.   Feed demand for coarse grains under baseline and alternative
(HIC) diet scenarios (thousand metric tons)**

Location	2000	2030 baseline	2030 HIC diet change
East Asia and Pacific	96.9	276.8	272.6
East Asia excluding China	12.0	33.3	31.9
China	84.9	243.5	240.7
South Asia	1.5	6.4	6.4
South Asia excluding India	0.9	2.8	2.8
India	0.6	3.6	3.6
Sub-Saharan Africa	7.8	19.0	18.8
Latin America/Caribbean	63.7	144.9	139.8
Brazil	30.4	68.0	64.3
East Europe/Central Asia	76.1	103.0	100.0
Middle East and North Africa	16.3	38.1	38.1
Developing countries	262.5	588.3	575.6
HICs	277.2	434.7	427.9
United States	158.7	242.7	240.6
World	539.7	1023.0	1003.5

Source: IMPACT model projections.
Note: HIC, high-income country.

4. Strategies to improve the nutritional status of the Bottom Billion

Beyond the diet change scenarios, we consider policy-focused interventions for improving the nutritional outcomes for the Bottom
Billion in the target regions. We chose two interventions (supply-side
and demand-side) of the food system to identify which approach
works better for closing nutritional gaps for the Bottom Billion. The
supply-side intervention boosts agricultural production, which in turn
increases food availability. The demand-side intervention boosts
incomes, increasing access to food even if the level of availability
remains the same.

Supply-side yield-enhancement intervention accelerates the baseline
levels of non-price-driven, technology-oriented growth in crop yields,
especially staple cereal commodities. This intervention illustrates the
importance of agricultural research and development (R&D) spending
and investments (International Assessment of Agricultural Knowledge
Science and Technology [IAASTD], 2009). Yield-enhancement intervention improves the Bottom Billion's agricultural production and can positively impact their household consumption outcomes.

Demand-side income-enhancement intervention helps improve income
that provides more money for food purchases. This type of intervention
for the Bottom Billion generates an additional policy-driven 0.5% of
GDP growth per year to accelerate the pace at which their households
can increase their nutritional intake.

Table 7. Impact of scenarios on world prices of commodities, difference relative to baseline case

	Beef	Pork	Lamb	Poultry	Eggs	Milk	Rice	Wheat	Maize	Other Grains	Soybean
Diet	−782	−480	−918	−671	−26	0	6	−7	−28	−13	−1
Yield	−6	−3	−5	−6	−2	−1	−11	−2	−5	−3	0
Income	19	4	22	7	2	0	−1	0	0	0	0

Source: IMPACT model projections.

5. Impacts on the nutritional status of the Bottom Billion

These two interventions provide a range of results that exist across the Bottom Billion. The difference in dietary patterns across these countries remains a primary determinant of their nutritional intake responses to policy-driven shocks. Table 7 shows the impact on global commodity market prices for livestock commodities relative to the baseline case.

A population's move toward a plant-based diet negatively influences livestock prices. The result is an increase in the prices of meat and dairy commodities. Increasing the Bottom Billion's income in this case does not result in an increase in price (and demand), as would occur by increasing the income of prosperous populations.

A population's move toward a plant-based diet affects all cereal prices and especially maize, which is a staple food crop for much of the Bottom Billion. Given the thin global market for rice (i.e., 6% rice vs. 40% maize traded in the global market), there is a shift from rice to wheat in some regions as incomes increase.

Price changes also have an impact on the recommended daily intake (RDI) of nutrients from various food commodities. Table 8 shows how various interventions affect the 2050 RDI levels of carbohydrate and protein RDI attainment.

In Africa, the yield-enhancement intervention has a positive effect on carbohydrate intake, while the income-enhancement intervention has a mixed effect. For the portion of the Bottom Billion populations located outside of Africa, both interventions have positive effects. The greatest gains are seen in Central America and Colombia, where maize is consumed as a major food grain. In Asia, where rice is consumed as a major food grain, the income-enhancement scenario has a positive effect due to rice prices.

When focusing on protein intake and the fulfillment of protein RDIs for the Bottom Billion, the effect from crop yield increases depends on livestock prices. In Africa and Latin America, the protein intake effect is positive for consumers since they purchase and consume more of those products.

Within our modeling framework, the determinants of child malnutrition are derived primarily from four key indicators: per capita calorie

Table 8.   Scenario impacts on achievement of RDI for carbohydrates and protein among the Bottom Billion (relative to baseline case)

		Carbohydrates			Protein		
		Diet	Yield	Income	Diet	Yield	Income
Africa	Benin	0.9%	0.6%	−0.1%	1.9%	0.2%	0.3%
	Burkina Faso	0.7%	0.4%	−0.7%	1.2%	0.2%	0.0%
	Burundi	0.9%	0.8%	−0.3%	0.7%	0.1%	0.1%
	Cameroon	1.6%	1.2%	0.3%	2.6%	0.3%	0.7%
	Central African Republic	1.1%	0.8%	0.0%	6.0%	0.3%	1.0%
	Chad	0.4%	0.4%	−0.2%	1.9%	0.2%	0.5%
	Congo	0.8%	1.0%	−0.2%	3.7%	0.3%	0.7%
	Democratic Republic of Congo (DRC)	0.9%	0.9%	−0.3%	0.8%	0.2%	0.1%
	Ethiopia	0.9%	0.3%	−0.1%	1.3%	0.1%	0.2%
	Côte d'Ivoire	1.1%	1.0%	0.2%	3.0%	0.4%	0.8%
	Kenya	0.7%	0.3%	0.1%	1.0%	0.1%	0.1%
	Madagascar	1.0%	1.4%	0.0%	2.2%	0.2%	0.6%
	Mali	0.5%	0.4%	−0.2%	1.6%	0.2%	0.2%
	Mauritania	0.6%	0.4%	0.9%	2.9%	0.2%	0.7%
	Malawi	1.2%	0.6%	0.0%	1.0%	0.1%	0.2%
	Mozambique	1.1%	0.9%	−0.1%	0.9%	0.2%	0.1%
	Niger	0.5%	0.5%	−0.1%	1.7%	0.3%	0.3%
	Rwanda	1.4%	1.1%	0.1%	1.3%	0.2%	0.4%
	South Africa	2.0%	0.7%	0.6%	3.0%	0.1%	0.6%
	Tanzania	1.2%	0.9%	−0.3%	1.1%	0.2%	0.1%
	Togo	1.2%	0.7%	0.2%	2.4%	0.4%	0.7%
	Uganda	1.6%	1.3%	−0.2%	2.0%	0.2%	0.4%
	Zimbabwe	2.4%	0.8%	0.9%	2.4%	0.2%	0.7%
Asia	Bangladesh	0.2%	0.5%	0.1%	0.7%	0.1%	0.3%
	Mongolia	0.5%	0.2%	0.5%	4.5%	0.1%	1.7%
	Myanmar	−0.1%	0.6%	0.2%	1.1%	0.2%	0.6%
	Nepal	1.0%	0.5%	0.6%	1.0%	0.1%	0.4%
	North Korea	0.4%	0.1%	0.4%	0.4%	0.1%	0.4%
	Southeast Asia	0.0%	0.3%	-0.1%	2.1%	0.1%	0.4%
	Sri Lanka	0.4%	0.6%	0.9%	1.9%	0.2%	0.8%
	Vietnam	0.4%	0.5%	0.5%	4.4%	0.1%	0.8%
	Central America and Caribbean	1.5%	0.9%	1.2%	3.7%	0.1%	0.3%
	Colombia	1.8%	1.4%	1.2%	1.7%	0.1%	0.0%

availability, access to clean drinking water, rate of female schooling, and the ratio of female-to-male life expectancy. Smith and Haddad (2000) established the link between malnutrition and these four indicators.

The IMPACT child malnutrition tracking methodology is implemented through prevention of child malnutrition as a function of per capita calorie availability (generated endogenously by the model), as well as exogenous projected rates of female schooling, shares of population with access to clean water, and ratio of female-to-male life expectancies (Smith & Haddad, 2000). Figure 1 shows the effects of reducing child malnutrition for the Bottom Billion. Partly because the number of

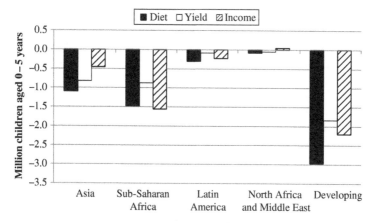

Fig. 1.   Scenario impacts on total child malnourishment in 2030 relative to baseline case (millions of children aged 0–5 years). Source: IMPACT model projections.

malnourished children is relatively smaller in Latin America, the Middle East, and North Africa, the impact of reducing child malnourishment in those regions is less significant than in South Asia and sub-Saharan Africa.

6. Implications for food security-focused policy for the Bottom Billion

The policy instruments for influencing consumer food choices and diet outcomes for the Bottom Billion are quite different than those for wealthier populations. Many challenges must be overcome to create food security policies that work for the Bottom Billion.

Supply-side yield-enhancement intervention has the smallest effect across all of the populations in the Bottom Billion as compared to demand-side income-enhancement intervention in the food balance equation. In terms of strategy, long-term agricultural productivity must be maintained to meet the challenge of feeding an additional 3 billion people by 2050 (FAO, 2010). A considerable lag exists between spending on agricultural R&D and the realization of higher crop yields (Beintema & Stads, 2010). Therefore, policy makers might prefer interventions focused on the demand-side drivers of food system change.

Animal-sourced protein consumption patterns are key in determining the evolution of price trends for meat and dairy products as well as the trajectory of commodities for livestock feed. Lower animal-sourced protein consumption could reduce the demand and price of meat and dairy products and free up volumes of plant-sourced protein (cereal) that would otherwise be diverted to livestock feed uses. The importance of changes in animal-sourced protein consumption behavior on market outcomes remains clear and presents a challenge for the way policies might influence demand-side factors, which are often the real drivers of changes in food systems. Thus, policy instruments should try to influence consumer preferences.

It is important to address the possibilities for influencing food consumption among the Bottom Billion. Promoting healthy diets through the direct intervention of government-sponsored feeding programs (e.g., food-aid relief efforts or school lunches) constitutes one such possibility. Better health and safety standards — such as those regarding proper food processing, packaging, and storage — need to be implemented. A policy focusing on safe foods can have a profound effect on human health. Reducing morbidity, as well as diseases that cause gastrointestinal ailments, can make macronutrients and micronutrients easier to metabolize.

Income-enhancement intervention has been effective in improving nutritional outcomes for some of the Bottom Billion. Ultimately, the issues that keep the Bottom Billion in chronic malnutrition are also those that keep this group impoverished. The factors delineated by Collier (2007) can be applied to the underlying causes of food insecurity. The multigenerational implications of poor feeding practices suggest future food insecurity (IFPRI, 2002). While we do not explicitly model the dynamics of this process, we see strong links among these factors.

Because poverty alleviation programs rely on stop-gap measures, short-term solutions for improving the nutritional status of the Bottom Billion are limited. The success of lifting the Bottom Billion out of poverty requires long-term policies geared toward economic development and growth.

7. Implications for policy processes

Food insecurity policies are difficult to design and carry out. This is because policies that move the system in a single direction can have both positive and negative impacts. For example, increasing livestock production to meet food demand has a direct impact on environmental greenhouse gas emissions, which have a long-term effect on climate (FAO, 2006; Nellemann et al., 2009).

In a similar vein, the way policy can address long-term demand-side food security is not always clear. Most agricultural policies that are aimed at the consumption side of the equation focus on the elimination (or imposition) of barriers to trade — whether in the form of tariffs or direct restrictions of trade movements — rather than anticipating long-term shifts or evolutions in supply and demand.

Significant attention has been paid to the supply side of agriculture as well as the investments needed for supply growth to keep up with demand growth. A great need exists for increased R&D spending from both public and private sources. Concurrent improvements in extension services and in marketing and distribution infrastructures are also necessary. These can come only from national governments and from allocations in public spending at the farm level.

8. Conclusions

In this chapter, we addressed the nutritional security attainment gap for the Bottom Billion. We discussed the key drivers of change in food systems and explored how supply-side and demand-side drivers can affect the dynamics of world food markets, especially food prices and consumption.

A strong shift toward a healthier diet will have significant impacts on the price and consumption of both animal-sourced and plant-sourced proteins. This will in turn produce a positive effect on protein, carbohydrate, and dietary fiber intake. Supply-side yield-enhancement interventions will help achieve target RDI levels, while demand-side income-enhancement interventions will increase food purchasing power of consumers.

The supply-side drivers of yield-enhancement influence policies that encourage production and the adoption of innovative technologies. Food safety regulation and labeling policies protect consumer health. Demand-side drivers of income-enhancement influence policies that encourage food security. While we do address all the important aspects of food security for the Bottom Billion, the analytical framework used in this chapter can be expanded in future work to gauge how policy can ensure future food security.

References

Beintema, N., & Stads, G. J. (2010, March). *Public agricultural R&D investments and capacities in developing countries: Recent evidence for 2000 and beyond.* Retrieved from http://www.asti.cgiar.org/pdf/ GCARD-BackgroundNote.pdf

Collier, P. (2007). *The Bottom Billion: Why the poorest countries are failing and what can be done about it.* Oxford: Oxford University Press.

Delgado, C. L., Rosegrant, M. W., Steinfeld, H., Ehui, S., & Courbois, C. (1999). Livestock to 2020: The next food revolution. *A 2020 vision for food, agriculture, and the environment.* Discussion Paper no. 28. IFPRI, Washington, DC.

Food and Agricultural Organization of the United Nations [FAO]. (2006). *Livestock's long shadow: Environmental issues and options.* Retrieved from http://www.fao.org/docrep/010/a0701e/a0701e00.HTM

Food and Agricultural Organization of the United Nations [FAO] (2010). *How to feed the world in 2050.* Rome: FAO.

International Assessment of Agricultural Knowledge Science and Technology for Development [IAASTD] (2009). *Agriculture at a crossroads.* Washington, DC: Island Press.

International Food Policy Research Institute [IFPRI] (2002). *Mexico progress: Breaking the cycle of poverty.* Washington, DC: IFPRI.

Msangi, S., & Rosegrant, M. W. (2012). Feeding the future's changing diets: Implications for agricultural markets, nutrition and policy. In S. Fan & R. Pandya-Lorch (Eds.), *Reshaping agriculture for nutrition and health* (pp. 65−71). Washington, DC: IFPRI.

Nellemann, C., MacDevette, M., Manders, T., Eickhout, B., Svihus, B., Prins, A. G., & Kaltenborn, B. P. (Eds.). (2009). The environmental food crisis: The environment's role in averting future food crises. United Nations Environment Programme, GRID-Arendal, Norway. Retrieved from http://www.ilo.org/global/What_we_do/Publications/Newreleases/lang−en/docName–WCMS_098503/index.htm

Popkin, B. M. (2006). Global nutrition dynamics: The world is shifting rapidly toward a diet linked with non-communicable diseases. *American Journal of Clinical Nutrition, 84*(2), 289−298.

Popkin, B. M. (2009). Global changes in diet and activity patterns as drivers of the nutrition transition. *Nestle Nutrition Institute Workshop Series Pediatric Program, 63*, 1−10. doi:10.1159/000209967

Rosegrant, M. W., Cai, X., & Cline, S. (2002). *World water and food to 2025: Dealing with scarcity.* Washington, DC: IFPRI.

Rosegrant, M. W., Paisner, M. S., Meijer, S., & Witcover, J. (2001). *Global food projections to 2020: Emerging trends and alternative futures.* Washington, DC: IFPRI.

Rosegrant, M. W., Tokgoz, S., & Bhandary, P. (2013). A new normal? A tighter global agricultural supply and demand relation and its implications for food security. *American Journal of Agricultural Economics, 95*(2), 303−309.

Ross, C. (2013, July 9). *The rise of chronic diseases in BRIC markets.* Retrieved from http://www.pmlive.com/pharma_intelligence/the_rise_of_chronic_disease_in_bric_markets_487936

Smith, L., & Haddad, L. (2000). *Explaining child malnutrition in developing countries: A cross-country analysis.* Washington, DC: IFPRI.

Stehfest, E., van den Berg, M., Woltjer, G., Msangi, S., & Westhoek, H. (2013). Options to reduce the environmental effects of livestock production: Comparison of two economic models. *Agricultural Systems, 114*, 38−53.

Westhoek, H., Rood, T., van den Berg, M., Janse, J., Nijdam, D., Reudink, M., & Stehfest, E. (2011). *The protein puzzle: The consumption and production of meat, dairy and fish in the European Union.* The Hague: PBL Environmental Agency.

World Bank (2013). Fish to 2030: Prospects for fisheries and aquaculture. World Bank Report no. 83177-GLB. The World Bank, Washington, DC.

World Health Organization [WHO] (2003). Diet, nutrition and the prevention of chronic diseases. WHO Report no. 916. WHO, Geneva.

17

Regional and National Rice Development Strategies for Food Security in West Africa

Eric J. Wailes[a], Alvaro Durand-Morat[a] and Mandiaye Diagne[b]

[a]*Department of Agricultural Economics and Agribusiness, University of Arkansas, Fayetteville, AR, USA*
[b]*Africa Rice Center (AfricaRice), Regional Station Saint Louis, BP 96, Senegal*
E-mail address: ewailes@uark.edu, adurand@uark.edu and m.diagne@cgiar.org

Abstract

Purpose — This chapter assesses the regional and national approaches to improving food security for rice consumption in West Africa.

Methodology/approach — Using the Arkansas Global Rice Model and the RICEFLOW frameworks, we examine the consequences of pursuing self-sufficiency in rice. National rice development strategies have been designed to double the 2008 rice production levels by 2018. The Coalition for African Rice Development and the Africa Rice Center have assisted 23 nations in developing national strategies. We evaluate the strategies of 15 nations for rice land expansion and intensification to increase yields for regional self-sufficiency.

Findings — West Africa accounts for nearly 25% of global rice imports. The elimination of rice imports reduces global rice prices. Results show that achieving self-sufficiency in West Africa is inefficient at the global level. However, if self-sufficiency makes domestic rice uncompetitive with imported rice, then West African consumers will demand a significant price discount for domestic rice, thus reducing benefits to producers and consumers.

Practical implications — Because of the partial equilibrium nature of this study, the consequences for diversification of West African diets are not explored. Although beyond the scope of this chapter, a coordinated policy sequencing approach toward enhancing productivity and quality of rice production — as well as increasing investment in infrastructure, institutions, and emergency food reserves — should be studied more thoroughly to achieve food and nutritional security for West Africa.

Frontiers of Economics and Globalization
Volume 15   ISSN: 1574-8715
DOI: 10.1108/S1574-871520150000015025

Keywords: Food security, rice, production levels, yield growth, self-sufficiency, West Africa

1. Introduction

Rice is an important staple food in all West African nations. In 2014, average per capita consumption of rice in the 15 Economic Community of West African States (ECOWAS) nations was 50kg, a 25% increase from 2008. Increased production has been unable to meet growth in consumption, forcing the region to rely on imports for 50% of its rice consumption. However, compared to other food commodities, global rice trade is one of the most distorted markets. This gives rise to price volatility and food security concerns. The 2008 global rice price crisis inspired ECOWAS to develop a regional food security strategy. Funded by a large number of international donors, the Africa Rice Center and the Coalition for African Rice Development (CARD) have embarked on both regional-based and national-based approaches using rice sector development strategies to achieve rice self-sufficiency.

Africans' livelihoods depend heavily on agriculture, with approximately 70% of the population living in rural areas and working in agriculture-related sectors. Agriculture, which comprises approximately 25% of Africa's GDP, accounts for the majority of Africa's exports (FAOSTAT, 2015). While both production and consumption of main staple crops are on the rise within the ECOWAS region, rice production has been unable to keep pace with rice consumption. Accordingly, rice imports from Asia and the Americas have been escalating steadily. The present rice self-sufficiency ratio is approximately 50%.

Widespread hunger and undernourishment are chronic problems for much of the population of West Africa. Although there is little disagreement on the magnitude and importance of food insecurity in this region, its causes and control are subject to considerable debate and research. Little progress has been achieved in reducing the prevalence of undernourishment (PoU) and the number of underweight children in West Africa, particularly since 2005 (FAO, IFAD, & WFP, 2015). West Africa is experiencing one of the fastest population growth rates in the world (2.7% in 2010) and the 2015 estimated population of 350 million is projected to double in 26 years (United Nations, 2013). Much of the population is mired in poverty. According to the World Bank (2015a, 2015b), 52% of the population in West Africa lives on US$1.25 or less per day. Expenditures on food and nonalcoholic beverages averaged 53% of final household consumption expenditures in 2009 (African Development Bank, 2012).

This chapter focuses on West Africa based on the ECOWAS economic integration and food security objectives.[1] From a food security perspective, particular attention is given to rice that contributes the largest share of energy to the West African diet (FAOSTAT, 2015). Historically, rice has been an important staple food in several West African countries and is becoming increasingly important in the other regional nations.

The ECOWAS region has become an important net importer to meet the growing demand for rice (Wailes & Chavez, 2015). Population growth and income growth combined push rice consumption growth ahead of productivity growth. While import dependency has made the ECOWAS region vulnerable to grain price fluctuations and supply shocks that originate in the rest of the world, rice imports have helped reduce food insecurity for the region. During the 2007–2008 global food crisis, international rice export prices spiked by nearly 300% and several key rice exporters imposed export bans. As a result, ECOWAS, national leaders, international research and donor agencies, and nongovernmental organizations have addressed food security concerns by increasing rice productivity, liberalizing trade, and developing regional food reserves.

We examine one of these approaches – increased production and self-sufficiency – as a means to address food insecurity in West Africa. Following the food price crisis of 2007–2008, the ECOWAS nations developed regional and national rice development strategies (NRDS) to increase domestic production (Africa Rice Center [AfricaRice], 2011). Strategies such as investment in institutions and infrastructure are expected to facilitate the expansion of rice production areas, particularly irrigated lowlands. Other strategies include the development of production technologies (e.g., certified seed systems) and cultural practices that improve low crop yields.

While the significant increase in rice imports has improved food security in West Africa, the volatile global rice market has raised concerns about dependency on rice imports (FAO, IFAD, & WFP, 2015). Economic integration of the West African countries is a fundamental goal of ECOWAS. Implementation of the Common External Tariff is one of the primary instruments for harmonizing ECOWAS member states to improve food security for the region.

In addition to self-sufficiency, ECOWAS is attempting to establish a regional emergency food security reserve system. Food reserves would eliminate short-term shortages and help stabilize food prices. Production

---

[1] The ECOWAS was established by the Treaty of Lagos in 1975. Members include Benin, Burkina Faso, Cape Verde, Côte d'Ivoire, Gambia, Ghana, Guinea, Guinea-Bissau, Liberia, Mali, Niger, Nigeria, Senegal, Sierra Leone, and Togo. Mauritania, once a member, withdrew in 2000.

and supply shocks induced by climatic events, international trade crises, and even the recent Ebola epidemic have resulted in both food shortages and price spikes. These shocks have been particularly devastating for the poorest segments of the population. With encouragement from the G20, ECOWAS initiated a food reserve collaboration with the West African Economic and Monetary Union and the Inter-State Committee for Drought Control in the Sahel. This resulted in the establishment of the Global Alliance for Resilience, a regional framework to coordinate national and regional food staple reserve stocks in the Sahel and West Africa (Global Alliance for Resilience [AGIR], 2013).

2. Food and nutritional vulnerability in West Africa

Beginning in 1990, West Africa has made good progress in alleviating caloric undernourishment in sub-Saharan Africa, with the total PoU in West Africa projected to decrease from 24.2% to 9.6% by 2016 (FAO, IFAD, & WFP, 2015). However, improvements have not been uniform across the region. For example, the PoU level in Burkina Faso, Guinea-Bissau, Liberia, Senegal, and Sierra Leone is projected to remain above 20% in 2016. Data in Table 1 show a 37% increase in total per capita calories for West African countries between 1981 and 2011. The availability of food staples – grains, roots, and tubers – accounted for 80% of the growth, with rice possessing the largest share of any food.

Table 1.   Growth in per capita consumption of West African countries (kcal/cap/day)

Year	1981	1991	2001	2011
Rice	264	304	324	391
Wheat	105	73	120	160
Maize	102	232	177	251
Millet	212	260	251	198
Sorghum	206	240	238	220
Other cereals	12	8	8	7
Cassava	181	269	274	262
Other roots and tubers	112	174	235	281
Sugar	90	71	97	97
Pulses	47	62	80	89
Oil crops	68	43	80	90
Vegetable oils	231	261	282	262
Fruits and vegetables	115	118	131	134
Meat	49	45	48	54
Other	172	142	162	192
Total	1,966	2,302	2,507	2,688

Source: FAOSTAT (2015).

Table 2.   ECOWAS rice production, consumption, and trade, 2000 and 2013

Variable	Units/Year	2000	2013	% Change
Area harvested	1,000 ha	4,457	6,326	42%
Yield	mt/ha	0.99	1.31	33%
Production	1,000 mt	4,408	8,293	88%
Per capita use	kg	34.0	50.0	47%
Total consumption	1,000 mt	7,901	16,370	107%
Imports	1,000 mt	3,802	8,050	112%
Net imports	1,000 mt	3,802	7,910	108%
Ending stocks	1,000 mt	1,078	1,604	49%

Source: United States Department of Agriculture, Foreign Agricultural Service [USDA/FAS] (2015).

Growth in rice consumption in West Africa since 2000 has been possible due to domestic supply, which has increased by 88%. Table 2 shows a 42% increase in area harvested and an average annual increase of 3.5% in crop yields per hectare. Despite the increase in production, rice imports have more than doubled, thus making the region vulnerable to the volatile world rice market (Wailes, 2005). The range of the import dependency ratio varies widely within the region, from 1% for Mali up to a high of 79% for Benin.[2]

The volatile rice market has led to a strong interest in more investment in domestic rice production, the development of a regional emergency food reserve, and the harmonization of trade policies. While ensuring adequate supplies of basic staples such as rice will not fulfill all the nutritional requirements in West Africa, it is a necessary step toward reducing undernourishment of the population (Lopriore & Muehlhoff, 2003). The remainder of this chapter focuses on the impact of the self-sufficiency approach envisioned in NRDS to help West Africa achieve greater food security in rice.

3. Alternative approaches to food security for rice in West Africa

In 2008, the Japan International Cooperation Agency and the Association for a Green Revolution in Africa established the CARD. The food security objective of CARD is to double rice production in West Africa by 2018 through institution building and coordination of donor

---

[2] The high import dependency for Benin is in part a result of the rice smuggled into Nigeria to avoid the country's high import duty.

assistance for the rice sector (AfricaRice, 2011). CARD and Africa Rice Center have assisted African nations in creating the NRDS. Table 3 provides a summary of the production objectives by 2018 for each of the West African nations.

Each of the ECOWAS countries has developed its own approach to expand its area harvested compared to its crop yield per hectare. Benin's strategy relies equally on expanding rice area, upgrading existing rice-growing areas, facilitating improved access to inputs, and improving post-harvest processing and storage (Republic of Benin, 2011). Burkina Faso's approach intensifies production to obtain higher crop yields rather than expanding production area (Burkina Faso, 2011). The Côte d'Ivoire strategy relies more on increased production area and less on intensification of production (Republic of Ivory Coast, 2012). Gambia possesses the most ambitious strategy: increasing production by 471%, primarily by improving crop yield by 270% and nearly doubling rice area (Republic of Gambia, 2014). Ghana's strategy envisions an increase in rice area and intensification of production (Republic of Ghana, 2009). Relative to production area and crop yield, Guinea requires only modest increases in production area and crop yield to achieve the target production by 2018 (Republic of Guinea, 2009). While no NRDS document is available for Guinea-Bissau, the study by Kyle (2015) is used to specify a reasonable increase in production area and intensification of rice production (Table 3). The NRDS for Liberia is ambitious, with expansion and rehabilitation in irrigated lowland area as well as intensification of upland rice areas. This strategy would increase crop yield from a very low level and increase production to a self-sufficiency level (Republic of Liberia, 2012). The strategy of Mali, which is already near self-sufficiency, is to expand newly irrigated rice land and to intensify production to create an exportable rice surplus of 1.5 million metric tons (mmt) (Republic of Mali, 2009). Among ECOWAS members, Niger has the smallest rice economy in West Africa. With no NRDS in place for Niger, IFAD is currently assisting Niger rice farmers in expanding production through irrigation technology and multiple cropping (The Guardian, 2015). Mechanization and better input markets will facilitate the expansion of land area under production. Nigeria is the largest rice economy in West Africa and the world's second largest rice importer. Its strategy includes expansion of production area by 40% and doubling crop yield (Federal Republic of Nigeria, 2009). Improvements of input markets and the delivery of extension services will create intensification. Senegal has the highest average crop yields in West Africa, so its strategy depends on production area expansion (Republic of Senegal, 2009). Sierra Leone's strategy relies on expanded production area, particularly lowlands and improved crop yield in all ecosystems – upland, lowlands, and mangroves (Republic of Sierra Leone, 2009). The NRDS for Togo is to expand lowland and irrigated areas and to intensify all ecosystems by improving input supply

Table 3. National rice development strategies, proposed production increases, West Africa

Country	Area Harvested (ha)			Yield per Ha (mt)			Production (1,000 mt)		
	2013	2018	Change	2013	2018	Change	2013	2018	Change
Benin	68	138	103%	2.06	4.30	109%	140	593	323%
Burkina Faso	137	192	40%	1.42	2.80	97%	195	536	175%
Côte d'Ivoire	450	1,430	218%	1.16	1.48	28%	500	2,116	323%
Gambia	65	100	54%	0.54	2.00	270%	35	200	471%
Ghana	220	375	70%	1.6	2.40	50%	352	900	156%
Guinea	1,100	1,325	20%	1.23	1.40	14%	1,355	1,855	37%
Guinea-Bissau	135	145	7%	0.94	1.30	38%	126	189	50%
Liberia	230	300	30%	0.65	2.40	269%	150	720	380%
Mali	605	1,087	80%	2.38	2.37	0%	1,438	2,576	79%
Niger	8	17	113%	3.25	4.00	23%	26	68	162%
Nigeria	2,500	3,500	40%	1.11	2.39	115%	2,772	8,365	202%
Senegal	107	327	206%	2.71	3.06	13%	290	1,001	245%
Sierra Leone	650	1,100	69%	1.22	1.78	46%	791	1,958	148%
Togo	51	67	30%	1.96	2.10	7%	100	140	40%
Total	6,326	10,102	60%	1.31	2.10	60%	8,270	21,217	157%

Source: PSD Online (USDA/FAS, 2015); Arkansas Global Rice Model (Wailes & Chavez, 2015).

chains (Republic of Togo, 2010). Of the West African rice economies, Togo and Guinea are closest to achieving their 2018 NRDS production targets.

4. Assessment of the NRDS of West Africa

Previous research has hypothesized that improving food security in Africa requires greater focus on upgrading rice value chains to enhance quality-based competitiveness of domestic rice relative to imports (Demont, 2013). Improving farm-level productivity may be insufficient to improve food security if domestic rice is inferior – or perceived by consumers to be inferior – relative to imports. In fact, expanding the supply of inferior domestic rice would make it cheaper than rice imports, which would decrease net returns. The projected changes in rice production across West Africa are unlikely to be achieved without massive funding and mobilization of resources (Table 3). Evaluating the economics of doubling rice production without upgrading rice value chains is beyond the scope of this chapter. Instead, we provide an assessment of the consequences for the West African rice economy and the larger impacts on the global rice economy if production targets are achieved by 2018. Our analyses makes two assumptions: (1) domestic and imported rice are fully substitutable and (2) domestic and imported rice are imperfectly substitutable.

The analytical framework is based on two global rice models: the Arkansas Global Rice Model (AGRM) and the RiceFlow model (Durand-Morat & Wailes, 2010; Wailes & Chavez, 2011). AGRM is an econometric structural model based on estimated equations of area harvested, crop yield, per capita consumption, trade, and stock behavior. All countries in the world are included either individually (44 major rice producing/consuming countries) or regionally to capture the rest of the world through six subregional groupings (Wailes & Chavez, 2011). Eight of the ECOWAS countries are individually modeled (Côte d'Ivoire, Ghana, Guinea, Liberia, Mali, Nigeria, Senegal, and Sierra Leone) and the remaining six (Benin, Burkina Faso, Gambia, Guinea-Bissau, Niger, and Togo) are aggregated in a regional model. AGRM is nonspatial and therefore the structure implies Armington demand elasticities for domestic and imported rice of infinity. The RiceFlow model is a spatial partial equilibrium model that specifies rice value chains for all rice producing and consuming countries or regions in the world. We use the RiceFlow model to impose Armington elasticities that reflect imperfect substitution between domestic and imported rice. The values for the Armington elasticities are taken from the GTAP 8 database (Hertel, McDougall, Narayanan, & Aguiar, 2012).

Table 4. *AGRM estimated market effect of National Rice Development Strategies, 2018*

Variable	Benchmark		NRDS Scenario		
	2013	2018	2018	Change	% Change
ECOWAS					
Area harvest (1,000 ha)	6,326	7,231	10,102	2,871	39.7%
Yield (mt/ha)	1.31	1.47	2.1	0.63	42.4%
Production (1,000 mt)	8,293	10,658	21,206	10,548	99.0%
Consumption (1,000 mt)	16,370	19,532	20,396	864	4.4%
Per capita consumption (kg)	50	52.4	54.8	2.32	4.4%
Net imports (1,000 mt)	7,910	8,910	−763	−9,673	−108.6%
Stocks (1,000 mt)	1,604	1,849	1,896	47	2.5%
World					
Reference price (US$/mt)	428	464	373	−91	−19.7%
Area Harvest (1,000 ha)	160,865	162,402	164,095	1,693	1.0%
Yield (mt/ha)	2.96	3.09	3.09	0	0.0%
Production (1,000 mt)	476,960	502,323	507,682	5,358	1.1%
Consumption (1,000 mt)	478,200	499,845	507,981	8,136	1.6%
Per capita consumption (kg)	66.5	65.9	67	1.1	1.6%
Net trade (1,000 mt)	37,722	39,031	35,290	−3,741	−9.6%
Stocks (1,000 mt)	107,067	113,729	106,517	−7,212	−6.3%

Source: USDA, *PSD Online*, and Arkansas Global Rice Model (Wailes & Chavez, 2015).

5. Results

AGRM results are presented in Table 4. Actual 2013 data for ECOWAS are consistent with the aggregation of the 2013 data in Table 3. Benchmark estimates for 2018 exclude NRDS. Differences in the benchmarks for 2013 and 2018 reflect a continuation of existing relationships among model variables (e.g., expanding ECOWAS rice area harvested and crop yield per hectare). Total consumption increases by slightly more than 3 mmt based on an increase in per capita consumption of 2.4 kg and an annual population growth for the region of 2.7%. Production increases by more than 2 mmt and net imports increase by 1 mmt to satisfy rice consumption growth.

The West African NRDS for area harvested, crop yield, and production targets are then imposed on the model to estimate (1) the effects on increased rice availability within the ECOWAS region and (2) the impacts on the world long grain reference price, global production, consumption, and trade. The change and percent change columns reflect the impacts. Consistent with the NRDS, rice production is doubled. Total consumption increases by only 4.4%. However, compared to the benchmark (2.4 kg), the increases above the 2013 per capita consumption doubles from 2.4 kg to 4.8 kg in the NRDS scenario. Net imports decline, as a trade reversal is projected for the ECOWAS region with a net export of 763,000 metric tons. It is worth noting again that this model assumes that domestic and imported rice are perfectly substitutable.

ECOWAS accounts for 23% of world net imports in the 2018 benchmark. Large country– or, in this case, large region – effects are transmitted to the rest of the world. Under the NRDS scenario, the ECOWAS region achieves self-sufficiency, which greatly impacts prices on the global rice market. The world long grain reference rice price decreases 20% from US$464/mt in the 2018 benchmark to US$373/mt under the NRDS scenario. With a lower international price, area harvested in the rest of the world decreases by 1.2 million hectares and production decreases by 5.2 mmt. This implies production efficiency losses in the rest of the world, as reduction of land yielding 3.1 mt/ha gives way to land yielding 2.1 mt/ha in the ECOWAS region. However, a US$91/mt decrease in the world rice price would equate to a large economic welfare gain of US$46 million for global rice consumers. Achieving self-sufficiency in West Africa probably would have dynamic costs for the stability of the global rice market, as the trade share of global consumption would decrease.

Table 5 presents the estimated results under the NRDS scenario using the RiceFlow model. The key result of this analysis is that with imperfect substitution between domestic production and imported rice, the

Table 5. *RiceFlow estimated market effects of national rice development strategies, 2018*

Variable	2013 Level	Benchmark 2018		NRDS Scenario 2018	
		Level	Change from 2013	Level	Change from benchmark
ECOWAS					
Production (1,000 mt)	7,777	9,432	21.28%	19,947	111.5%
Consumption	15,726	18,846	19.84%	20,385	8.2%
Net imports	8,041	9,505	18.21%	576	−93.9%
From India	3,525	4,152	17.79%	26	−99.4%
From Thailand	1,836	2,327	26.74%	287	−87.7%
From Vietnam	1,086	1,256	15.65%	239	−81.0%
From other	1,594	1,770	11.04%	24	−98.6%
Wholesale price (long grain white rice)	564	550	−2.48%	298	−45.8%
World					
Global trade	36,986	41,231	11.48%	32,765	−20.5%
Thailand	6,593	7,816	18.55%	5,850	−25.2%
India	10,148	11,521	13.53%	7,911	−31.3%
Vietnam	6,747	7,244	7.37%	6,219	−14.1%
Export prices Free on Board long grain white (US$/ton)					
Thailand	525	503	−4.19%	492	−2.2%
India	398	384	−3.52%	380	−1.0%
Vietnam	446	435	−2.47%	433	−0.5%

Source: RiceFlow Model (Durand-Morat & Wailes, 2011).

ECOWAS domestic price decreases by nearly 46% while world reference prices for exporters decrease 2% or less. Imports into ECOWAS decreases from 9.5 mmt to only 5.76 mmt. The loss of the West African market requires adjustment by exporters. This adjustment is achieved through reduction in rice production, with a presumable shifting of resources into production of other agricultural commodities.

The important economic consequence of implementing self-sufficiency under NRDS is that owners of ECOWAS rice land are trapped into negative returns. Thus, self-sufficiency production levels can only be sustained by large transfers from the government to landowners. Because domestic wholesale price declines by US$252/mt, consumers within ECOWAS benefit from an increase in total consumption of 8.2%, as well as from lower rice prices. However, a large part of this decrease reflects the discount necessary to switch from higher-quality imported rice to lower-quality domestic rice.

6. Conclusions

This chapter provides an assessment of the consequences for the West African rice economy, and the larger impacts on the global rice economy, should self-sufficiency in rice production be achieved by 2018. Food insecurity remains an important concern for the region. West Africa is dependent on rice imports for half of its consumption. National strategies have been developed to achieve self-sufficiency. Using the AGRM and RiceFlow models, we find less than compelling the benefits for self-sufficiency. Expansion of rice production displaces nearly 25% of global rice trade, thus undermining production in more efficient rice producing export countries such as India, Thailand, and Vietnam. Benefits to West African consumers include lower rice prices. However, if domestic rice is not competitive with or substitutable for imported rice in terms of quality, then much of the price reduction reflects discounts for the lower-quality product. We find that returns to rice land actually becomes negative in West Africa and that maintaining self-sufficiency would require large public support expenditures. We conclude that achieving food security through self-sufficiency is inefficient. Improvements in productivity and expansions in production based on comparative advantage should be studied in conjunction with sequencing rice trade liberalization and the development of emergency reserve stocks.

References

Africa Rice Center [AfricaRice] (2011). *Lessons from the rice crisis: Policies for food security in Africa*. Benin: Cotonou. Retrieved from http://www.africarice.org/publications/Lessons%20from%20the%20 rice%20crisis.pdf

African Development Bank. (2012). A comparison of real household consumption expenditure and price levels in Africa. *Office of the Chief Economist*. Retrieved from http://www.afdb.org/fileadmin/uploads/ afdb/Documents/Publications/Household%20Consumption%20 Report.pdf

Burkina Faso, Ministry of Agriculture, Water and Fisheries. (2011). *National rice development strategy*. Retrieved from http://www.ricefor-africa.org/images/stories/PDF/burkina_faso_en.pdf

Demont, M. (2013). Reversing urban bias in African rice markets: A review of 19 national rice development strategies. *Global Food Security, 2*, 172−181.

Durand-Morat, A., & Wailes, E. J. (2010). *RiceFlow: A multi-region, multi-product spatial partial equilibrium model of the world rice economy* (Staff Paper SP 03). Fayetteville, AR: University of Arkansas. Retrieved from http://purl.umn.edu/92010

Durand-Morat, A., & Wailes, E. J. (2011). *Rice trade policies and their implications for food security*. Retrieved from http://purl.umn.edu/ 103818

FAOSTAT. (2015). *Food balance sheets*. Retrieved from http://faostat3. fao.org/

Federal Republic of Nigeria, National Food Reserve Agency. (2009). *National rice development strategy*. Retrieved from http://www.inter-reseaux.org/IMG/pdf_NRDS_FINAL__National_rice_development_ stategy_.pdf

Food and Agriculture Organization of the United Nations [FAO], International Food for Agricultural Development [IFAD], and World Food Program [WFP]. (2015). *The state of food insecurity in the world 2015. Meeting the 2015 international hunger targets: Taking stock of uneven progress*. Rome, FAO. Retrieved from http://reliefweb.int/sites/ reliefweb.int/files/resources/a-i4646e.pdf

Global Alliance for Resilience [AGIR]. (2013). *AGIR − Sahel and West Africa regional roadmap*. Retrieved from http://www.oecd.org/swac/ publications/AGIR%20roadmap_EN_FINAL.pdf

Hertel, T. W., McDougall, R. A., Narayanan, G. B., & Aguiar, A. (2012). Behavioral parameters. In G. B. Narayanan, A. Aguiar, & R. McDougall (Eds.), *Global trade, assistance, and production: The GTAP 8 database*. West Lafayette, IN: Purdue University. Retrieved from https://www.gtap.agecon.purdue.edu/resources/download/7047.pdf

Kyle, S. (2015). Rice sector policy options in Guinea-Bissau. WP 2015-01. Cornell University, Ithaca, NY. Retrieved from http://www.dyson.cor-nell.edu/research/researchpdf/wp/2015/Cornell-Dyson-wp1501.pdf

Lopriore, C., & Muehlhoff, E. (2003). *Food security and nutrition trends in West Africa: Challenges and the way forward.* Retrieved from http://ftp.fao.org/es/esn/nutrition/ouagafinal.pdf

Republic of Benin, Ministry of Agriculture, Livestock and Fisheries. (2011). *National rice development strategy for Benin.* Retrieved from http://riceforafrica.org/downloads/NRDS/benin_en.pdf

Republic of Ghana, Ministry of Food and Agriculture. (2009). *National rice development strategy.* Retrieved from http://www.riceforafrica.org/images/stories/PDF/ghana_en.pdf

Republic of Guinea, Ministry of Agriculture and Livestock. (2009). *National strategy for the development of rice growing.* Retrieved from http://www.riceforafrica.org/downloads/NRDS/guinea_en.pdf

Republic of Ivory Coast, Ministry of Agriculture. (2012). *Revised national rice development strategy for the Cote d'Ivoire rice sector (NRDS) 2012–2020.* Retrieved from http://www.riceforafrica.org/downloads/NRDS/Cote_dIvoire_en.pdf

Republic of Liberia, Ministry of Agriculture. (2012). *National rice development strategy of Liberia: Doubling rice production by 2018.* Retrieved from http://www.riceforafrica.org/downloads/NRDS/LNRDS.pdf

Republic of Mali, Ministry of Agriculture. (2009). *National strategy for the development of rice growing.* Retrieved from http://www.riceforafrica.org/downloads/NRDS/mali_en.pdf

Republic of Senegal, Ministry of Agriculture. (2009). *National strategy for the development of rice cultivation.* Retrieved from http://www.riceforafrica.org/downloads/NRDS/senegal_en.pdf

Republic of Sierra Leone, Ministry of Agriculture, Forestry and Food Security. (2009). *National rice development strategy.* Retrieved from http://www.riceforafrica.org/downloads/NRDS/sierraleone_en.pdf

Republic of Gambia, Ministry of Agriculture. (2014). *National rice development strategy.* Retrieved from http://www.riceforafrica.org/images/stories/PDF/gambia_en.pdf

Republic of Togo, Ministry of Agriculture, Livestock and Fisheries. (2010). *National rice development strategy.* Retrieved from http://www.riceforafrica.org/downloads/NRDS/Togo_En.pdf

The Guardian. (2015). *IFAD to mechanize rice, cassava production in Niger.* Retrieved from http://www.ngrguardiannews.com/2015/05/ifad-to-mechanise-rice-cassava-production-in-niger/

United Nations (2013). *World population prospects: The 2012 revision, volume II: Demographic profiles.* New York, NY: United Nations.

United States Department of Agriculture, Foreign Agricultural Service [USDA/FAS] (2015). *PSD Online.* Washington, DC: USDA.

Wailes, E. J. (2005). Rice global trade, protectionist policies, and the impact of trade liberalization. In M. Ataman Aksoy & J. C. Beghin (Eds.), *Global agricultural trade and developing countries* (pp. 177–194). Washington, DC: World Bank.

Wailes, E. J., & Chavez, E. C. (2011). 2011 updated Arkansas global rice model. Staff Paper 01. University of Arkansas, Fayetteville, AR. Retrieved from http://purl.umn.edu/102650

Wailes, E. J., & Chavez, E. C. (2015). International rice outlook, baseline projections, 2014–2024. Staff Paper 01. University of Arkansas, Fayetteville, AR. Retrieved from http://purl.umn.edu/199846

World Bank (2015a). *Poverty and equity databank*. Washington, DC: World Bank. Retrieved from http://povertydata.worldbank.org/poverty/region/SSA

World Bank (2015b). *Africa development indicators*. Washington, DC: World Bank. Retrieved from http://data.worldbank.org/data-catalog/africa-development-indicators

ACKNOWLEDGMENTS

We would like to thank all of those who contributed to this volume entitled *Food Security in an Uncertain World: An International Perspective*. This work was made possible through funding provided by the Ben Hill Griffin, Jr. Endowment, and by the National Institute for Food and Agriculture (USDA Multistate Research Project, S-1062). We especially would like to thank Carol Fountain for managing our overall project on food security. We would also like to thank Carol Fountain, H. Carole Schmitz, Carolyn Bradley, Michael Rowin, and Dwayne J. Haynes for their editorial assistance. Without their tireless effort, this project would not have been possible.

Printed in the USA/Agawam, MA
December 29, 2015

628517.017